T3-BNW-799

# Dreams of Equality
## Women on the Canadian Left, 1920–1950

Joan Sangster

M&S

BRESCIA COLLEGE
LIBRARY
57259

# For Kate and Laura

Copyright © 1989 by Joan Sangster

All rights reserved. The use of any part of this publication reproduced, transmitted in any form or by any means, electronic, mechanical, photocopying, recording, or otherwise, or stored in a retrieval system, without the prior consent of the publisher is an infringement of the copyright law.

**Canadian Cataloguing in Publication Data**
 Sangster, Joan, 1952-
  Dreams of equality

 (The Canadian social history series)
 Bibliography: p.
 Includes index.
 ISBN 0-7710-7946-X

 1. Women in politics – Canada – History.
 2. Right and left (Political science). I. Title.
 II. Series.

 HQ1236.5.C3S3 1989      320.530971      C88-094897-3

Printed and bound in Canada

McClelland & Stewart Inc.
*The Canadian Publishers*
481 University Avenue
Toronto, Ontario

# Contents

## *Abbreviations*

| | |
|---|---|
| CAC | Consumers Association of Canada |
| CASD | Committee to Aid Spanish Democracy |
| CCF | Co-operative Commonwealth Federation |
| CCL | Canadian Congress of Labour (CIO) |
| CCW | Canadian Congress of Women |
| CCYM | Co-operative Commonwealth Youth Movement |
| CGIT | Canadian Girls In Training |
| CI | Communist International |
| CIO | Congress of Industrial Organizations |
| CLDL | Canadian Labor Defence League |
| CLP | Canadian Labor Party |
| CLWF | Canadian League Against War and Fascism |
| CPC | Communist Party of Canada |
| DLP | Dominion Labour Party |
| EYWA | East York Workers Association |
| FCSO | Fellowship for a Christian Social Order |
| FOC | Finnish Organization of Canada |
| FSU | Friends of the Soviet Union |
| HCA | Housewives' Consumers Association |
| ILGWU | International Ladies Garment Workers Union |
| ILP | Independent Labour Party |
| IUNTW | Industrial Union of Needle Trades Workers |
| IWA | International Woodworkers of America |
| LPP | Labor Progressive Party |
| LSR | League for Social Reconstruction |
| MWUC | Mine Workers Union of Canada |
| NCDR | National Council for Democratic Rights |
| NCW | National Council of Women |
| NDP | New Democratic Party |
| NUWU | National Unemployed Workers Union |
| PWA | Progressive Women's Associations |
| RILU | Red International of Labor Unions |
| SCM | Student Christian Movement |
| SDPC | Social Democratic Party of Canada |
| SPC | Socialist Party of Canada |
| SPNA | Socialist Party of North America |
| TLC | Trades and Labour Congress |
| UE | United Electrical Radio and Machine Workers of America |
| UFA | United Farmers of Alberta |
| UFC | United Farmers of Canada, Saskatchewan Section |
| ULFTA | Ukrainian Labour-Farmer Temple Association |
| WIDF | Women's International Democratic Federation |
| WIL | Women's International League for Peace and Freedom |
| WJC | Women's Joint Committee |
| WLL | Women's Labor League |
| WUL | Workers Unity League |
| YCL | Young Communist League |
| YWCA | Young Women's Christian Association |

# Preface

"The degree of emancipation of women is the natural measure of general emancipation of society,"[1] declared Charles Fourier, a French utopian socialist of the early nineteenth century, in his historic treatise on socialism. From the time of the utopian socialists, the emancipation of women has been investigated, debated, explained, and even attempted by socialists and, later, Communists, who, despite their doctrinal differences, have agreed that women were accorded an inferior political, social, and economic role in society. Women have also played a part in the building of socialism, though the socialist movement has seldom made women's equality its central priority. Indeed, even the major theoreticians on the "woman question" were men: after Fourier, Marx, Engels, and Lenin became the most influential thinkers until the women's movement in recent years produced a renaissance in socialist-feminist thought.[2]

These recent theoretical perspectives have stimulated exciting new international scholarship on the history of women and socialism. In the Canadian context, however, little has been written on left-wing women or on the intersection of socialist and feminist politics.[3] While historians of Canadian women have concentrated on middle-class feminism and the lives of working women, historians of the left have centred their inquiries on questions of ideology, party leadership, and labour relations that not only exclude women but also often assume either rigidly social democratic or Communist conclusions.[4] A few accounts have dismissed women's contribution to socialist parties as negligible; in general, though, the subject has simply encountered a resounding silence.

Although hidden from written history, women were an important force in the making of Canadian socialism and communism.

7

Within the left, there did exist a sexual division of political labour, and women were seldom represented in "prestigious" jobs as union organizers, party theoreticians, or national spokespersons. Women, however, comprised an indispensable army of local educators, electioneers, and grassroots workers who helped to create the foundation upon which socialism could be built. There were important ideological differences between the Communist Party and the social democratic alternative, the Co-operative Commonwealth Federation (CCF), but one thing they shared was the acceptance – sometimes a mere tolerance – of separate women's organizations, serving a variety of purposes, from traditional auxiliary work to feminist social action. Although women's committees generally remained subject to party control, they were also the living product of women's perceived needs, their ideas about women's social role, and even their feelings of oppression. And without this energetic commitment to women's self-organization, the woman question would have remained almost entirely dormant and lifeless in both parties.

At the time, of course, few socialists and even fewer Communists would have accepted the label "feminist." Some survivors of the suffrage movement did consciously carry the spirit of feminism into the CCF. But the political world view of most radical women, especially Communists, was shaped by their experiences of class and economic exploitation and by a re-education in socialist theory that rejected the "sexual antagonism" presumed to be characteristic of feminism.

Nonetheless, there was an element of feminism in the political beliefs and practices of these women who, in their own way, tried to expose and alter women's social and economic inequality. Undeniably, they sometimes shied away from reproductive issues and showed reluctance to challenge directly women's subordination in families and even male prejudice within socialist parties. Yet, in forging a link between women's experience of class and gender oppression, these women were developing a nascent tradition of feminist-socialism and, in doing so, they were exploring territory largely untouched by the earlier suffrage advocates. In the post-suffrage decades, in fact, when the liberal women's movement lay weakened and fragmented, much of the dynamic debate on the woman question was found in leftist circles.

This book is about these female pioneers within the Canadian left. Retrieving the history of women socialists is, I believe, an important task for contemporary socialist-feminists if we are to understand what historical conditions encourage, or stifle, women's radicalism. In order to answer this question, we need to understand the past ideas, insights, mistakes, and limitations of early activists on the left. We need to recover women socialists' vision of the New Jerusalem, ask if it was similar to men's version of socialism, and document the roles women assumed in socialist parties, assessing how these approximated the division of labour and ideology of women's role in the wider society. We need to discover how socialists perceived the woman question, what their solutions to oppression were, how successfully they organized women, and what impact autonomous women's committees had within the left. Finally, we must weigh how woman's economic life and role in the family intersected with and influenced her politics. And however partial the efforts of these early socialist activists may appear from the perspective of contemporary socialist-feminist politics, they must be viewed with some understanding of the meaning that ideas and activity had for people in their own time and social context.

By recovering our political ancestors, "we seek a past which does not maintain our subordination by exclusion or distortion." At the same time, our task is not to draw absolutist "history shows us" conclusions[5] or to overromanticize past female heroines. Rather, as Sheila Rowbotham argues, we need to maintain a constant dialogue between our quest for historical evidence and the criticisms that emerge out of our contemporary feminist concerns.[6] We want, ultimately, to develop an ongoing relationship with the past, which is sympathetic yet critical, building a complex picture of women's "dreams of equality."

When I first began this book, I was afraid there would be few sources on an earlier generation of socialist women. Women's involvement in the grassroots rather than the leadership, the secondary nature of the woman question within the left, and the CPC's Leninist mode of organizing, as well as its persecution by the state, all seemed to make my task problematic. Moreover, such sources as the radical press and oral history, though valuable and rewarding, were also selective and partisan. However, as I gathered more and more material revealing the rich and detailed history of women on the left, I had to limit the scope of my work. My first chapter offers a brief review of early socialist organizing in Canada and socialist theory on the woman question. In subsequent chapters I have examined only two manifestations of the Canadian left: the Communist Party and the CCF, and I have ended their story in the 1950's, a period of retreat for both parties, before the radically altered political climate of the New Left of the 1960's. Their stories are generally told separately, though they did overlap in ideas, converts, organization, and, increasingly, in hostility. Moreover, I have concentrated primarily on two regions of Canada, Ontario and the West, leaving the tale of socialist women in Quebec and the Maritimes to regional historians already working on similar projects.

While writing this book, I have received important financial, scholarly, and moral support. My initial research was aided by a SSHRC doctoral fellowship and a research grant from Trent University helped to defray my translation costs. This book has been published with the help of a grant from the Canadian Federation for the Humanities, using funds provided by the Social Sciences and Humanities Research Council of Canada.

Many people helped make this book a reality. When I began work on this project as a Ph.D. thesis, my supervisor, Richard Allen, provided intellectual interest and moral support. McMaster colleagues Bernice Kaczynski, Richard Rempel, and Carolyn Gray, and, at Trent, Keith Walden, were important listeners and advisers. Karen Teeple provided help with oral history, while Lynda Yanz, Debbie Field, and Wayne Roberts engaged me in useful discussions on women's labour history. Other colleagues across Canada offered research advice, shared sources, and let me read their unpublished work; thank you to Kathy Arnup, David Frank, Craig Heron, Linda Kealey, Susan Radosovic of the UFAWU, and Nolan Reilly, and to the members of my feminist history discussion group, Ruth Frager, Franca Iacovetta, and Janice Newton. Veronica Strong-Boag, Greg Kealey, and Linda Kealey read my manuscript and offered useful suggestions for change, while two translators, Mauri Jalava and Wally Lewyckyj, provided indispensable help in exploring the lives of Finnish and Ukrainian women.

The inspiration for this book owes a special debt to two groups of people. For the women I interviewed, I have profound gratitude. They welcomed me into their lives and generously shared their pasts with me, and although I did not always agree with their political priorities, I respected their past activism and their continuing dedication to social change. Secondly, I want to thank socialist and feminist friends in Hamilton, Brandon, and Peterborough, particularly women from the McMaster Women's Centre and Hamilton Working Women, for their interest in my work, their criticisms, questions, discussion, and personal support. They helped me to ask new questions of the past and enriched my understanding of feminism and socialism. Thanks in particular to Donna Jowett, Joanna Sargent, Janet Tulloch, and to two important women who have been close friends and collaborators: Margaret Fischbuch and Margaret Hobbs.

Last, but not least, I want to thank my family, especially David Poole, for his respect for my work and his unfailing emotional support. To our daughters, Kate and Laura, I also owe a debt of gratitude. Their presence did not hasten the completion of this book, but they did inspire me to try to understand and explain the dream of women's equality, in the hope that their lives might be enriched by this history.

I

# Theory and Practice: Early Canadian Socialists Explore the Woman Question

Women who embraced the Communist Party's revolutionary message, or who resolved to reform society through the CCF, were part of an ongoing Canadian socialist tradition that had concerned itself with the woman question as early as the turn of the century. Communists' and CCFers' understanding of women's oppression was shaped both by these established, indigenous traditions and also by new intellectual and international currents of the 1920's and 1930's. The Communist Party followed in the path of the earlier Marxist Socialist Party of Canada (SPC) and the Social Democratic Party of Canada (SDPC), with its emphasis on class inequality, class conflict, and the revolutionary transformation of society. The CCF, a more eclectic and predominantly social democratic alliance, drew in some Marxists but also attracted labourites, Christian socialists, Fabians, and radical farmers. Established socialist traditions and new theoretical insights shaped but never determined the CPC's and CCF's initial approach to women's inequality; as both parties matured, their views on women were altered by international forces, political pragmatism, and, importantly, by the actions of women within each party.

### Revolutionaries Explore the Woman Question

Immediately after World War One, the Canadian socialist movement was dramatically transformed by the establishment of a new revolutionary party, the Communist Party of Canada, formed primarily from the SPC, the SDPC, and the small Socialist Party of North America (SPNA). Since its beginnings in 1903, the SPC had promoted a dogmatic brand of Marxism that officially rejected electoral reform, trade union work, and international debate, appropriately earning the party the label "impossibilist." The SPC's impossibilism, along with its authoritarian, centralized organization, resulted in the creation of two splinter groups: the SPNA, which carried on in the impossibilist tradition, and the SDPC, which became the popular alternative to the SPC, promoting a platform of "reform now, revolution later." Strong support for the SDPC came from former Finnish and Ukrainian locals of the SPC that had become dissatisfied with the SPC's inflexible English leadership and opted for a more localized and ethnically tolerant socialist movement.[1]

The leadership of the new Communist Party was also predominantly English-speaking, but the membership was drawn heavily from a constituency of Finnish, Ukrainian, and Eastern European Jewish immigrants. Informally allied to the Communist Party were three cultural organizations that had their roots in the pre-war left: the Finnish Organization of Canada (FOC), the Ukrainian Labour-Farmer Temple Association (ULFTA), and the (Jewish) Labor League. Despite this important link between immigrant groups and communism, the Party cannot be analysed solely in terms of ethnic "peculiarities." Communism was an "alternative ideology which, for specific, historical reasons, including class and culture, found political support from these European immigrants."[2]

The Communist Party was the product not only of indigenous socialist organizations but also of faith and hope in a new international revolutionary movement, the Communist International (CI). Founded by Russian Bolsheviks in 1919 to provide a Marxist, revolutionary alternative to the discredited Second International, in its infancy the CI functioned partly through democratic debate. But by the early 1920's it was indisputably led by the Communist Party of the Soviet Union. Canadian Communists, however, accepted this control and the conditions of allegiance demanded by the CI *precisely* because they welcomed attachment to the successful Russian Revolution and the Soviet Communist Party.[3]

Through the International, Canadian Communists acquired a new window on the woman question. Previously, Canadian socialists had read August Bebel's *Woman Under Socialism*, or occasionally Frederick Engels's *Origin of the Family*, to decipher the meaning of the woman question. This Marxist theory was interpreted differently in the actions of the SPC and the SDPC. The SPC was undoubtedly the most ambivalent toward the woman question: on the one hand, it supported women's suffrage bills, but then it downplayed female suffrage as a bourgeois measure, secondary to the more important revolutionary demands for women's economic independence and class equality for all people. The SPC generally held to a rigid class perspective, refusing to acknowledge the special oppression of women, and its paper, the *Western Clarion*, sometimes portrayed women as intellectually inferior and inherently conservative. Although a few SPC women accepted this pejorative view of women as "passive, clinging to religion and . . . a drag and fetter on the movement," [4] there were certainly some voices of female dissent in the SPC, arguing that the SPC's ideological rigidity and its failure to attract women were precisely the reasons why separate women's groups and more discussion of the woman question were needed in the Socialist Party. [5]

The debate over the importance of women's suffrage to socialists was probably one reason for the SDPC's split from the SPC. Like its parent, the SDPC viewed class inequality as the fundamental cause of women's subordination, but it favoured immediate reforms to alleviate women's suffering and promoted autonomous organizations for women, like the Finnish women's "sub-branches" and sewing circles. [6] SDPers were known to repeat some of the arguments of middle-class maternal feminists that women's moral superiority and domestic concerns should be the basis for their political participation, but the SDPC's strong emphasis on the economic exploitation of working-class women set it firmly apart from most middle-class feminists of the pre-war period.

Within both the SPC and SDPC, women's primary contribution was their grassroots support work. Most socialists, argues Linda Kealey, saw women as secondary and dependent workers; they feared women's labour would threaten male jobs and thus promoted the ideal of the family wage. Motherhood was always presumed to be women's natural and desired career, though a brave minority of activists, like Helena Gutteridge, combined a feminist and socialist analysis to demand complete choice and equality for all women in all spheres of life. Women's participation in socialist and labour organizations, and their militancy, did increase during the war years, and especially during the labour revolt of 1919. Linda Kealey demonstrates that the crises of the war period and the state's defence of capitalism mobilized labour and socialist women as never before to defend the economic viability of the working-class family as well as women workers' right to organize. While socialist women often "subsumed women's interests in broad labour concerns" or justified their roles in maternalist rhetoric, they did show a new awareness of gender inequality and a growing consciousness of the need for women's public, political action.[7]

After 1919, the Communist Party offered women radicalized by the war and the labour revolt not only a new organizational home but also a revised Marxist-Leninist view of the woman question. In its loyalty to Marxism, the CPC resembled the SPC and SDPC, but the Communist Party gave more emphasis to Marx's work, and especially to Frederick Engels's *Origin of the Family, Private Property and the State*, and it added crucial lessons from Lenin.

Marx's writings specifically on women are not substantial; his major legacies to later socialists were his discussion of the sexual division of labour and his materialist analysis of woman's status in society and her role in the changing forces of economic production. Marx attributed woman's inferior status primarily to the class system, though he emphasized the very antithetical experiences of bourgeois and working-class women. Professing disdain for the "corrupt and rotten bourgeois morality"[8] of the bourgeois family, Marx nonetheless decried the assault on the more idealized working-class family by industrial capitalism. In his polemical writing, Marx waxed indignant on the toll factory work took on the family. Yet, fundamental to Marx's analysis, and crucial to the Communists' reading of Marx, was his contention that woman's entry into wage labour held out the possibility of transforming woman's role in society and emancipating her through involvement in the class struggle.

Marx's ideas on the family were later expanded by his colleague, Frederick Engels, in *Origin of the Family, Private Property and the State*, a book that became the cornerstone of the CPC's educational work on the woman question. First published in 1884, *Origin of the Family* challenged prevailing Victorian and Christian ideas by arguing that the family was not an unchanging, "natural" institution, but that, rather, it had evolved historically in response to the way people earned their livelihood. Engels made extensive use of anthropological work, which suggested that matriarchal societies had preceded patriarchal ones. The emergence of private property, he argued, led to monogamous marriages in which men could identify their children and pass on property to them, producing a patriarchal society in which women were sexually subject to men. Unable to escape his Victorian context, Engels criticized and then excused monogamy. Poten-

tially, he said, monogamy was a positive advance, which introduced the modern possibility of "individual sex love."[9] Women's
subjection, therefore, was not intrinsically linked to monogamy,
only to monogamy as it existed in capitalist society. Finally,
Engels, too, stressed that women's entrance into the work force
provided the conditions for women's participation in the class
struggle and, thus, for their eventual freedom.

In the nineteenth century, Engels's analysis represented an important liberation from previous theories of gender inequality, for
it saw women's oppression as a consequence of historical forces
rather than biology. Contemporary critics, however, have questioned his use of anthropological sources and his imprecise discussion of the family and the sexual division of labour. Recently,
socialist-feminists have extended his analysis of monogamy and
domestic labour much further.[10] Whatever the criticisms of
Engels – and there are many valid ones – the fact of his extensive
influence remains. For Canadian Communists, Engels's work
spawned a number of significant maxims. First, women's oppression was directly related to the system of private property and
could only be addressed with the abolition of capitalism. Second,
women's involvement in productive labour outside the family was
an essential step toward their participation in the class struggle.
Lastly, Engels's work implied that, with the end of capitalism,
the preconditions for new sexual and family relationships were
established: monogamy could find a more equal, loving form in
the Communist future.

Engels's conclusions formed an important part of August Bebel's *Woman Under Socialism*, a book used, especially in the
1920's, in the Communist Party's educational work. Bebel's writing appealed not necessarily because of its original argument but
because it synthesized information on working-class women and
socialist ideas in a readable, sometimes inspiring manner. Bebel,
for instance, reiterated Engels's thesis regarding the supplanting
of matriarchy with the rise of private property, dramatically declaring that "woman was the first human being that tasted bon-
dage, woman was a slave before the slave existed."[11] Like Marx,
Bebel stressed the irreconcilable differences between bourgeois
and working-class women, and he decried the exploitation of
women wage-earners and the destruction of the family. For Communist readers, Bebel reaffirmed the tenet that the woman question was inseparable from the question of capitalism and that
"only in connection with each other can the two reach final

solution."[12] Moreover, Bebel's conclusions about the bourgeois basis of the feminist movement substantiated the idea that a revolutionary working-class women's movement was the only true vehicle for women's emancipation.

The latter conclusion was central to Lenin's writing on the woman question, which became a significant influence on Canadian Communists' strategic deliberations. Women's emancipation, Lenin emphasized in the Marxist tradition, was possible only with the abolition of private property. Leadership for the women's movement, he further argued, must come from *inside* the Communist Party, not from separate, possibly "bourgeois" women's organizations. The Communist Party, Lenin explained frankly to German socialist Clara Zetkin, saw the organization of women as an expedient means of furthering the revolution: "we must have . . . committees, sections or whatever . . . with the specific purposes of rousing the broad masses of women, bringing them into contact with the Party and keeping them under its influence. . . . This is . . . a practical revolutionary *expediency*."[13]

Lenin's advocacy of separate agitational work among women also emanated from his belief that women, isolated amidst domestic drudgery, were more politically "backward"[14] than men. Although this derogatory view of women was quite common among socialists, Lenin at least emphasized the necessity of relieving women of their confining domestic labour and of eradicating "male supremacy" from within the Communist movement. Overall, however, Lenin's definition of the woman question remained an economistic one. On questions of sexuality and marriage, his views were circumscribed, in part, by the prudery of his times. He was contemptuous of the sexual double standard but also scathing in his rejection of demands for "free love." (He chastised his own mistress, Innessa Armand, for her advocacy of free love, saying the idea was "bourgeois and decadent!"[15]) His hostility to Alexandra Kollantai's writing on marriage revealed, at heart, a lack of sympathy for any questions relating to women's sexual oppression by men.

Lenin's approach to the woman question was an amalgam of established Marxist principles, Marxism altered by cultural influences, and sheer political pragmatism. His views reaffirmed the Marxist emphasis on the primacy of class struggle, the dangers of bourgeois feminism, and the importance of women's participation in wage labour. Finely attuned to the Russian situation, his prescriptions for organizing women stressed the need for a

working-class women's movement, guided absolutely by the vanguard Communist Party. Lenin sometimes indicated that other
Communist parties should use pragmatic flexibility in applying
Bolshevik principles to political organizing. In Canada, Leninist
theory was, to a limited extent, modified by the historical development of the Communist Party. Yet, the Canadian Party also
repeated Leninist directions verbatim and labelled these the ''correct'' methods of organizing. The appropriateness of Leninism
for Canadian conditions was never questioned, nor was its economistic framework ever challenged. The limits put on women's
self-organization, in Lenin's insistence that women be guided by
the Communist Party, meant that women were never architects
of their own liberation; they were always directed by the agenda
of a male-dominated Party leadership. Finally, as the Communist
Party evolved, Leninism was used not simply as a political strategy in itself, but as an effective means of implementing advice
from the Communist International, which came to reflect, first
and foremost, Stalin's political priorities.

### Social Democrats Explore the Woman Question

While the Communist Party's interpretation of the woman question paid homage to Marx, Engels, and Lenin, the CCF's diverse
theoretical ancestry included labourism, agrarian radicalism,
Marxism, Fabianism, and Christian and utopian socialism. In the
pre-war socialist movement, labourism had constituted an influential current, peopled especially by British working-class immigrants and trade unionists who embraced various political
traditions, including Christian socialism and British ''Lib-Lab-
ism.'' Labourism, argues Craig Heron, was a somewhat ''diffuse,
unsystematic'' ideology, but one that did have an anti-monopoly
critique of capitalism and a democratic, egalitarian view of good
government.[16] Labourites were class-conscious but less hostile to
the state than Marxists, and hence they placed their hopes in the
gradual process of electoral change, usually through the local
Labour Party or ILP (Independent Labour Party).

   Women labourites shared this class-conscious and reform-minded
critique of capitalism and often wedded it to a maternal feminist
argument that understood women's domestic role to be the key
rationale for their political participation. With middle-class feminists, labourite women made common cause on issues like mothers' allowances, but labour women's strong working-class

perspective and links to the trade union movement also separated them from these liberal feminists. Like the SDPC, local labour parties often spawned women's auxiliaries or, later, Women's Labor Leagues, which acted as support troops for the larger labour movement. Though labourite women appeared less concerned than Marxist parties with the theoretical debate over the woman question, they were still active in the front lines of day-to-day organizing, aiding women workers trying to unionize and working-class housewives battling to defend their families' standard of living.[17]

Like labourites, radical farmers brought to the CCF a belief in the efficacy of peaceful, parliamentary change, as well as established traditions of autonomous women's farm organizations. Expressing feelings of western exploitation and distrust of monopoly capitalism and of the two old-line parties, agrarian radicals in the CCF had some affinity with the earlier Progressive movement. Women in the pre-war Progressive farm movement had been strong advocates of women's self-organization and female suffrage, and, like many urban, middle-class feminists, in their campaign for the vote they often invoked arguments of women's higher moral calling, domestic duties, and the need to preserve Anglo-Saxon traditions. Nonetheless, they had eschewed absolute alliances either with urban feminists, who were sometimes viewed warily as women with "business" sympathies, or with labour women, who might be perceived as radical socialists. In the twenties and thirties, farm women's organizations regrouped and each province developed its own traditions of women's political activism and self-organization; in Saskatchewan, many women eventually joined the larger United Farmers of Canada, while in Manitoba and Alberta, distinct women's organizations were affiliated to the United Farmers movement. It is important to remember that farm women remained only potential recruits to the CCF, and in the 1930's only a radical minority of the organized rural women actually joined the party.

Agrarian radicals who did join the CCF believed, just as the earlier Progressives had, that the economic exploitation of both men and women rural producers by the banks and big business lay at the heart of the rural crisis. As Irene Parlby had succinctly put it, "tariffs, not men"[18] were the problem for farm women. At the same time, farm women, who experienced common hardships, especially in the domestic sphere, exhibited strong gender, as well as class, loyalties.[19] Moreover, male spokespersons for the radical agrarian current in the CCF pointed to a suitable "separate sphere" for farm women, in part a reflection of the persisting sexual division of labour found in farm families. These ideas were well illustrated in William Irvine's *The Farmers in Politics*, a book used in CCF educational work. Irvine echoed the view that economic conflict and injustice lay at the root of farm women's problems, but he added that women, because of their idealistic, spiritual nature, tended to "approach political problems from a different angle."[20] For instance, women's maternal concerns engendered a strong loyalty to the home, encouraging them to concentrate on questions relating to the young, such as education. While this idea of separate spheres obviously limited the role of women in the larger farm organizations, it did accord them a place as "junior partners"[21] in the agrarian movement and justified the existence either of their own organizations or of assured places in the larger farm movement, which women then used to address their female concerns, needs, and, sometimes, their feelings of subordination.

Influential within both agrarian radicalism and labourism was the philosophy of Christian socialism, a tradition of major importance to the CCF. The roots of Christian socialism were found in the pre-war Social Gospel movement, described by Richard Allen as an attempt to move beyond individual salvation and apply Christian principles to the reform of society. As the Social Gospel movement began to disintegrate in the 1920's, its most radical strain persisted as Christian socialism, which increasingly embraced secular politics rather than the organized church as the means to realize the Kingdom of God on earth.[22]

While secular by definition, socialism for Christian CCFers was still a religious ideal. As CCFer Rev. Salem Bland argued in *The New Christianity*, the capitalist system had to be transformed for it was essentially "rapacious and heartless" and the antithesis of "the Golden Rule . . . and Christian Brotherhood."[23] In the 1930's strong echoes of *The New Christianity* were found in the publications of the Fellowship for a Christian Social Order (FCSO), an organization of ministers and lay people whose aim was to transform "a capitalist system . . . fundamentally at variance with Christian principles."[24] The FCSO traded leaders and ideas with the early CCF and gave direct aid to the party's youth wing, the Co-operative Commonwealth Youth Movement (CCYM). These Christian socialists imparted a moral and ethical discourse of considerable strength to the CCF. While they usually rejected a

Marxist analysis and revolutionary methods, Christian socialists could also be quite critical of piecemeal change, for their vision of the New Jerusalem encompassed an absolute and total regeneration of society on moral terms.

Although Christian socialists nominally supported the idea of egalitarian social relations, they were not especially interested in exploring the origins and nature of women's oppression. Except for a few radicals like Nellie McClung, Social Gospellers had tended to overlook power relations between the sexes, stressing instead principles of human co-operation and the "Brotherhood of Man." The Social Gospel tradition for the most part embraced a traditional view of womanhood: women may have been spiritually equal before God, but on earth they were relegated to a separate sphere shaped by their roles as mothers, wives, and charity workers.[25] In the 1920's and 1930's, a younger generation of Christian socialists in such organizations as the Student Christian Movement and FCSO became more conscious of the need to democratize gender relations. Buoyed by their wartime leadership in the student movement and by women's new legal rights, women began to take more prominent roles in progressive Christian organizations.[26] By the 1930's, therefore, the Social Gospel's idea of woman's separate maternal sphere was to some extent modified and expanded by an emphasis on the egalitarian Brotherhood of Man.

Co-operation and brotherhood were themes in the utopian socialist tradition, also an influence on the early CCF. CCF reading lists included books on Owenism and many party members were deeply influenced by Bellamy's classic utopian novel, *Looking Backward*. The primary appeals of Bellamy were his moral critique of capitalism and his faith in rational, co-operative, and peaceful change. The greed and inefficiency of capitalism, Bellamy emphasized, had not been abolished by revolution, but rather by humanity's awareness of an impending crisis and its co-operative efforts to create a planned, efficient society. In Bellamy's utopia, women are "separate but equal" citizens: they work in the public sphere but perform jobs suitable to their weaker physical abilities, and their highest calling and career is still motherhood. Despite his more radical pleas for women's economic independence and the socialization of housework, Bellamy tried to assure his reader that relations between the sexes would not be adversely altered under socialism, for romantic marriage and the nuclear family could remain sacred. Many CCF women found Bellamy's support for women's economic equality and right to work inspiring. But this feminist impulse in *Looking Backward* was offset by Bellamy's more traditional, Victorian ideas, exalting woman's moral and maternal character and offering her a corollary separate sphere of activity.

The CCF was also influenced by British Fabianism, which, like Bellamy, promoted a brand of socialism stressing efficient and centralized state planning. Fabian ideas in Canada were most strongly represented in the League for Social Reconstruction (LSR), a depression-born association of intellectuals that attempted an educational campaign against the inequalities and inefficiencies of monopoly capitalism. Although references to the LSR as the sole "brain trust" of the CCF may be exaggerated, its influence was considerable.[27] The political world view of the LSR's professional and professorial constituency was articulated in *Social Planning for Canada*, the LSR book that became an essential part of CCF educational offerings in the 1930's. *Social Planning* provided both a rational indictment and moral censure of the wasteful and inhumane capitalist system; the solution, it went on, was cooperative ownership and state planning, to be effected by peaceful, parliamentary change. Like the British Fabians, the LSR put much stock in centralization and social engineering – an emphasis on expertise and leadership values that may have militated against a sympathy for feminist ideas. Indeed, a major concern with women's oppression was never a central part of the Fabian tradition. Some CCF women in the 1930's and 1940's, argues Susan Walsh, were influenced by George Bernard Shaw's *An Intelligent Woman's Guide to Socialism*, especially its critique of prejudice against women in public life. But as Walsh points out, Shaw, like Bellamy, never questioned that women's "primary" role was motherhood.[28]

Other early British Fabians, such as Beatrice Webb, had been positively disinterested in the "less intellectually prestigious"[29] question of women's inequality. With the founding in 1908 of the socialist-feminist Fabian Women's Group, some of this ambivalence was challenged. But in the wake of World War One, this group curtailed its activities. Perhaps this was one reason its influence was not apparent in the Canadian LSR. Some important LSR research did document women's economic exploitation, but the League did not delve deeply into the questions of gender inequality or women's role in the socialist movement. It is important to concede, of course, that women in the LSR were a minority within a small organization. Thus, women's small numbers, as well as the absence of Fabian feminist mentors, and perhaps, in some cases, their own successful careers, all militated against the LSR's exploration of the woman question.

Some LSR intellectuals incorporated Marxist ideas into their eclectic reform philosophy, but Marxism in itself was also an important influence on the CCF. Remnants of the older SPC became a vocal minority within the party in urban Ontario and B.C. in particular. Their view of the woman question, not dissimilar to that of the earlier Marxist socialist parties, emphasized the economic exploitation of women, the primacy of class action, and the need to organize women as wage-earners. There is little evidence, however, that they saw the woman question of critical importance, in theory or in practice. There were few concerted attempts by SPCers in the 1920's to organize women socialists, though by the 1930's Marxists in the SPC and CCF came to accept autonomous women's organizations. In short, the Marxist tradition brought to the CCF a sharp awareness of women's economic exploitation, but it did not yield a strong, consistent reflection on the theory of women's oppression or a solid practice of women's self-organization.

### Conclusion

The formation of the Communist Party of Canada and later the CCF offered Canadians two new paths to socialism, the first stressing Marxism and connection to the Russian Revolution, the second an eclectic alliance of utopian ideals and pragmatic social democratic traditions. Both parties inherited traditions of theory and practice that shaped their understanding of women's social role and women's oppression. Marxist and Leninist theory and, ultimately, guidance from the first "Marxist" experiment, the Soviet Union, informed the Communists' views of gender inequality. Both these influences emphasized the imperative of a revolutionary transformation of society to achieve meaningful equality for women. Since women's oppression was an outgrowth of capitalist social relations, women's redemption could only come through their entry into social production, their participation in the class struggle, and, eventually, the destruction of a class system. Moreover, women's struggles had to be located within the larger working-class movement, always guided by the "correct" leadership of the Communist Party.

The CCF inherited a number of intellectual traditions, which produced a less clear-cut – even contradictory – understanding of women's oppression. Marxists in the party, for instance, had a heightened awareness of women's economic exploitation but felt some antipathy to separate women's organizations; yet, such organizations were already a firm part of the labourite and agrarian traditions. This eclectic socialism of the CCF may not have produced a coherent ''theory'' of women's oppression; but the party did inherit some tried-and-true strategies for organizing women, including semi-autonomous women's groups. Despite this acceptance of women's self-organization, as well as agreement that women were set apart by their moral and maternal character, the CCF, like the Communists, did not believe that women were oppressed by men but rather by an economic system that brought in its wake women's subordination. Thus, for both parties, only solidarity between the sexes could usher in women's emancipation.

Importantly, neither the CCF nor the CPC remained rigidly bound to these inherited traditions. During the next decades, Communists' and socialists' treatment of the woman question was also shaped by changing international influences, the norms and values of Canadian society, and the organized actions of women within both parties. In its first decade of existence, the CPC paid most attention not to Marxist theory but to the directives of thè politically minded Communist International, while the early CCF, despite its lack of interest in the woman question, was forced by feminists within its ranks to address some crucial questions of gender inequality.

# The Communist Party Confronts the Woman Question

The initial platform proclaimed by the nascent Communist Party of Canada in 1922 made no specific mention of gender inequality or woman's role in the revolutionary movement. Within two years, however, the Communist Party of Canada (CPC) had altered this oversight by setting up a Women's Department and spearheading the formation of a national organization for working-class women, the Women's Labor League (WLL). The Communist Party's approach to the woman question was conditioned primarily by its response to the advice of the Communist International, or Comintern, and secondly, by the Party's own analysis of the needs of working-class women. In the last resort, the advice of Soviet Communists was refracted through the prism of local traditions, ideas, and realities. While the CPC's ethnic complexion and its emphasis on a class analysis of women's oppression signified continuity with the pre-war socialist movement, Communists also sought to transcend their past, embracing a new social and sexual order that included the emancipation of women. And although the CPC remained a weak force within Canadian political life of the 1920's, its agitational work on women's issues did mark out new parameters of thought and action for Canadian socialism.

Admittedly, the woman question never became a central priority for the Communist Party, a consequence of internal Party failings and external social pressures. Despite the Communists' connection to the "successful" Russian revolution, their vision of a new order for women remained marginal – even within their own movement. Although many noble convention resolutions declared the need to organize women, the Party itself mirrored some of the formidable structures of inequality and oppression facing women in wider Canadian society.

### International Advice and Canadian Responses

During the twenties, the influence of the Comintern on the Canadian Communist Party in regard to the woman question was very powerful, in part because the International was generally the guiding influence on its member parties, but additionally because reforms within Russian society appeared to herald major, inspiring advances toward women's emancipation. Soviet women were accorded political equality, registration of civil marriage was instituted, abortions legalized, and a new family law code established women's equal status in marriage. In 1919, the Soviet Communist Party set up the Zhenotdel, a women's section that attempted educational work – everything from literacy classes to conferences for working women – to draw women into political activity. The barriers to its work were immense: Zhenotdel workers had to contend with the economic chaos and poverty of post-revolutionary Russia; male hostility, even from within Communist circles, to women's political activism; and firmly entrenched cultural barriers to women's emancipation, especially in the peasant villages and in the Muslim East. Despite these obstacles, the Zhenotdel waged a highly successful educational campaign, "achieving in its work, a major impact on Soviet society, especially in the cities."[1] Contemporary Bolshevik leaders, however, became increasingly alarmed at the Zhenotdel's "feminist tendencies" and in 1929, when the Central Committee Secretariat of the Party was reorganized, the Zhenotdel was effectively eliminated. Its demise, of course, was linked to the triumph of Stalinism and the liquidation of any organizations that might threaten the centralized party-state.

To North American Marxists and even to some socialists and liberals, who had been concerned primarily with transforming the productive process and according women political equality, the Russian example initially appeared to be a beacon of hope. Within the Canadian Communist Party the Russian reforms stimulated new discussion of gender inequality and the organization of working women. From *The Communist International* and *Imprecorr*, Canadian Communist leaders gleaned information on Zhenotdel activities, conferences, theses, and Bolshevik resolutions on the mobilization of women. Directives from the International Women's Secretariat of the Communist International urged the establishment of a Communist women's organization in Canada, and

Soviet reforms in marriage, divorce, and abortion laws fostered similar debates in Canada, opening up women's issues that had rarely been discussed by the pre-war socialist movement and, indeed, were rarely discussed in the subsequent history of the Communist Party.

The recommendations for the organization of women made by the International Women's Secretariat essentially represented traditions already part of the Canadian left: the unionization of wage-earning women and the establishment of support groups for working-class housewives. After the Party decided to work openly in 1922, a Women's Department was set up to co-ordinate these activities. The first director, Florence Custance, remains a vaguely defined figure in Communist history, in part due to her early death in 1929. Born in England and trained as a school teacher, Custance emigrated to Canada with her husband, a carpenter, and she became involved in the labour movement as a leader of the Amalgamated Carpenters of Canada Wives Auxiliary. By the time of World War One she was deeply involved in the Socialist Party of North America, and in 1919 she was a participant in the secret Guelph Convention that established the CPC. In the 1920's she occupied strategically important Party positions and headed the Canadian Friends of Soviet Russia. A somewhat reserved intellectual rather than an "agitational" leader, Custance also became the driving force behind the organization of the Communist women's movement. In May of 1922, shortly before she left for the fourth Comintern Congress in Moscow, Custance's Women's Department announced its existence with a public meeting attended by about 200. *The Worker* sporadically carried news of the Women's Department until a regular women's column, co-ordinated by Custance and entitled "The Working Women's Section," began to give more frequent coverage to the woman question. Finally, in 1926, Custance initiated *The Woman Worker*, a separate newspaper written by and for the Women's Labor Leagues.

Following repeated directives of the International to set up a working-class women's organization to be guided by the Party, Custance turned her energies also to the Women's Labor Leagues (WLLs). The Labor Leagues followed in the tradition of the pre-war SDPC Finnish sewing circles and took their name directly from existing WLLs, which had been established as adjuncts to labour parties and socialist groups, sometimes with links to the trade union movement.[2] Gradually, Custance and other Communist

*Designed by a Finnish* WLL *correspondent, the cover of* The Woman Worker *depicted a woman holding a book, symbolizing Knowledge, and a flame, representing Enlightenment: both were necessary "to help working women in their struggle and problems of life."*

women began to join and form their own WLLs, and in 1924 a federal WLL apparatus for the growing movement was established at a conference in London, following that year's Trades and Labour Congress convention. Elected national secretary at that conference, Custance announced that the leagues would enjoy some local autonomy, although they would be guided by the general goals of the larger Federation of WLLs.

Much to its chagrin, the federation was denied formal affiliation to the TLC, supposedly because its members, as housewives, were not "producers." Custance drew strong applause from women delegates when she retorted that male trade unionists "lived in the Middle Ages" and should "wake up" to the fact that WLL members "are women who cook, sew, wash, scrub, and who perform duties necessary to the whole process of production."[3] The presence of Communists like Custance on the WLL executive, however, was likely the true reason for some TLC members' hostility to the leagues. Rejection of the WLLs by the TLC was a disappointing setback for Custance, for affiliation had been part of the Party's larger United Front scheme to work within and influence the labour movement. At the local level, some WLLs had more success with this strategy. In 1924, for example, the Toronto WLL affiliated with the Toronto and District Labour Council, and over the next three years it earned praise from trade union men. But in 1927 this amiable relationship ended abruptly with the WLL's expulsion from the Council. A campaign against the league was led by socialist Jimmy Simpson, who had heartily endorsed the WLL in 1924 but now objected to its Communist membership.[4]

The Women's Labor Leagues, like the larger CPC, also tried to play a role in the young Canadian Labor Party (CLP). In the early 1920's labourites participated in some local WLLs and contributed to *The Woman Worker*. WLLs in turn attended Labor Party conventions and successfully lobbied for resolutions on issues like "no cadet training in the schools," which most socialists and labourites alike supported. Only in 1927, however, were Communists able to dominate the resolutions agenda, and this was a shallow victory, as labourites had decided to abandon the CLP, leaving Communists to occupy its shell. In the West, the WLLs also participated in the Western Women's Social and Economic Conferences, initiated by labourite Beatrice Brigden in 1924. In the first few years, the WLLs easily carried motions from their own program, such as demands for better minimum wage laws. But by the late 1920's, Communist women became increasingly disturbed by the Conference's reformist viewpoint and its paternalistic concentration on issues like sterilization of the "feeble-minded." Unable to mould a majority that was Marxist and Communist in outlook, the WLLs eventually withdrew from active participation.

By 1927, the WLLs had become predominantly Communist in outlook. Only a minority of WLL women were Party members, but most were willing to accept political guidance from the CPC's Women's Department. As the number of Labor Leagues grew to thiry-seven at the end of 1927, they also came to reflect the ethnic strengths of the Communist Party, with Finnish leagues outnumbering the English-speaking ones. Jewish, Ukrainian, and Finnish women were also organized through their respective ethnic organizations: the Jewish Labor League, the Finnish Organization of Canada, and the Ukrainian Labour-Farmer Temple Association. Finnish and Jewish women, however, participated in Labor Leagues that were loosely, sometimes closely, linked to the Party's Women's Department. Ukrainian women, on the other hand, belonged to the Women's Section of the ULFTA, answered to ULFTA's Central Committee, and usually had less contact with the English WLLs.

### Organizing Women Workers

Whatever the organizational differences based on ethnicity, there was basic agreement on the overall perception of the woman question. Capitalism, emphasized the first WLL constitution, had created two kinds of labour: "household drudgery and wage labour . . . both of which were essential to the maintenance of capitalism."[5] Revolutionaries, Custance argued, must therefore fight for women's right to organize and for equal pay, as well as for the protection of mothers and children. Moreover, "working class women must struggle for equality along with men of their own class, refusing to be used as scabs or wage-reducers" and unswayed by the false arguments of the feminist movement. Sex, it was stressed, was "a minor question compared to the class struggle . . . we must first take up the struggle against capitalist tyranny which keeps our husbands chained to uncertainty and us to worry and desperation . . . and our children to want."[6]

Throughout the 1920's these basic tenets – the economic exploitation of women and the imperative of unified revolutionary action – were stressed again and again. Pre-war socialist parties had taken a similar approach, but the Communist Party was distinguished by its new emphasis on the woman question and by a measure of sympathy for women's *particular* oppression within capitalism. *Worker* articles, for instance, emphasized the necessity of bringing the "most oppressed" group – women – into revolutionary politics, to help them "work out their own emancipation."[7] *The Woman Worker*, unabashedly political, proclaimed its intention to forgo all the traditional "fashions, recipes and sickly love stories" of other women's papers. It kept its promise and concentrated on women's struggle for "equal duties and rights with men" as well as women's specific "fight against customs, traditions, and superstitions which have kept them chained to passive roles and conservatism."[8]

The WLLs were the centerpiece of the Communist Party's attempts to put its theory on the woman question into practice and were intended to join together women in the home and women in the work force, a task the Party immediately found problematic. Young and/or single women cadres, with their greater freedom to travel, were more likely to be active as organizers for the Young Communist League (YCL) or as industrial agitators, while it was the married "Party wives," tied closely to home and family, who concentrated on the support work associated with the WLLs. The Labor Leagues, explained one Finnish woman, were made up of women like her mother who "mainly did fund-raising and social affairs" along with an "important attempt at political education."[9] That "The WLLs were for the housewives, not the women in the factories"[10] became the common perception. Ironically, in keeping with predominant social norms, many homemakers might be charged, especially in the absence of their travelling revolutionary husbands, with the difficult tasks of feeding and clothing the family, but not with the task of political and labour organizing. In Britain, one historian argues, a very sharp separation existed between the "cadres" and the "Party wives," with the latter held in some contempt by the former.[11] In contrast, the Canadian WLLs occasionally did draw both groups together, but even though the two groups were not hostile, differences *did* exist. And clearly, the Party lamented the housewife composition of the WLLs, for according to advice from Moscow, as well as traditional Marxist thinking, the mobilization of wage-earning women should have priority.

To facilitate this work with wage-earning women, the CPC's Women's Department studied the economic, legal, and social status of working women and published its findings in the foundling WLL leaflet. The vast majority of wage-earners, the WLL document declared, laboured in unskilled jobs, often without even the protection of the minimum wage. Low wages, long hours, and unsafe working conditions were convincing indications of the necessity to unionize these women: a Comintern directive was hardly needed to encourage revolutionaries' disgust with the lot of Canadian women workers.

Desperate working conditions, however, do not necessarily make unionization an easy prospect. Custance believed there were four substantial obstacles to the Party's work with wage-earning women, including the influence of religious, social, and pacifist organizations like the YWCA, which "pose as protectors of the working girls"; the organized welfare programs of factories; to a certain extent the misleading protection of the minimum wage laws; and, lastly, the fact that "women do not take wage-earning seriously" but see it as a "temporary necessity" before marriage.[12] Whatever the presumed consciousness of working women, the structural realities of their work lives – seasonal and unskilled work, small workplaces, and a high turnover – did mitigate against their organization. Furthermore, women could draw little aid from the established trade union movement, for the conservative TLC, weakened by the 1921-22 depression, membership losses, and employer overtures and offensives, had little or no time for the concerns of working women.

The Party's initial trade union strategies, however, also tended to exclude women. In the early 1920's the Red International of Labor Unions (RILU), a Comintern organization, urged its member parties to work within established trade unions. Women's marginal status in the union movement meant that they were easily by-passed by these strategies, which concentrated on areas of established radical support, such as mining and lumbering. Other suggestions for organizing wage-earning women were similarly inappropriate: the Comintern's repeated advice to initiate "mass delegate meetings from the factory nuclei"[13] of activist women belied the Canadian reality of an extremely weak radical presence in most women's workplaces. Finally, organizing new locals of unions was a time-consuming and expensive enterprise that the small, poorly funded Women's Department was ill-equipped to pursue on its own. Ultimately, if the wage-earning woman failed to take herself seriously, so, too, did the CPC. In its self-criticism, the Party openly admitted its efforts with working women were lacking: "the material at the disposal of the Party to carry on this," reported Custance in 1927, "has been up to the present limited and weak. Therefore, much that could have been done, has been left undone."[14]

Despite these failures, the Women's Department did give attention to the plight of working women in its own press. The "Working Women's Section" and later *The Woman Worker* abounded with personal and second-hand descriptions of the day-to-day existence of working girls and women, often followed by an analysis of women's wage labour under capitalism written by Custance or perhaps by Becky Buhay, a young organizer fast growing into a Party leader. The problems of working women were also debated in *Kamf*, *Vaupaus*, and *Robitnysia*. The *Kamf*'s Women's Section, for example, printed the tale of a Jewish garment worker describing the speed-up and unhealthy conditions in her Montreal factory. In reply, Buhay pointed out that terrible conditions could only be effectively combatted with a union, and that the "false consciousness" of the author's fellow French-Canadian workers should be faced squarely with gentle reprimands for their frivolous ways. Sometimes advice like this lectured working women, telling them, for instance, to eschew "charm and personality" courses at the YWCA and "thoughts of catching Prince Charming" and instead to educate themselves to the class struggle.[15] Still, letters were not always greeted with paternalism; they were given encouraging, though simple advice: keep on fighting for your rights, organize a union, and find support in the revolutionary movement.

The Women's Department also developed a campaign to expose the violations and inadequacies of the minimum wage laws, thus "showing the ineffectiveness of government protection as compared with that of unions."[16] In the fall of 1924, for instance, the Toronto WLL pursued evidence that the Willard Chocolate Company, which had prosecuted girls for stealing fifty cents worth of candy, was falsifying its time cards and that the Minimum Wage Board had only taken steps when the workers secured a lawyer. Even then, the Board urged no publicity, supposedly for the sake of Willard's. This famous Chocolate case became a labour cause célèbre, but despite WLL and Labour Council pressure, public hearings did not produce a conclusive conviction of the employer. Nevertheless, the CPC continued to press home the message that the Minimum Wage Board was essentially afraid of business, and that the government was hardly a "neutral" body acting to protect women. The Women's Labor Leagues produced evidence at the annual Board hearing to show that the suggested "minimum" wage could barely support a working woman, and that it often became the "maximum" wage for women. Across Canada, newly organized WLLs also took up cases of minimum wage abuse; the campaign was visible in Vancouver, Montreal, Winnipeg, and Regina, where an Employed Girls Council, initiated by the WLL, had some small successes in pressuring the government to close loopholes in the legislation. Florence Custance played a pivotal role in the Ontario effort, making useful alliances with local Labour Councils and the Canadian Labor Party. Her effort even earned her praise from the labourite paper, *The People's Cause*, which commended Custance's stubborn persistence in tracking down employers who were ducking the law.[17]

Finally, in the later 1920's, a few WLLs were also able to spark the creation of social and support groups for young working women. In such cities as Sudbury and Toronto, for instance, Finnish Communists established organizations for Finnish maids. Though not officially trade unions, these organizations did aim to improve the work lives of domestics, while also offering social and recreational activities. Once an economic downturn set in, they tried to prevent "unscrupulous" employment agents such as an infamous Lutheran minister in Toronto, from taking advantage of unemployed Finnish women by offering them jobs at low wages. "Maids," cried out one circular in *Vapaus*, "join the membership of Finnish maids organization, where you have no bosses, no clerical hirelings, only yourselves . . . we will strengthen our mutual enterprises and act for our education, and amusement too."[18]

### Organizing Housewives

The second aim of the CPC's Women's Department was to mobilize women in the home by setting up housewives' auxiliaries that would aid men's struggles and concurrently develop women's revolutionary consciousness. Communists strongly believed that working-class women were a conservative influence on their families; like Lenin, they saw women, isolated amidst domestic drudgery, as easy prey for the illusory myths of a capitalist society. "Women," wrote Custance in a Women's Department report, "are almost entirely under capitalist class influence, through the church and the newspapers."[19] Nowhere was this more boldly stated than in the Ukrainian press, which claimed that women

were poorly educated, sometimes illiterate, their class consciousness low, and their knowledge of politics in general and Marxism
in particular almost non-existent. Indeed, ULFTA set up a separate
newspaper for women, *Robitnysia* (*The Working Woman*), specifically as an educational tool to "bring women up to the level
of men." Unlike the Finnish or English Communist papers, *Robitnysia* saw illiteracy as a major obstacle in its work among women,
indicating that Ukrainian women did have more serious barriers
to political involvement than many other Party women. *Robitnysia*
was concerned not only with teaching women to read, and the
fundamentals of Marx, but also with basic scientific education.
A popular science section including articles such as "Charles
Darwin" and "Where Did Man Come From?" was designed to
wean women away from superstitious and religious interpretations
of natural phenomena.

Communists were especially concerned that wives of trade
unionists be made sympathetic and active supporters of their husbands in struggle, for "women can determine the fate of a strike,
make, or mar men's morale."[20] While the Party recognized the
essential role that women played in labour struggles, it also projected a simplified view of working-class women that placed women
at polar ends of the political spectrum. Women were supposedly
suspicious of social change and socialism, but when their revolutionary consciousness was raised they became militant fighters,
even more militant than men. "Will women speed the liberation
of society or be the bulwark of reaction?"[21] was the classic question asked by the Communist press. As Dorothy Smith notes,
"working-class women are portrayed either as 'backward' or as
salt of the earth heroic figures; both are polar positions along a
single dimension."[22]

How do we explain this extremely prevalent view of women's
"innate" conservatism? It is possible, first, that women's apathy
or cynicism was interpreted as conservatism or, second, that this
view of women as "backward" was simply the product of strong
male prejudices that female Party leaders, such as Becky Buhay,
were not hesitant to criticize. Ukrainians, she once charged, "have
the old peasant attitudes on this question [of women]. . . . They
say a woman talks too much and can't be trusted. . . . In Lethbridge . . . they even suspended a woman from the meetings."[23]

At the same time, it is possible that women were less interested
in politics because of the material realities of their lives and the
powerful ideological message that women "belonged in the home."

If Ukrainian women lacked the opportunity to learn how to read, if Jewish women were shut out of union drives, if Finnish and English women were pressed to finish their domestic work in the home – by definition a never-ending job – then it is hardly surprising that they had little time for the Party.

Despite fears of female conservatism, women, it was believed, *could* be radicalized. Housewives were reminded of the limited material conditions of their lives, the drudgery of endless domestic labour, the meagre wages of their husbands, and the limited opportunities facing their children. In a short story published in *The Worker*, two working-class housewives talk over the fence about the effects of war and unemployment on their homes. The narrator's husband, a veteran, is unemployed: the "British Vampire," his wife explains, "took his best and left him no will to fight."[24] The story's final message is clear: the role of a housewife was to bind her husband and family together despite and against an unjust, exploitative capitalist society. Stories and poems, some of which were made into plays, were also found in *Robitnysia*, depicting arguments to drive home the realities of class and the need for homemakers to join in the fight against injustice. In one story a housewife demonstrates to her husband that his unwillingness to let her join a women's organization plays into the hands of the bosses; other stories portrayed the suffering of mothers who could not feed their children, whose sons were exhausted by work, or whose daughters had to resort to prostitution to make ends meet.

Communists assumed that women in the home did understand in a personal way the consequences of unemployment, low wages, and rising prices. Thus, the task of the Party was to "make the personal, political," and to this end, homemakers were frequently appealed to on consumer and peace issues. The Communist press reflected the prevailing notion that men were the breadwinners, while women supervised the family budget; rising consumer prices were therefore seized on as a potentially radical issue for homemakers. Similarly, articles on peace, which had a high profile in *The Woman Worker*, tried to personalize international issues by appealing to women on the basis of their maternal instincts. The peace appeal also attempted to expose war as a consequence of capitalist economics and imperialist expansion, but the materialist theme was intertwined with the maternal one. Not only will you lose your sons, these articles pointed out, but you will lose them in a war that will bring you hunger and capitalists greater profits.

While *The Woman Worker* urged its readers to reject the liberal pacifism represented by the United Nations Organization and the Women's International League for Peace and Freedom (WIL), it shared the WIL's emphasis on maternalism, though shaping it into a class-conscious mould. Associated with the anti-war cause was the campaign to remove military training from the schools, thereby eliminating the capitalist and militarist indoctrination of working-class youth. In keeping with United Front tactics, the WLLs tried to link forces with other reformers on this issue, and Custance attempted herself to run for the Toronto School Board, including ''no cadet training'' in her platform.[25]

As well as appealing to working-class women on issues of bread and peace, the Party encouraged women's active support for the labour struggles of their menfolk. Though women sometimes played a crucial role in strikes, it was difficult to sustain their involvement in ongoing political organizations, so *The Worker* and *The Woman Worker* used their columns to publicize numerous examples of wives' militancy, and to encourage their further political action. During a cross-country tour for *The Worker*, Becky Buhay found herself in the midst of a coal miners' strike in Alberta. She helped the wives organize a support group that clashed more than once with police. After the most violent exchange on the picket line, eighteen women were injured, one suffered a miscarriage, and many were jailed and sentenced on charges of rioting. *The Worker* followed their cases, which Buhay used as inspiring evidence that women, when aroused, could be excellent revolutionary fighters: ''the women's defiant attitude was the greatest surprise to the authorities who expected tears, supplications and general weakness, but they discovered before long that women were made of sterner stuff.''[26]

### The Family and Reproductive Rights

Although economic issues, especially the family wage and the workplace, were central to the Communist Party's approach to work among women, it did not totally ignore reproductive issues or women's subordination in the family. Some Party leaders, but particularly Custance, were aware of the important writings of Bolshevik Alexandra Kollantai on love, marriage, and the family, though Kollantai's ideas were probably reinterpreted or dismissed by the end of the decade, as she fell out of favour in Russia. In their discussion of women's role in the family, Canadian Communists wrestled with lingering patriarchal traditions and new revolutionary ideas. Working-class women were idealized and commended for their selfless devotion to home and motherhood, but Communists also criticized a society that tied women to "household drudgery" and argued that to be truly free, women had to be relieved of the degrading labour of "providing services to others, . . . living by the sufferance of one's husband."[27] "Complete freedom is impossible as long as men are the privileged sex," continued another article on this topic, and women were advised to "break through their bonds of timidity and through self assertion help to achieve their own emancipation."[28]

Canadian Communists were certainly sympathetic to Leninist conclusions about the need to liberate women from domestic toil, but it was never clear *how* that would happen. As late as 1925, after most Russian communal kitchens had closed, they were referred to positively in the Canadian Communist press. By the end of the decade, however, they were largely forgotten; the socialization of domestic labour never became a major point of discussion for the Party.

The CPC also wrestled with the issues of birth control and abortion. A call for mothers' clinics, which were to dispense birth control, was part of the first WLL platform, though Communists always carefully placed the demand for birth control within a class analysis, rejecting neo-Malthusian justifications for control of working-class births. Poverty, Florence Custance reminded her readers in *The Woman Worker*, was not due to the size of the population but to the distribution of wealth, and fewer births would not solve the poverty problem.[29] The Party's approach to reproductive issues was also influenced by the example of the U.S.S.R., which had legalized abortion and birth control to provide immediate economic and physiological relief for working-class women. Like the Soviets, the CPC stressed the health benefits to working-class wives, rather than presenting birth control as the inalienable right of every woman, though the latter view may have been held by some Communist women. Statistics showing maternal ill health and a high incidence of maternal and infant mortality, for example, were often used to buttress the WLL's arguments for mothers' clinics. Emma Goldman's more radical libertarian perspective on birth control was resolutely rejected; in 1927, her Canadian speeches on birth control were ignored by the Communist press. Rather, the Party promoted its own class analysis, which stressed the right of the working-class family to make their own decisions about family size, and working-class wives' need for relief from the physical burdens of constant childbearing.

While quite different from the contemporary feminist rationale for reproductive control, the Communist Party's support for mothers' clinics was still a small crack in the wall of silence existing in Canadian society in the 1920's. Unlike the United States, Canada had not yet produced a birth control movement of any substance, and given the persisting medical, clerical, and legal opposition to birth control, the subject was largely taboo. Despite the illegality of disseminating birth control information, women were eager, even desperate, to obtain this information, and abortion was sometimes attempted as the last resort in fertility control. Pressure from rank-and-file women was clearly one impetus to the Party's discussion of the subject. Immediately after an article on birth control appeared in *The Worker*, an Alberta comrade responded by insisting that birth control was "an essential information for working-class women in the here and now . . . an indispensable psychological aid to working-class marriage,"[30] and he urged the Party to devote more space to the subject. In the columns of *The Woman Worker* the issue was even more hotly debated, and Custance noted that concern with birth control was a major drawing card for women's interest in the WLLs.

Rank-and-file letters to *The Woman Worker* indicated the wide parameters the birth control debate assumed. In its first issue *The Woman Worker* reprinted a speech given to a Vancouver WLL, which took the radical line "that every woman should have the right to decide when to have children."[31] The subsequent responses of readers, however, revealed the persistence of more conservative eugenicist ideas within the WLLs, paralleling their strength in the wider society. One Toronto member challenged religious objections to birth control but then went on to argue for a "scientific view," saying "we can no longer breed numerically without thinking about intelligence and quality of offspring."[32] The most extreme eugenicist wrote in, warning that forcing women into childbearing might "breed race degeneracy." The writer drew proof for her contention from the "fact" that the "priest-ridden Poles, Slavs and Italians have weak and sickly children."[33] Although these views were printed in *The Woman Worker*, editorials tended to downplay eugenics, and they completely rejected any hint of neo-Malthusian support for birth control.

In terms of political action, some local WLLs pressed city governments for mothers' clinics and lobbied the Canadian Labour Party to place birth control in its platform. While the Labor Leagues were successful in making mothers' clinics part of the CLP policy, they were less successful in gaining wider public attention or government sympathy. Toronto League members described being literally "laughed at" by local government officials during one lobbying attempt; the issue, tersely commented a WLLer, "is not supported by the Establishment."[34] But even within the Party, there was some hesitancy to embrace the birth control cause. *Robitnysia* simply avoided the issue, and after the establishment of *The Woman Worker*, so, too, did *The Worker*. Though *The Worker* editors may have felt that birth control was a "woman's issue," this meant that there was little wider Party discussion and recognition of the seriousness of WLL demands for mother's clinics.

The issue of abortion was also dealt with by the Party, though in a secondary, quiet manner. Abortion, too, was analysed from a materialist perspective that stressed the immediate needs and social reality of working-class women. Readers were sometimes reminded of new access to abortion in the Soviet Union, and similar liberalization was recommended for Canada. But abortion was described as an unpleasant and unfortunate practice, resorted to only in capitalist societies or a Communist society in transition. The author of a rare article on abortion maintained that "we are for less and less abortions; they could be reduced to a minimum with birth control information made available."[35] Still, the writer continued, the laws should be reformed, for they were routinely disobeyed by doctors and women, to the danger of women's health and life. Although different in content from later feminist arguments stressing women's right to choose, the CPC's occasional calls for liberalization were very radical in a time when church, state, and the medical profession would barely countenance discussion of the topic. This intense opposition, along with the Party's own ambivalence, may be the reason that the year 1927 saw the last major discussion of abortion in the CPC press for many years.

### International Mentors and Local Opponents

Articles in the Communist press dealing with abortion, birth control, and women's role in the family often drew dramatic comparisons between the oppression of Canadian women and the constantly improving lives of Russian women. While the Communist press primarily pointed to women's equal political status and economic independence in the U.S.S.R., attention was also given to women's new sexual autonomy and the emergence of an egalitarian family life. Marriage laws, "no longer made only to benefit men," and the accessibility of divorce were destroying the patriarchal family, the press claimed. With the disappearance of sexual inequalities, the double standard, and economic dependence, Russian women were said to "feel like they are real human beings . . . equal to male workers."[36] Reports of Soviet life were especially vocal about the new Russian motherhood: "with the availability of birth control, aid to pregnant women and modern creches, we have abolished women's subordination," declared one optimistic author.[37]

It is difficult to assess how thoroughly these optimistic views of Soviet life were assimilated by Communist women. Certainly, leaders like Becky Buhay displayed an intense admiration for Soviet life, even in private letters written during her visits to the U.S.S.R.[38] Surely, however, romantic pronouncements on the U.S.S.R. also served to obscure the complexity of women's oppression and the extent to which it was embedded in both Russian and Canadian society. Of course, one-dimensional *Worker* articles may not have reflected Communists' private experience of altered sex roles and the family.

Within the Party, new forms of relationships and family arrangements were accepted, although only to a limited extent. In the pre-war socialist movement, Finnish women had turned a critical eye to marriage, and Finnish Communists were known to opt for common-law liaisons rather than legal marriages. They made a political point of rejecting Church-sanctioned relationships: "we didn't believe in that religious hocus pocus," remembers one Finnish comrade; "when we were married our friends gave us a party . . . or you might put an ad in the paper with our friends' greetings and congratulations."[39] As a result of such experimentation, some members must have experienced the difficulties of living out female "independence" in a sexist society. The rejection of traditional relationships potentially had a tragic side: dominant social norms in the 1920's still saw such relationships as immoral, and in their defiance of these norms women could be hurt.[40] Moreover, not all ethnic groups in the movement shared a positive view of sexual experimentation. The Ukrainian press had little sympathy for alternative relationships: the women's paper made it quite clear that one rationale for women's self-organization was the creation of "a new morality" to "root out habits of darkness . . . [including] promiscuity."[41]

Overall, information on women in the U.S.S.R. still had a substantial impact on Communist Party members, creating feelings of international solidarity and Party loyalty. Building on a long-established tradition of internationalism within the socialist movement, the CPC helped to galvanize anger about women's exploitation abroad, draw lessons about women's opposition to capitalism, and create hope and support for Communist movements of resistance. The struggles of Communist women in the Third World, the U.S., and Europe figured highly in the press: the stories of American textile workers battling southern police or of impoverished Chinese workers became rallying points for Communist loyalty, forging a definition of the movement as just, militant, and destined to victory.

In Canada, International Women's Day was used to enhance international solidarity and to publicize the struggles of Canadian women. In the 1920's this day became a major event, celebrated in public meetings that were themselves international in character, encompassing one, two, or three language groups. From small, towns like Blairmore, Alberta, to urban centres like Toronto, Finnish, Ukrainian, Jewish, and English women's groups created International Women's Day events that combined rousing political speeches, solidarity greetings, and musical entertainment. In Sudbury, reported one account, the "lady comrades worked ceaselessly on an inspirational program in English, Ukrainian and Finnish." The evening festival began with a march to the stage by the women comrades, showing "how women in a united mass step forward to demand their rights." Then the women sang "that ravishing workers song, the Internationale, in different languages," and there followed a program including Ukrainian mandolin orchestras, choirs, solos, Finnish poetry readings, and speeches given in each language,[42] detailing the rise of women in Russia and the women's movement in Canada. These meetings often publicized a list of women's demands coincident with the Party program, stressing the organization of women workers and the need for mothers' clinics and better minimum wage laws.

The tasks of Communist women were not only set out in the framework of an international struggle but were counterposed to the unacceptable political aims of Canadian middle-class feminists. By the 1920's, the resolution of the suffrage issue had dispersed much of the pre-war feminist movement, but such women's religious and reform organizations as the YWCA and the National Council of Women were still active. The Communist leadership feared the influence of these groups on working-class women, who, they believed, might be easily patronized and swayed by their social "betters" and thus have their attention deflected from class issues. Rank-and-file Communists shared these worries. Finnish WLLer Mary North complained to *The Woman Worker* that working-class women in her Alberta mining town too naively accepted the opinions expressed in bourgeois women's magazines, which pandered to women with articles on fashion and movie actresses, while Glace Bay activist Annie Whitfield bemoaned the local church's influence on working-class women. *Robitnysia*, in particular, addressed what it believed to be the dangerous religiosity of working-class women. These fears were grounded, in part, on realistic observations of women's participation in non-political groups and on the numbing influence of anti-socialist and anti-feminist popular magazines and movies in the 1920's. At the same time, many of the warnings about women's participation in middle-class culture again embraced the old adage that women's natural deference made them easy prey to counterrevolutionary influences.

To counter the danger posed by middle-class organizations, the Communist press tried to expose the misguided, bourgeois views of women's reform groups. In 1927, *The Woman Worker* ridiculed the NCW's efforts to have women senators appointed and denounced the NCW's attack on socialist Sunday schools and its resolution to "investigate communist education"[43] in Canada. In 1925, at a large Toronto meeting initiated by the WLL to discuss the "protection of womanhood," Florence Custance laid out the WLL's case for the unionization of women workers. *The Worker* contrasted Custance's comments with those of Mrs. Huestis, a former suffragist, who claimed that prostitutes made an "immoral" choice of occupation, having already "succumbed to the lure of commercialized entertainment and pretty clothes." It was clear, retorted *The Worker*, that middle-class women were interested in moral reform and "protection for the feeble-minded," but they did not understand that for working girls the real issues were good wages and unionization.[44] There was little to quibble with in *The Worker*'s characterization of the paternalistic attitudes of reformers like Mrs. Huestis, but its biting comments didn't solve the CPC's basic problem that many women joined non-political or moderate reform organizations rather than the WLLs.

Hence, following the Party's United Front strategy of limited, but critical, participation in non-Communist groups, the Women's Department occasionally included news items on women's reform groups in *The Woman Worker* and, most importantly, tried to maintain contacts with women in labourite, farm, and peace organizations in the hopes of drawing them into the Communist movement. The Women's Labor Leagues, for instance, were interested in linking up with women's farm organizations, although they were hesitant to support farm women already allied to local Councils of Women. The National Council of Women, *The Woman Worker* tried to convince Saskatchewan women in the United Farmers of Canada, was "well-intentioned" but was basically anti-labour and patronizing to working girls.[45] *The Woman Worker* did print a reply from the farm women, which argued that the Local Council was its "only contact with urban women"[46] and assuring *The Woman Worker* that farm women still had "independence of action." But Custance made sure that she had the last word, once again counselling the dangers of alliances with privileged middle-class feminists unaware of the daily realities of exploitation suffered by farm and working women.

### The Women's Labor Leagues

As the WLLs were slowly influenced by the Comintern Congress of 1928, their opposition to women's reform groups sharpened. Until 1930, however, and the immersion of the Labor Leagues in the Workers Unity League, the WLLs comprised a unique experiment in Canadian Communist history. Although generally controlled by the Party, they constituted an organization separate in name and identity from the CPC, with a membership that went beyond Party members and a structure that allowed a degree of local autonomy. When the Federation of WLLs was founded in 1924 it was far from assured that the leagues would prosper. Custance's task was not an easy one: she depended on local Party officials for organizational aid, and few district functionaries had the time or inclination to organize Women's Labor Leagues. In 1924, Custance later noted, there was pessimistic speculation about the WLLs' future, and for two years they made slow progress, gaining little support from "our men in the labour movement."[47] The leagues' failure to gain affiliation to the TLC probably made them even less important in the eyes of many Communist labour leaders.

*A Finnish Women's Labor League in 1929 was awarded a prize for its efforts on behalf of the American socialist paper for women,* Toveritar. (National Archives of Canada, C 111013)

Despite this apathy and pessimism, the WLLs expanded from ten to thirty-seven in 1927 and, according to the *The Woman Worker*, to sixty in 1929. This expansion can be attributed in large part to Custance's organizational skills and hard work, and also to the existence of a stimulating and provocative women's newspaper, for, as Custance noted, *The Woman Worker* sustained and extended the Labor Leagues with its wide selection of fiction, educational material, and the inspirational reports from sister leagues. The highly ethnic character of the Communist movement also pointed to the essential role that the CPC's sibling associations, the Finnish Organization of Canada and the Jewish Labor League, played in encouraging WLL activity. As Mary North pointed out, *The Woman Worker* was sold and read concurrently with the Finnish-American equivalent, *Toveritar* (*Woman Comrade*). The Finnish leagues, influential because of their sheer numbers, drew on strong traditions of women's self-organization rooted in the pre-war socialist movement. During the 1920's they also had their own organizer, Sanna Kannasto, a socialist orator and writer from the Lakehead area, who had worked as an organizer for the SPC and SDPC. Kannasto, ''a small bit of a woman, with piercing eyes'' and a "fiery" orator's tongue, was even viewed with some trepidation by the local WLLers, who saw her militant style as a marked contrast to that of many women, especially the "cool, undemonstrative Finns." Kannasto did education work for the FOC, even taking in promising young female comrades for intensive study. One such student spent two weeks at Kannasto's farm, trying to learn public speaking and socialist theory: "a lot of the Theory," she later quipped, "went right over my head."[48]

The Finnish leagues critiqued their own failure to break out of their ethnic enclaves, though overall the Finnish and Jewish leagues had closer contact with the Women's Department than did Ukrainian women, who were primarily tied to ULFTA. Before World War One, few Ukrainian women were full-fledged members of the Ukrainian Social Democratic Party. The Russian Revolution and the founding of ULFTA, however, stimulated new interest in women's organization, and out of Ukrainian Women's Committees to Aid Famine Victims in the Soviet Russia grew the first locals of the "Workingwomen's Section of the Labour-Farmer Temple." By 1923, there were fourteen such women's locals, and the following year *Robitnysia* was launched. This women's paper was edited by male leadership from the ULFTA, who naturally set the political agenda and provided the ideological framework for the discussion of the woman question. Indeed, when it was first established, there were frequent reader complaints that some *Robitnysia* articles were simply reprints from the *Ukrainian Labor News*. *Robitnysia*'s own editors, in turn, muttered that they were expending too many columns teaching uneducated women the most basic questions about how to build a women's organization. Despite evidence of paternalistic control, the paper began to gradually provide an outlet for women anxious to express their political views, often for the first time.

All these varieties of Women's Labor Leagues consisted largely of housewives and were firmly structured around language groups. When directives came from the Comintern in the mid-1920's to "Bolshevize" the Party, that is, establish membership around factory rather than language groups, they had little impact on the WLLs. Becky Buhay noted that the CPC work among women should be conducted in "purely proletarian circumstances,"[49] perhaps a critical reference to the WLLs' failure to change their language orientation. It was a failure that could only reinforce the CPC leadership's disinterest in the WLLs.

Yet, the WLLs did fill a necessary purpose: based on a socially acceptable auxiliary model, they answered the needs of women who were less proficient than male Party members in English, who were not eligible for trade union membership or welcomed as Party cell members. Most Labor Leagues divided their time between self-education and fund-raising. They held euchres and bazaars, sponsored May Day dances and anniversary festivals for the Russian Revolution, donating their proceeds to local Communist causes or to organizations like the Canadian Labor Defence League (CLDL), which looked after the legal defence of radical trade unionists and Communists. In fact, the WLLs were encouraged by the CPC to affiliate to the CLDL, perhaps because the CLDL was eager to use the WLLs' proven fund-raising talents. The Saskatoon Ukrainian women's local, named after Alexandra Kollantai, spent a major portion of its time on basketball events, dances, and raffles, raising as much as $1,000 a year, a substantial sum in the 1920's.[50]

Also in the auxiliary tradition, the Women's Labor Leagues initiated summer camps, usually organized along language lines, for Communist youth. Women's involvement in this work was partly the consequence of housewives' flexible work schedule during the summer, but it was also linked to the strong identification of women with the maternal task of socializing the youth for the future. "We are growing older," *Robitnysia* reminded its readers, and we "must replace today's comrades . . . and where will they come from, if we do not raise them ourselves?"[51] This identification of women with maternal roles did circumscribe women's role in politics, just as the earlier maternal feminism had limited the parameters of women's political participation. Nonetheless, youth education was important: the Party needed to augment its ranks, and youth camps helped to counter values taught in the public schools with an alternate ideology that could sustain the loyalty of Party children, perhaps even draw in new recruits.

Internally, league activities were directed toward their members' own education: the women spent time reading books, discussing current events, and improving their understanding of socialism. In northern Ontario a travelling library of radical books was circulated among towns, while the Ladysmith branch of the women's section of the FOC attempted to initiate its own in-house, handwritten newspaper, *Kipinä* (*Sparks*). Though the editors sometimes had trouble gathering articles, the women could look on their dilemma with humour; at the next meeting, they once reported, "the *Kipinä* paper will be read even if it does not have one article in it."[52] The Ladysmith branch also sponsored internal discussions on a wide range of topics. As members carefully sewed crafts to sell at fund-raising events, they debated: "Does woman belong at home or in politics?" or, more revealing, "Does the marriage law secure women their livelihood or oppress them as slaves?" In both cases, apparently, the women affirmed the latter proposition.[53] Some leagues rotated their officers every three months so that all members could gain leadership experience; others offered oratory lessons to develop the skills of women reluctant to speak in public. By meeting weekly to discuss books, commented one member, "we have been able to develop our own understanding and skills: we are no longer asking our men how we should think."[54] For women living in families where men's activities and opinions were considered of primary importance, this self-confidence was an achievement.

Although Party officials sometimes commended WLL work, they more frequently lamented the leagues' failure to recruit wage-earning and English-speaking women. At the same time, they were at a loss as to how to change the WLLs, especially when women's work was not high on their priority list. Party leader Jack McDonald claimed that "for two years, the Central Executive Committee never devoted one meeting to discussion of work among women. The Central Committee gave absolutely no attention to women's work."[55] Ironically, the large proportion of housewives in the leagues, which so concerned the CPC leadership, gave some question to their stereotype of "housewife conservatism." Interestingly, although *The Woman Worker* did echo the fear that housewives were "backward," it also contained alternative opinions voiced by rank-and-file WLLers. One correspondent pointed out that women's educational opportunities – "their opportunities to learn the truth – were fewer, and that working-class men, too, were conservative, due to the influence of the press, school, and church."[56]

A similar response came from some Ukrainian women in re-action to the "porcupinism" debate that raged in the pages of *Robitnysia* in the late 1920's. The term "porcupinism" was taken from the name of an author, Tymko Izhak, who penned a fierce diatribe in the paper against women's organizations, claiming that women, who were weak, unintellectual, and unproductive in the economy, should simply concentrate on being "man's helper."[57] Porcupinism, an apt synonym for male chauvinism, was actually endorsed by many letters from self-confessed porcupines, which the editors chose not to print, indicating how entrenched stereotypes of female backwardness were in some sections of the Party. The article, however, was likely composed deliberately to provoke women's opposition, and it did just that. Women readers responded in anger to Izhak's accusations. One group of letters accepted the label of female backwardness, but then tried to turn it to advantage, to argue for women's release from their isolated, domestic imprisonment. It was precisely because women were so behind ideologically, they said, that they needed to become active in their own organization and thus "develop confidence and enlighten themselves." "To be in the same organization as men," wrote another, "would be again to subordinate our thoughts and wishes to men."[58] Women readers were even more critical of Izhak's claim that women's work was unproductive. They provided long lists of women's crucial labour to the family; "at the end of the day," concluded one miner's wife, "you, my husband have worked your shift and for this you have your pay, but you, woman, where is your pay?"[59]

These Ukrainian women, like the WLL correspondents, were attempting to express their female experience of the world within a class perspective. Although *Robitnysia* and *The Woman Worker* never deviated from an overall emphasis on class struggle, they did provide a forum for the voices of working-class women who felt they were accorded an inferior status, treated "like toys or slaves"[60] by their menfolk. Some even implied that women were the scapegoats for class and patriarchal relations: "women are forced into an authority relationship with husbands who have grown to think they are the bosses in the home, and boss wives, as bosses boss them."[61] Florence Custance offered some sympathy for women suffering within marriage, but she immediately counselled them not to misdirect their anger against men. In the long term, she tried to show, "there are no easy cures for sexual inequality in marriage . . . we must see the basic causes of inequality. . . [capitalism] . . . . Thus, if women want more than a truce, if they want true freedom, the struggle against capitalism must take precedence."[62]

Social issues like prostitution and alcoholism were also presented within a class analysis, yet with some reference to the immediate suffering of women. Very occasionally, writers in *The Woman Worker* would refer to the white slave trade as "an outlet for male licentiousness."[63] More often, though, editorials attributed prostitution to poverty and low wages. Similarly, alcoholism was often portrayed as a consequence of the alienating capitalist work world, although its tragic effects on working-class households, and especially on women, were noted. In *Robitnysia*, some references were even made to wife-battering, a phenomenon middle-class reformers had usually linked to alcoholism but the left-wing press rarely mentioned. There was not complete consistency in readers' assessments of such issues as alcoholism; but overall, such "moral" issues never assumed the focal position in the WLLs that they had taken in the pre-war women's movement.

Although the Women's Labor Leagues generally followed the views of the CPC on social and economic issues, they did develop a small measure of autonomy, just as recommendations of the International Women's Secretariat were modified to fit Canadian conditions. In the coal-mining districts of the Crows Nest Pass, WLLs existed in close alliance with the Communist-dominated Mine Workers Union of Canada (MWUC). Wives and daughters of miners made up the bulk of Labor League membership for, as Mary North pointed out, "naturally . . . we are housewives for jobs here are only in mining and are hardly even accessible to the man."[64] The Crows Nest leagues concentrated on building an auxiliary to the MWUC and, for a while, on raising money for the Labour Party of Alberta. Their numerous social and fund-raising endeavours cited in *The Woman Worker* had political as well as financial importance, for union picnics and May Day dances were crucial stimulants to Communist solidarity; the atmosphere created by the women provided a social glue that helped to cement and sustain political allegiances.

In the northern Ontario WLLs, members were often the wives of primary resource workers or single domestics drawn in by the Finnish connection. As in the Crows Nest Pass, birth control was not an important public issue, indicating that *The Woman Worker*'s vocal stance on birth control did not reflect the views of all the WLLs. "Our members," recalled one woman from the Lakehead, "were extremely embarrassed when Sanna Kannasto insisted on talking about sexuality and birth control to the Finnish women's meetings."[65] The B.C. Finnish leagues also pursued activities linked to their ethnic identification; in Vancouver, they organized Finnish domestics, while in Sointula, once a Finnish utopian socialist community, they helped run the local co-operative store. Isolated by the Rockies, the B.C. WLLs held regional conventions, passing resolutions that were then pressed on the local Labour Party or on civic and provincial governments. Particular local and ethnic concerns were evidenced by calls for legislation permitting civil marriage, a reflection of the anti-church views of the Finnish leagues.

Alberta and northern Ontario WLLs sometimes sponsored regional conventions as well, but this practice was often forgone by the larger urban leagues of Toronto and Montreal, with their higher membership numbers and easier access to the Party's organizational machinery. In Toronto, the WLLs had a major hand in editing *The Woman Worker* and, during Custance's illness in 1928-29, kept the magazine going. The Toronto leagues were active in union support work but lacked the single-union emphasis of an area like the Crows Nest Pass; they helped with a boycott campaign during a bakers' strike, as well as a YCL effort to organize York Knitting Mills. In keeping with its urban setting, the Toronto WLLs, like those in Montreal and Regina, spent a large amount of time on the minimum wage campaign, and in Toronto they lobbied for mothers' clinics. Urban leagues also had greater opportunities to join with other Communist organizations, co-sponsoring rallies and demonstrations, such as the large defence meeting the Montreal WLL held for Sacco and Vanzetti.

The measure of local autonomy enjoyed by the WLLs was in part a consequence of the Women's Department's flexibility and concern for local conditions. But it was also the result of Party disinterest and default. Communication problems arising from language differences, geography, and Party disorganization were all factors creating the diversity of the league experience. After the 1929 CPC convention, questionnaires were sent out to the Labor Leagues to ascertain their membership and activities; the central office apparently had scanty records of the WLL network. This was partly a result of disarray in the wake of Custance's unexpected death, as Custance had been compelled to run a "one woman department."[66] In the final analysis, though, it was also a reflection of the peripheral status of the woman question within the Party.

### Conclusion

Within the Communist agenda, the woman question remained a secondary priority; nevertheless, its significance had increased since the time of the pre-war left. The CPC's new initiatives in work among women were primarily inspired by the example of

Soviet Russia and directives from the Comintern. To Canadian Communists, the impressive transformation of women's status in Russia implied both the value of the U.S.S.R.'s strategic suggestions and, if imitated, the possibility of similar successes. The Party attempted to build a Marxist and Leninist women's movement that was firmly rooted in the same political goals as the revolutionary movement, stressing economic issues and the primacy of class-based political action. The Women's Department focused its agitational efforts at the unique exploitation of women under capitalism, and while some Party goals, such as the unionization of women, were never fulfilled, other initiatives, like the minimum wage campaign, were more successful in exposing women's inequality under capitalism. By the end of the decade, the Party had grown, though women still constituted a small minority of the membership, and the WLL members tended to be party wives, not the desired newcomers from the factories.

Although economic issues formed the core of the Communist program, birth control and family life were not ignored, partly because of the impact of Soviet reforms, but also because of the keen interest of Canadian women in reproductive control and sexual autonomy. In lobbying for mothers' clinics or in doing their auxiliary work, the WLLs were involved in the socialist movement at a different level, and sometimes with a different rationale, than male members. WLLs provided women with a separate space to build their confidence and explore socialist issues from a woman's perspective. Their auxiliary work gave important support and sustenance to the movement; unfortunately, it also kept women in a sex-stereotyped domestic role that isolated them from power and perpetuated women's secondary status in the Party. With the notable exception of Florence Custance, and later Becky Buhay and Annie Buller, women were not represented in the Communist Party's seats of power. In fact, if only one family member could buy a Party card, it was to the "head of the household." As one comrade remembers,

> Woman's place was in the home. It's all right to organize women, men would say, but not my wife! So, when it came to going to a meeting, the men would go. It was more important. The men were the "brains." The women were in the kitchen. But they still supported so many causes.[67]

At the same time, domesticity was used as a radicalizing tool:

demands for bread and peace were rallying cries used to mobilize
women in their socially accepted roles as wives and mothers.

Because Communists largely adopted the ideal of a family
wage, women's political consciousness was interpreted in the
context of their domestic activities. Women's domesticity, of
course, was a double-edged sword. It might lead women to radical
politics; but it was also perceived as the cause of their conservatism. Though it is true that women were less likely to join the
Party, their "reactionary" mentality did not keep them tied to
the kitchen, as the "porcupines" claimed. Women's leap into
sustained political activity was precluded by illiteracy, material
impoverishment, family responsibilities, the unwelcoming attitudes of male Party members, and the same anti-socialist pressures
that kept working-class men from joining the Party. Moreover,
women may have been radicalized on issues like birth control,
while men were drawn in by trade union concerns. However, the
Party's peripheral interest in such women's issues as reproductive
control – a direct consequence of the CPC's brand of Marxist-
Leninism, as well as persisting patriarchal prejudices – inevitably
gave men's issues the weight of prestige and importance within
the Party.

Although woman's role in the family was seen as crucial to
her political understanding, it was not analysed as critically as
her role in production, nor was it judged to be central to her
oppression. While the problems of working-class housewives were
sympathetically explored, in the final analysis, women's maternal
role was accepted, even sentimentalized. *The Woman Worker* did
not embrace a dogmatic economism that rejected *all* issues of
women's sexual subordination; but the solution to sexual oppression was always seen in class terms. This emphasis on the necessity of revolutionary working-class solidarity would soon become
of paramount importance to the organization of women during
the next period of the CPC's evolution.

# 3

# Red Revolutionaries and Pink Tea Pacifists: Communist and Socialist Women in the Early 1930's

With the onset of the Great Depression, the Communist Party's ties to Russia disrupted, then altered, its work among women. After 1928, the Comintern predicted (quite correctly, as it turned out) economic doom for Western capitalism and new opportunities for Communist organizers. In the face of this economic crisis, Canadian Communists were advised to adopt a more militant, revolutionary line. For the Women's Department, this meant new emphasis on the organization of women wage-earners and unity with working-class men in the intensifying class struggle. The Party restructured and limited the Women's Labor Leagues, criticizing them for their reformist auxiliary work and housewife composition. Instead, it seemed, the Party hoped to recruit more female "red revolutionaries." The net effect of this strategy was to downplay women's specific oppression and erase any traces of feminism from the Women's Department, while enhancing the CPC's prevailing disposition to stress the primacy of class struggle.

While the Communist Party attempted to tighten its control over the Women's Labor Leagues, social democratic women were scattered among various socialist, labourite, and farm organizations. Though disparagingly referred to as "pink tea pacifists" by the Communists, these socialist women were gradually increasing their political profile in the 1920's and early 1930's, accumulating valuable skills and experience they would later incorporate into the CCF.

## International Advice and Canadian Dilemmas

In 1928 the Comintern, now dominated by Stalin, argued that the capitalist West was on the verge of a "Third Period" of intense economic and political crisis. Moreover, Communists, having veered dangerously toward reformism, had to reinstate a revolutionary political praxis. Comintern documents described a world divided into two irreconcilable camps – the capitalist powers and the socialist Soviet Union – and predicted that, in crisis, the capitalist class in the West would resort to violence against the U.S.S.R. and against their own working-class. "Little do people realize," announced Canadian Communist Stewart Smith when he returned to Canada from Moscow with this new line memorized, "that in a very short time the streets of Toronto will be running with blood."[1]

The full impact of the Comintern's new thinking was not felt until 1929-30, as confusion about the directions for change, leadership resignations, and ethnic differences all complicated the transition to the Third Period. The 1929 national convention in Toronto was a stormy affair, rife with faction fighting. One Party faction initially opposed the new Comintern directives, and Finnish and Ukrainian delegates accepted them only reluctantly, fearing revolutionary activity would result in deportation of their members and the loss of their property. Dissenters accepted the Comintern orders grudgingly, but expulsions and resignations continued. Deep divisions between the Central Committee and the language associations persisted into 1930, until Comintern envoys helped paper over political differences. The Communist Party thus entered the Third Period weakened by division and severe membership losses; by 1931 numbers had fallen to an all-time low of 1,300. As *Robitnysia* tried to put it tactfully: "in the turn to the class struggle, weaker elements . . . fell out, and a sturdier element . . . remained."[2]

During the early 1930's the CPC also encountered intensified police and state harassment. This may have been provoked, in part, by Communists' combative rhetoric and tactics, but it was also the product of a growing fear on the part of federal, provincial, and municipal governments regarding social disorder led by the CPC. In Toronto, an ex-army man and fervent anti-Communist ideologue, Chief of Police Draper, established a "Red Squad" to spy on the Party, forbade meetings in any language but English, and tried to prevent Communists from speaking in public at all. In response to this breach of civil liberties, the Communists adopted an old Wobbly tactic: the free speech fight. In the street confrontations and court trials that followed, the Communists sometimes exposed police brutality and judicial prejudice; however, because the Party contemptuously rejected any alliances with socialists, labour, or liberals, their struggle often remained an isolated one.[3]

The "Communist-Police War," as the *Globe* called it, did give some women the chance to prove themselves true "red revolutionaries." In one large Queen's Park demonstration, a YCLer, Lil Himmelfarb, tried to walk to the speakers' platform only to be thrown down by the police, who knocked out her front teeth. Other YCL women took their turns soapboxing on street corners or leading street demonstrations. In one such "battle of the Amazons," as Lita-Rose Betcherman has dubbed it, the police tried to stop Communist Jeanne Corbin, "a skinny, but determined figure in an unbecoming toque," from leading a column of two hundred marchers down College Street. The police, the *Star* reported, pushed her several times:

> Arrested by the irate officer, [Corbin] was taken into custody and shoved in the back of a cruiser. . . . Of the six others arrested, four were women, including three YCL flappers, Dora, Edith and the bloomered Diana, described by one policeman as the "worst of the lot".[4]

Other cities also used law-and-order tactics to combat communism and, in 1932, eight of the CPC's national leaders were arrested under Section 98 (forbidding sedition) of the Criminal Code. With their imprisonment, part of the Party's apparatus disappeared underground. Both the necessity of underground work and Communists' militant tactics now made it difficult for many women to participate in Party activities. Those involved in the Toronto free-speech fights were usually YCLers or single Party leaders like Becky Buhay. The YCL "Amazons" noted above shunned fines and opted for jail sentences, revealing both youthful zeal for the cause and a desire to prove equality of the sexes in all revolutionary endeavours. Most of these young women were aware of the risks they were taking. A YCL organizer in Sudbury, Taime Davis, helped organize a May Day demonstration, using tactics the Party knew might provoke counteraction. Not only did Communists call for the destruction of capitalism, they also liked to thumb their noses at Canada's Anglophile elite. A bylaw, Davis explained, said that all public processions had to carry a Union Jack:

> So we decided not to. We were that sectarian then. . . . But it was a Red Flag for the bulls. The police attacked us and beat

up the guys. Some were deported. I didn't get beaten because I didn't fight back. But I got fifteen days.[5]

Women with families were not expected to take such risks (though some did); instead of going to jail for the night, it was assumed they had to be home to feed their children. Women's familial roles set clear boundaries on their political activities; as party wives they were usually limited to petitioning against Section 98 and raising funds for Party leaders' defence funds. Though important, this work did not create the appropriate history or image for future Party leaders.

### The Woman Question and the Women's Labor Leagues

The new Third Period strategies had never focused directly on the need to redefine the woman question; nevertheless, the Comintern's directives did have important repercussions on the Party's work among women. The official Comintern program contained an impressive platform on women's equality, though within the Soviet Union the wide-ranging debate on women's issues had actually been silenced. By 1929, the Soviet Zhenotdel had been circumscribed, its work totally subordinated to Communist Party interests. Birth control was less accessible, and discussion of issues like family law reform was replaced by praise for women's role in boosting production, reflecting the government's obsession with industrialization rather than a deep concern for women's emancipation.[6] In Comintern circles, a major concern was the need to rally women's peace movements behind the U.S.S.R.'s strategic interests.

These Soviet and Comintern priorities were soon mirrored in the CPC. In 1929, a Comintern letter sternly ordered the Canadian Party to devote more attention to women industrial workers and to abandon the "bourgeois pacifist"[7] tone of the WLLs in favour of organizing women against a Western war waged against the Soviet Union. In the upcoming Western economic crisis, the Comintern also predicted, women would suffer wage cuts, speed-ups, and super exploitation as cheap labour. The Canadian Communist Party should thus organize these women workers and vigilantly oppose any "militarization of women"[8] who might be used in war production. Although the stock market crash in the fall of 1929 soon substantiated predictions of economic crisis, fears of a militarization of women were less plausible, as social democratic peace groups, such as the Women's International League for Peace and Freedom, were prospering and there was no substantial increase in women's employment in war industries.

Economic concerns now predominated in the Communist press, issues like birth control and the family were more rarely mentioned, and women were exhorted to "stand shoulder to shoulder with working-class men against capitalism."[9] The demise of *The Woman Worker* in 1929 further exacerbated this economistic emphasis, for *The Woman Worker*'s latent sympathy for women's oppression now found little outlet in the main Party paper, *The Worker*. Yet, it was not only the existence of a separate paper for women that had encouraged discussion of women's equality in the 1920's: it was also the ideological bent of the Party.

In 1930, *Vapaus*, the Finnish paper, decided to introduce a women's column, after the popular American socialist paper, *Toveritar (Woman Comrade)*, was banned from the mails by the Canadian government. This column included information on Finnish women's branches, political editorials, and advice on child-rearing; but, overall, it, too, emphasized the importance of the class struggle and a revolutionary consciousness. The Ukrainian *Robitnysia* also reflected the changing political winds. *Robitnysia*'s poetry and fiction became socialist realism writ large, with less lyrical and more heroic, programmatic material, increasingly written by male rather than female authors; the popular science section was reduced; and political and strategic recommendations were augmented. Previously, women had been encouraged to send in reports of their internal, usually cultural, activities; now, these "petty" reports were rejected for tales of exploitation in the lives of women workers.[10] In both the Ukrainian and English papers, articles on the Soviet Union emphasized the equal role of Russian women in industrial production. Tim Buck even argued that Soviet women's new status was reflected in the fact that they were "ready to stand in volunteer detachments of the Army."[11] Clearly, the militarization of women was considered detrimental only when it was promoted by capitalist states.

The Party drew up plans to implement the Comintern recommendations by reorganizing the Women's Department, directing its energies to three areas: trade union work, the mass (or ethnic) organizations, and opponent organizations. Trade union work soon came under the jurisdiction of the Workers Unity League, the new Communist-led trade union centre. The ethnic organizations were slated for a major overhaul, as the CPC hoped to defuse women's loyalties to their Finnish, Ukrainian, and Jewish parent organizations and instead direct their efforts to the "common struggles of women workers," essentially a continuation of earlier, unsuccessful attempts to bolshevize the Party. Finally, the Party's goal was now to be a United Front from below, which, translated, meant uniting the working class under CPC auspices alone and rejecting alliances with all other labour and socialist "opponent" organizations.

Rival women's organizations, whether they were conservative, liberal, or social democratic, were considered dangerous, but Communists portrayed social democrats, in particular, as an insidious threat, lulling working-class women into the false security of "social fascist" reforms. In 1931, for example, the Party was told by the Comintern to stage protests over the upcoming Women's British Labour Party Conference, contrasting the labour conference with a Communist women's meeting being held in Czechoslovakia. The latter conference, claimed the memo, was truly concerned with organizing working-class women; the former used pacifist and reformist phrases to disguise its true imperialist aims and delude women into thinking the Labour Party stood for economic equality for women. In Canada, commented *The Worker*, the same dangers existed: "the Macphails, Brigdens, Woodsworths" were to be exposed as sentimental idealists and "false friends of the working class."[12] Such denunciations alienated the Communist Party from some working-class people and earned the CPC the undying hatred of many social democrats.

The WLLs, too, were targeted for reorganization. The year 1929 marked a natural dividing point in the history of the Labor Leagues, for Custance, too ill to make her report to the 1929 convention, died suddenly in July of that year. The Women's Department quickly fell into disarray, for Custance alone had overseen "her beloved Labor Leagues." Since Custance's death, lamented the Finnish WLLs in Sudbury, "the Centre has been completely paralyzed . . . her work was totally neglected and our organ, *The Woman Worker* . . . died with Custance."[13] The next year the Women's Department began to find its feet again; English and Jewish leagues in Toronto elected an interim executive, including Alice Buck as secretary, and probably made up of women supporting the reigning Tim Buck leadership faction in the Party. This Toronto group sent out inquiries to all the known WLLs asking about their composition and activities, and not surprisingly, responses only substantiated the Comintern's criticisms that the

Labor Leagues were dominated by housewives involved in reformist auxiliary work.

In order to place the WLLs on a correct revolutionary footing, the CPC put them under the leadership of the Workers Unity League. The leagues would now answer to trade union organizers already burdened with what was seen as more important organizing work. They were to receive strict guidance from the WUL; were to pay half of their dues to the WUL; and were to operate under a new WUL constitution. Since the Workers Unity League was run largely by men unacquainted with the Party's work among women, this reorganization meant less autonomy and a somewhat condescending attitude toward the WLLs. Yet, many of the tasks outlined in the WLL's new constitution were similar to previous league activities: they were to ''work for the organization of women workers, against imperialist war, and for the struggles of housewives.''[14] Their activities, however, were posed in the methods and vocabulary of Third Period thinking; anti-war activity, for example, was equated with the ''defence of the U.S.S.R.'' and strike support was allowed only for those ''revolutionary'' unions recognized by the Party.

Some local WLLs resisted this reorganization, voicing apprehensions about the lack of consultation involved and demanding to know the merits of affiliation to the WUL. One league suggested a convention to debate the new strategy, indicating that Custance's attempts to build a strong federation of women had perhaps worked too well, as this Labor League quite self-confidently challenged the Party leadership. Resistance especially came from the Finnish stronghold in Sudbury. Already embroiled in battles with the Party's English-speaking leadership, Finns resented the English and Toronto domination of the interim WLL executive. In *The Worker*, an English Party organizer in Sudbury even took the side of the local leagues, arguing that the order to put the WLLs under the Workers Unity League did not make sense, for the WLLs, ''composed largely of housewives,'' were distinct from the ''economic centre''[15] of the WUL. Local WLLers agreed and added angrily that ''the question was decided without knowing how this was done, in areas where there are few Party members in the Leagues and where affiliation is not understood.''[16]

The 1931 Party Plenum, however, gave unequivocal reaffirmation to the new policy, and reluctantly the Labor Leagues accepted the Party line. By the spring of 1931 the rebellious Sudbury locals acquiesced and, like other leagues, offered ritualized resolutions of self-criticism for their past mistakes. Yet, it does not appear that affiliation to the WUL fundamentally altered the WLLS. Most Labor Leagues were still composed of home-makers and were ethno-centred. In 1933, the Sudbury district concluded that reorganization of the WLLS into several small "block" committees had resulted in more lively and confident participation of its members, but the district also noted that the WUL boards governing the WLLS had not worked well and that the leagues were still "essentially language organizations."[17] Under the WUL, some leagues did concentrate more time on organizing women wage-earners. Yet, their work bore a striking resemblance to the support work done during the 1920's. The WLLS in the Crows Nest Pass, for instance, were still concerned with their union auxiliary, while in northern Ontario Finnish WLLers tried to draw "servants and hotel workers . . . into household organizations . . . as well as the Unity League."[18]

Similarly, the Women's Section of the ULFTA had been pressured to take the "left turn" with mixed results. In 1931, a prominent ULFTA leader opened the debate in *Robitnysia* by lashing out at the Women's Section, charging it had failed so miserably to organize women workers that it might as well be liquidated. Trying to rouse women to revolutionary action, he concluded condescendingly, was "like throwing peas at the wall."[19] In response, many familiar arguments were brought out to defend the Women's Section: the solution was not to abolish but to strengthen women's organizations, and men who derided women's work were also to blame for the situation. Approvingly noting that the women were engaged in some hearty self-criticism, particularly for their ethnic isolationism, *Robitnysia* editors further encouraged women to subject themselves to the leadership of the Communist Party, to root out petit-bourgeois influences, including incessant "gossip" in some locals, and, most importantly, to involve Canadian-born working women in the current "revolutionary stirrings of the proletariat."[20] Some local women's sections of the ULFTA apparently were still not enthusiastic. In one meeting at which women were being urged to join the "shock brigades" and "face the Masses," a critic charged, "no one uttered a single word. . . . Some members were so enthused that they fell asleep, while others listened to the silence."[21] Over the next few years, women were repeatedly accused of dragging their feet, or, in the old paternalistic paradigm, of "lagging behind the men." The reluctance of Ukrainian women to embrace the "turn" was due in part to their occupational segregation – as housewives – from wage-earning women. Yet, over the next few years, these women, too, effected some changes in their political work: they were to be found on picket lines, in relief committees, and at demonstrations. Some would get arrested for their efforts and their "robkorky" (*Robitnysia*'s correspondents) would dutifully report these militant activities. Despite this important support work, however, the women "failed" in their major assignment: to recruit wage-earning women. This is mentioned primarily in their self-criticism, as something that was "not done."

Whatever the official emphasis on recruiting women from the factories, some ethnic women's groups continued to pursue other political priorities, such as consumer activism. In Toronto, for example, housewives in the Jewish WLLs mounted a successful boycott of kosher butchers who raised their prices in 1933. Like earlier boycotts organized by Jewish housewives in New York City, this strike radicalized homemakers around their daily concerns, though consumer activism, of course, did not question the division of labour that assigned domestic work to women in the first place.[22] Still, in the view of the female participants, argues Ruth Frager, the Toronto boycott was a courageous act, for in those days, a former WLLer remembered:

> the people [didn't] realize that women could do a thing like this – to go on the picket line, and have a fight with the butchers, and go to court . . . "What do you mean you're going out on strike? You're going to fight with the butchers, with the men?" I [said:] "Why not?"[23]

Party officials may have been more interested in organizing women workers, but they could hardly ignore such an important grassroots protest. Other leagues might also pursue projects unconnected to Party priorities, such as the Vancouver WLL's public meeting demanding legal access to birth control. Indeed, in British Columbia, a dedicated British-born organizer, Annie Stewart, helped to organize new leagues in the early thirties, so that the WLLs remained a vital force well into the Popular Front. The barriers posed by geography, language, and indifference to work among women still allowed a small measure of latitude for local WLLs.

In the long run, however, Custance's death, intra-party battles, reorganization under the WUL, and the demise of *The Woman Worker* all hurt the Federation of WLLs. By insisting that the WLLs were only to participate in the economic struggles of revolutionary unions, the Party isolated the leagues from potential recruits involved in other labour struggles. Ultimately, the Labor Leagues were caught in a no-win dilemma. The Comintern-inspired critique of the WLLs denigrated their reformist auxiliary work, but the CPC offered few workable directions for change and gave little time to the upkeep of the WLLs. In the early 1930's some Labor Leagues persisted and even augmented their membership, but, increasingly, new women's organizations were established. As a result, by mid-decade the national federation of WLLs had diminished in size, and the leagues Florence Custance had so carefully nurtured gradually receded from Party history.

### New Female Leadership: Annie Buller and Becky Buhay

With Custance's death and the reorganization of the WLL came a new generation of female leaders. Julia Collins, wife of Party leader Sam Carr, assumed the title of women's director of the Workers Unity League, while Becky Buhay and Annie Buller, at different times, managed the Party's Women's Department. And it was Annie Buller and Becky Buhay who, more than any other women, came to symbolize female leadership in the CPC for the next thirty years.

Born in 1895 to Jewish parents in Russia, Annie Buller came to Montreal as a child and attended school there until she was fourteen. From her first job in a tobacco stripping factory she moved into the garment industry and from there joined a retail store, where her talents as an astute businesswoman helped her rise to the position of buyer.[24] By World War One, Buller was involved in the Montreal socialist movement and had met her lifelong friend, Becky Buhay. Their relationship quickly blossomed: Annie, Becky wrote privately, "gave me courage and strength [when we met]. . . . I was starved for love and appreciation [and] she made me believe in myself." Buller, in turn, was attracted to Buhay's feminist sensibilities and her intellectual gifts. When Annie left Montreal for New York in 1919, Buhay mourned the deep "void" in her life, the loss of "wonderful days and nights together . . . our heart to heart talks . . . with feelings never before expressed." Over the next decade, their friendship was cemented by the "socialist cause they loved so well"[25] and by their close working relationship in the Party's overwhelmingly male leadership. Their friendship would endure long separations

*Becky Buhay and Annie Buller, Montreal, 1927.*
(Rue Studio, Communist Party of Canada,
National Archives of Canada, PA 127602)

and inner party battles: luckily, Buller and Buhay generally stood
together in these battles, for in 1929 Becky Buhay was separated
by faction fighting from her own brother, Michael.

Becky and Michael Buhay had come to Canada as working-
class Jewish emigrants from Britain. Both were already versed in
socialist ideas when they arrived as teenagers. They had grown
up in London's East End in a family sometimes solely supported
by a strong-willed mother, who encouraged Becky and her brother
to attend the ILP socialist Sunday schools. After emigrating, Becky
worked in her own trade, as a photo refinisher, then in the tobacco
and garment industries. She began to organize for the Amalgamated Clothing Workers Union of America, during the war joined
the SDPC, then went to New York to attend the Rand School of
Social Science, a radical educational centre. Buller joined her
there and both became active in American socialist politics; in-

deed, Buhay's high profile led to government surveillance and her hasty return to Montreal in late 1919.

On her return to Canada, Buhay, deeply affected by the Winnipeg General Strike, joined the One Big Union, attending its inaugural convention in Port Arthur. Soon back in Montreal, she, Buller, and Bella Hall Gauld helped organize the Montreal Labour College, modeled vaguely on the Rand School and the British Plebs League. By 1922, both Buller and Buhay were deeply involved in the Party. Buller moved to Toronto in the mid-1920's to become business manager of *The Worker*; Buhay stayed in Montreal, rejoined the needle trades, and organized her garment shop. In 1929 Buhay, by then relocated at Communist Party headquarters in Toronto, succeeded Custance as secretary of the Canadian Labor Defence League and head of the Women's Department. Buller, who briefly took over the Women's Department in 1930, devoted her time to *The Worker* and to trade union work, especially the newly formed Industrial Union of Needle Trades Workers (IUNTW). In this capacity – as a union organizer – she rushed to the scene of the Estevan strike in 1931 to lead the miners and their families in the demonstration in which three miners were shot by the RCMP. In the arrests that followed, Buller was charged with inciting to riot, and despite an eloquent, self-conducted defence, she was sentenced in 1933 to a year in jail. Buhay, too, had her own salient experiences with the police. In the middle of a public meeting during the free-speech fights, the police raided the theatre, whisked the speakers off the stage, and dropped the curtain. Buhay, not one to be easily silenced, crawled under the curtain and began to denounce the police to an enthusiastic audience. Suddenly, she began to faint and was grabbed by Tim Buck; she had finally been silenced by police tear gas.[26]

Buller and Buhay joined the CPC in its youth, and by the Third Period their loyalty to the Party, as well as their close friendship, had been forged. Like many Communists, their political commitment was reinforced by the comradeship they enjoyed with like-minded radicals who were often beleaguered by a hostile state and treated with social disapprobation. And it is significant that the latter was often expressed in anti-Semitic terms,[27] for this racism may have drawn Jewish radicals like Buller and Buhay closer together. Becky Buhay's letters to Annie during a western tour for *The Worker* underscored the political and emotional bonds the two friends shared. Travelling by train, sometimes on a gruelling eighteen-hour schedule, with no money for a sleeper, billeted with poor families, and often reduced to inadequate food, Becky found strength in the idealism she attached to her work and the moral and sisterly support gleaned from Annie's letters. Interspersed with Party business, they exchanged birthday wishes, gifts of embroidery, and political gossip, all the while reassuring each other of the value of their political endeavours.[28]

No other women in the Party's history occupied the strategic positions or commanded the lasting mythology that Buller and Buhay did. Buller's talents were her ability to rouse an audience and her business and organizational acumen; Buhay's were her grasp of theory and her educational talents. Both women were also determined and ambitious and could hold their own in factional fighting. Although Annie Buller claimed to be less confident in theoretical matters than Buhay, she could be aggressively single-minded over an issue; the more critical called it "domineering," especially if she was giving advice on their personal lives. In contrast to Custance's more reserved manner, Buller and Buhay were "agitational" leaders who had to sacrifice many of the comforts of a personal life for the constant rounds of speaking, travelling, and even imprisonment associated with their political careers.

Buller was married in the 1920's to Harry Guralnick, an activist in the Jewish Labor League, and they subsequently had one son. These emotional attachments, Buller once explained to her friend, poet Joe Wallace, were important to her, although her more "hard-boiled comrades"[29] took a dim view of her emotional priorities. Since other female activists sometimes found Buller's single-minded devotion to the Party difficult, or undesirable to emulate, it is hard to imagine what these comrades expected from a woman revolutionary. Buhay, in contrast, remained single, though in the early 1930's she and Tom Ewen lived together in a common-law relationship. Unfortunately, while Ewen's four children remained fond of their surrogate mother for many years, Tom himself left an unhappy Becky after five years.

Other female activists also grew to political maturity during the late 1920's, although none rivalled the pre-eminence enjoyed by Buller and Buhay. Bella Hall Gauld, a fellow organizer of the Montreal Labour College, was active on the Montreal scene for two decades, but her frail health and backroom organizational work meant she was less prominent in the Party. Brought up in a western middle-class family with a strong religious orientation, Gauld was influenced by J.S. Woodsworth and found her early vocation in the Settlement House movement. Her Christian liberal beliefs gave way, after her education at the Rand School and during the Winnipeg General Strike, to a belief in Marxism, and in the 1920's she joined the CPC and took a large role in the local WLL, the CLDL, and the Pioneer movement.[30]

Bessie Schacter, a Montreal garment worker originally from the Ukraine, and Pearl Wedro, a fur worker of East European extraction, also initiated a lifelong commitment in the 1920's. Schacter, who was a founding member of the Amalgamated Clothing Workers Union in Montreal, had been part of the Montreal Labour College circle, while Wedro was drawn to the CPC through her interest in trade unionism and connections to the Jewish socialist movement.

More prominent in the CPC in the early 1930's was Jeanne Corbin, a French emigrant who came to Tofield, Alberta, with her homesteading family but soon moved to Edmonton; at eighteen, she joined the Young Communist League, supposedly after witnessing the Alberta mining struggles of the 1920's.[31] Corbin was already under RCMP surveillance when she was attending Victoria High School in Edmonton; investigators claimed she was trying to recruit other students to the YCL, though with no success, and that she was teaching revolutionary propaganda to children in the ULFTA in her spare time. Corbin, the police continued, was rather "forward," a serious "agitator" with no time for bad habits like smoking or drinking; indeed, at all the YCL functions, she didn't even dance, noted one police informer. Jeanne attended normal school and taught for a while but her politics probably cost her her job: the RCMP made sure that the Department of Education licensing authorities were aware of the whereabouts of this most "dangerous" young woman.[32]

To the Party, on the other hand, Corbin was a prize recruit: clever, determined, and bilingual, Corbin was "discovered" by Becky Buhay at an Alberta Communist summer school and was immediately persuaded to come to Toronto to join the staff of *The Worker*. Corbin helped establish a French Communist paper and organized longshoremen in Montreal, then worked in northern Ontario with the CLDL and as a union organizer for miners and bushmen. A year's imprisonment after her involvement in the Noranda strike of 1934, however, led to problems with tuberculosis and Corbin's retirement into a sanitarium, where she died, long forsaken by her family, in 1944.

*Jeanne Corbin emerging from Queen's Park
during free speech rally, October 19, 1929.* (City
of Toronto Archives)

### The Women's Delegation to the Soviet Union

One of Becky Buhay's first tasks as new head of the Women's
Department in 1930 was to lead a women's delegation to the
U.S.S.R. Encouraged by the Comintern, the Canadian Communist Party organized an official women's tour, which the Wom-
en's Labor Leagues aided by raising money and managing local
publicity work. The primary purposes of the delegation were to
help build support for the U.S.S.R. in Canada, especially through
local branches of the Friends of the Soviet Union (FSU), and to
advertise the new equality of Soviet women and contrast it to the
continued exploitation of Canadian women.

The selection of delegates for the trip, the Party claimed, was
held in large conferences of enthusiastic workers across the coun-

try. In reality, however, a Toronto committee made the final choices, and although the WLLs raised money for the project, some grumbled unhappily about it. A Finnish WLL in B.C. voiced its disapproval by pointing out that the $2,000 needed for the delegation could be better spent in Canada. Northern Ontario Finns were more than disgruntled, objecting to a campaign that had been initiated without their consultation and a process of selecting delegates that had "left aside" Finnish and Ukrainian women.[33] They offered a counterproposal for a national convention of WLLs in a circular considered so oppositional that orders came from Party headquarters to "ban"[34] the offending pamphlet.

In the final selection, however, deference was paid to the language associations, for a young Finnish domestic from northern Ontario, Elsa Tynjala, was chosen, along with a ULFTA activist from Alberta, Annie Zen. From Cape Breton, the Party chose a homemaker and WLL activist, Annie Whitfield, while the two trade union representatives were Pearl Wedro and Bessie Schacter. On its return, the CPC hoped to escort the women on a triumphant cross-country tour, "with mass campaigns, the calling of conferences and demonstrations . . . utilizing the women's witness of the U.S.S.R. to build support for the FSU and the WUL."[35]

The Party's grandiose expectations, however, were not realized. Successful meetings were held in some large cities, but the delegation's personnel disappointed the Party. Buhay, the most experienced politician, had been greatly impressed by the "Fairy Tale Land"[36] she found in the U.S.S.R., but she was too ill to tour for the Party. Annie Whitfield refused to join the planned tour after Montreal, insisting on returning home for "domestic reasons."[37] Her silence, however, may have reflected an earlier disagreement with the Party. During the delegation's stay in the U.S.S.R., Whitfield did not immediately admit admiration for Russian socialism, and it took a number of additional educational tours before she changed her mind. Tom Ewen, also in Russia at the time, reported to Tim Buck that Whitfield was causing problems, threatening to "tell the truth when she gets home – whatever 'the truth' is''; Stewart Smith later reported that these problems with Whitfield "had been cleared up."[38]

Zen and Tynjala, most comfortable within their own cultural milieu, also frustrated the Party with their reluctance to write articles or speak in English. In the end, only Pearl Wedro and Bessie Schacter fulfilled the Party's hopes and became active in the FSU and WUL after their return from Russia. Although *The*

*Worker* gave substantial coverage to the delegation's favourable experience of the "socialist fatherland," internally the Party frankly admitted that "it had failed to make any concrete organizational gains from the project."[39]

### Unemployment Work

Following the delegation to the U.S.S.R., the WLLs became involved in the unemployment campaigns led by the WUL and its affiliate, the National Unemployed Workers Union (or Association) NUWU. The CPC's Women's Department asked local Communist organizers to have WLL members visit employment agencies and leaflet the streets in order to reach unemployed female workers. Local functionaries, however, seldom paid much attention to such directives, and so the major role of the Labor Leagues was gathering signatures for the CPC's petition for non-contributory unemployment insurance. Indeed, the Women's Department seems to have accepted this role, informing the local leagues in 1931 that one of their most important tasks on International Women's Day was to do a house-to-house canvass for petition signatures.

The Party also tried to set up a women's section of the NUWU, encompassing housewives and workers, but progress from 1930 to 1932 was very slow. Privately, the Party admitted it could not effectively compete with non-political women's organizations. In Calgary, Communists criticized reformers who were training unemployed women for domestic service, but they conceded that their own attempts to reach unemployed women had been unsuccessful; in Winnipeg, their attempt to entice unemployed women away from the recreational and social Girls Commercial Club into a more militant organization was also a failure. Sometimes, too, the Party was hampered by its exaggerated Third Period reasoning. When a women's section of NUWU was established in Vancouver in 1931, its members, largely wives of the unemployed, passed resolutions calling for immediate necessities such as free milk in the schools, only to be told that they should take a more "revolutionary"[40] line. Protests over unemployment or relief could take on gestures of uncompromising sloganeering. Referring to relief officials as "child starvers" might be dismissed as strong rhetoric; rejection of all labour aldermen as "well nurtured old ladies who never show any courage"[41] both alienated labour support and was sexist in tone.

By 1932, however, the Party was altering its approach, and the newly formed unemployment councils were not seen as "revolutionary" vehicles as much as practical instruments to push for unemployment and social insurance.[42] A growing number of unemployment and relief protests, which addressed specific local complaints and drew on grassroots anger against the welfare system, began to yield fruit. Women took an active part in many of these local protests, sometimes forming their own women's welfare rights organizations. In East Windsor, for example, a delegation of the wives of the unemployed presented a list of demands to City Council, including the right to buy any commodity they wished and more money for their families' clothing. Encouraged by a sympathetic alderman, Tom Raycroft, the women persisted in pressing for an end to relief vouchers, backing up their demands with regular deputations to City Hall. Similarly, in Burnaby, the local WLL led a delegation to city officials, demanding more adequate medical aid for families of the unemployed.

In Alberta, local relief protests became such common occurrences that the Premier secretly worried that "with Communist activities . . . any policy of cutting off relief would result in widespread disorder."[43] In the fall of 1932, the Alberta Communist Party organized a province-wide hunger march to Edmonton, calling for unemployment insurance, cancellation of farm debts, and free medical and dental aid. In Edmonton a small contingent of women marchers was caught in the battle with police instigated by frightened local authorities. Meanwhile, a much larger group of Ukrainian women prepared food for the marchers in the local Ukrainian Labour Temple, which the police had already raided in search of weapons. Finding only the women serving turkey dinners to the paraders, the police "saved face" by announcing that the Temple contained massive quantities of food, proving that the "Red" hunger marchers were not really hungry people after all. Nevertheless, the hunger marchers did find some public support, even from local labourites embarrassed by the indifference to the march displayed by Edmonton's Labour mayor.[44]

In some neighbourhoods, ethnic loyalties were also utilized by CPC members to unify opposition to relief regulations and eviction orders. By drawing on her Ukrainian contacts Winnipeg ULFTA member Kay Hladiy quickly organized support for local unemployed families. In one instance, she remembered, the Ukrainian group mounted an "eviction strike" in which all the assembled sympathizers bid one or two cents for an evictee's furniture, effectively stopping the auction.[45] It was these kinds of local struggles, not the sectarian rhetoric of the Third Period, that occasionally won reprieve for the victims of unemployment and slowly augmented respect for the Party.

The main thrust of the Party's unemployment and relief work with women came to focus on the wives of the unemployed. The National Unemployment Council repeated the well-established dictum that women's political understanding was drawn from domestic and personal experiences, and that women, usually conservative, could be radicalized on this basis. The Party tried to appeal to women on the basis of their role as household manager and their concern for their families: "women," explained *The Worker*, "could be fighters, especially since they are the ones who must stretch the family budget and . . . deal with the insulting relief regulations about purchasing."[46] In order to recruit more housewives on welfare the Party suggested organizing women's relief auxiliaries, with a list of demands such as hot school lunches (now appropriately "revolutionary"), better milk vouchers, care for pregnant women, and the right of wives to collect relief.

Communists, however, did not expend significant energy organizing unemployed women wage-earners. The difficulties reaching these women, of course, were immense. Aside from a constant fear of being penalized for relief activism, Communists also had to contend with the problematic nature of the unemployed "work force." Unemployment was a fluid state, with some workers drifting in and out of jobs, in and out of cities. Often isolated and preoccupied only with personal and family survival, the unemployed did not necessarily see their condition as a social predicament. The prevailing hegemony of ideas of individualism and self-help was crucial in reinforcing workers' self-blame and isolation. For women, too, these pressures were even more complex. Women's wage labour was not fully sanctioned by society and, as unemployment mounted, there were public attempts to discourage women, particularly married women, from taking jobs away from men. The depression, complained the CPC, was leading to the unfortunate, reactionary refrain that women should be "sent back to the kitchen."[47] Widespread discrimination by relief authorities against single women further impeded recruitment to a welfare rights group, for women were usually forced to move out of the city, in with family, or take low-paid domestic work. As Marjorie Cohen notes, "the plight of working women in the

Depression was not taken seriously. . . . It was assumed that a woman always had a man to protect and support her.''[48] Yet these same assumptions to some extent influenced the CPC. The Party's sporadic attempts to organize single women on relief and reject the back-to-the-kitchen solution for unemployment revealed a latent current of sympathy for women's oppression. Overall, however, the Party was much less concerned with the woman wage-earner than it was with protecting the family wage, aiding woman's role as household manager, and organizing the male unemployed. Despite regular self-criticism of its meagre efforts with unemployed females, the Party never really overcame its own indifference to this group. Like society at large, the Party came to stress the plight of the "lost (male) youth" in the relief camps, not the young woman, denied relief and forced into a low-paying domestic job.

### Women and the Workers Unity League

The Communist Party's highest priority in its work among women was its intent to organize women into the "revolutionary" unions of the Workers Unity League: the Marxist lesson that women's involvement in wage labour was the key to their revolutionary consciousness was now completely taken to heart. Established in 1930, the WUL concentrated its efforts on organizing new industrial unions, and by 1935, concludes Ian Radforth, it had organized many unskilled workers, helping to lay the basis for the Canadian CIO. Initially, the League set out unrealistic plans to colonize women's workplaces, such as the needle trades, textiles, and the food industry, to issue radical workplace newspapers, then to prepare the ground for mass strikes. In reality, organizing was a more painstaking and difficult proposition, and not until 1933 did the WUL experience significant growth; by then, "improvements in the WUL's weak organizational structure, an economic upturn and a curb on the League's ultra-left language stressing imminent class war''[49] all improved the WUL's prospects.

Especially in the early years, internal problems plagued the WUL: there was a shortage of paid organizers, few comrades available to infiltrate women's workplaces, and for those, like the ardent Young Communists who attempted to organize the Silknit textile factory in Toronto, dismissal quickly followed their agitational activities. Nor was the WUL able to easily intervene in "spontaneous working-class struggles," as the Comintern had advised. In 1929, for instance, a militant strike at Hamilton's Canada Cottons was initiated by women workers protesting newly imposed speed-up measures. The Communist press immediately cited the strike as proof positive that the Comintern's prophecies of speed-ups were accurate. But the actual workers rejected Party involvement in the strike.[50] Furthermore, there were times when the Comintern's prophecies did not fit the Canadian labour situation: cheap female labour did not always replace male labour, as was predicted, because some employers hired men to avoid paying the minimum wage to women. Last, but not least, because the WUL sometimes set up "dual" unions that challenged existing internationals, there was bitter strife between the TLC and the WUL, a fact that wasted precious time and energy on sectarian inter-union rivalry.

There were also immense external obstacles to union organizing, especially the ever-present spectre of economic depression and a host of repressive state measures used against trade unionists, including the imprisonment and deportation of union radicals. Moreover, the female workers the Party hoped to contact, like the workers at Canada Cottons, were often young, temporary, sojourners in the work force with a high turnover rate and little experience with unions. The only increasing female occupation in the depression was domestic service, known to be an organizer's nightmare.

Still, Party attitudes also contributed to difficulties in organizing women. Some Party organizers shared with their enemies in the TLC the unstated understanding that women were "secondary" earners, less important to industrial organizing strategies. Annie Buller, a WUL organizer for the needle trades, once lamented that she had seen a "complete lack of organization work among women,"[51] while Pearl Wedro, even more critical, claimed that women were simply prevented from taking a leading role in union work:

> Usually in unions women took a backward [sic] seat. And they weren't elected, and they were kind of looked at as people who paid their dues, they come and go . . . even in progressive-led [CP] unions, a woman's chances are less than a man's . . . if I was a man I think I would have been placed with the highest responsibility. . . . But that was not the case.[52]

The difficulty of integrating women into trade union work was compounded by the ultra-left atmosphere of the early 1930's.

How many women, after all, could accommodate their lives to the imperatives of union organizing, which often necessitated travelling alone, separation from one's family, and the possibility of jail terms? Women did not fit easily into the transient, rough-and-ready, tough image associated with union organizers. For some young female activists, the Party's revolutionary stance was appealing; the Third Period saw the recruitment of cultural radicals Dorothy Livesay and Jean Watts and trade union organizer Ann Walters, a second-generation Finn in her early twenties who went from the YCL to organizing textile workers in small-town Ontario. Nonetheless, the intense demands of Third Period organizing also tended to divide women into Party "cadres" and "wives." Livesay, recalling her Party work in the early 1930's, illustrates this dilemma very well:

> The young organizer for whom I wrote pamphlets had two children and a wife who was "unpoliticized" and left behind in the kitchen whilst we were at meetings. Such were the dichotomies I found in male-female relationships in the thirties. . . . In theory, we were free and equal comrades on the left. In practice, our right hand was tied to the kitchen sink.[53]

Although few women became trade union organizers, we must also assess Communists' success in organizing rank-and-file women into new unions. Here, the WUL record is more impressive, for the League filled a decided vacuum in the Canadian labour movement. As jobs disappeared in the early thirties, the TLC's organizational work collapsed and the international unions clung desperately to their existing membership. Undaunted by the depression, the WUL, motivated by political zeal, eagerly stepped into this breach. For women workers in particular, the WUL offered potential salvation; though historically ignored by the craft unionists, the WUL publicly proclaimed its intent to devote itself to the doubly exploited – women and youth.

A significant amount of WUL energy was devoted to the needle trades, in which there existed a tradition of union militance encompassing both sexes and drawing on a strong Eastern European, Jewish-socialist presence in the industry. Indeed, the needle trades seemed one of the most promising areas for the organizing effort, save for the Communists' intent to fight social democratic trade unionists as well as the employers. The WUL union, the International Union of Needle Trades Workers (IUNTW), had its first major confrontation with Toronto employers in 1931, and it was a rout for the employers, in part because of inadequate WUL preparation but also because Communist attacks on the rival ILGWU proved suicidal. In the first five-day strike held in the bitter January cold, 300 dressmakers walked the picket line demanding better pay and shorter hours; but within days the strike was defeated. This defeat, claimed the IUNTW, was the result of ILGWU workers who crossed the picket line – hardly surprising as their leaders were being denounced as "fascists and gangsters."[54] Barely a month later the IUNTW itself opposed an ILGWU strike, and in the end the main losers were the workers who failed to gain their wage increases.

In subsequent years, however, WUL organizers wisely directed more of their efforts toward the unorganized, and by 1934 twelve IUNTW locals existed across Canada, some promoting a new, more democratic system of internal union representation.[55] The WUL's successes began to cause the internationals anxiety, even prodding the ILGWU leadership out of its organizing lethargy. In 1933, ILGWU officials pressed their union headquarters for more organizing funds, pointing to the IUNTW's "prestige" and advances with previously unorganized workers as a cause for concern.[56] The IUNTW was particularly effective in Winnipeg, where in 1933 the union led successful strikes against subcontracting; by 1936, the IUNTW was still the major garment union in the city. Elsewhere, of course, the union had setbacks. In Montreal in 1934, the IUNTW mounted a general garment strike that brought thousands of Jewish and French-Canadian women into the streets. The strikers' demands for better wages, however, were never obtained, though the union did temporarily disprove the view that language barriers and French-Canadian culture made these women workers "unorganizable."[57]

In the garment industry, argues John Manley, the IUNTW displayed more sympathy for women workers than the internationals ever had. Ruth Frager, however, is more critical of the IUNTW's attitudes toward women. She maintains that organizers never questioned the ghettoization of women into unskilled jobs and never appealed to women with special organizing methods or a platform promising to eradicate discriminatory benefits, dues, and wage structures.[58] Clearly, the instructions of the Women's Department to use special methods to draw women into unions and to advance more women into union leadership often went unheeded by union leaders more preoccupied with what they saw as the "important" task of organizing the unorganized. Frager's own interviews with Jewish workers offer some explanation for the persisting inattention to gender inequality within these radical unions. Union men were understandably content with the existing sexual division of labour, and women, she points out, identified primarily with their class and ethnic group. They were more concerned with anti-Semitism than with gender oppression and rarely challenged the existing division of labour within the factory or even their own double burden of domestic and wage work.[59] Thus, the Third Period line of working-class unity did have a reasonable appeal to women whose consciousness was shaped largely by their experiences of wage labour in an exploitive, nativist society.

The WUL also had some successes in other areas of female employment, often conducting strikes that brought temporary gains or prevented wage cutbacks, though falling short of union recognition. At the Mercury Mills in Hamilton a WUL-sponsored strike against speed-up measures resulted in company threats to move the textile factory to Woodstock. Fearing loss of their jobs, many workers returned to work and the union went unrecognized. Nonetheless, the strike could be considered a "draw" as workers remained WUL members and there were improvements in piece work and no discrimination in rehiring. Indeed, WUL strikes were not all "reckless ventures," as the TLC claimed. Ian Radforth argues that the Ontario WUL had the same rate of success/compromise as the international unions. And, unlike the TLC, the WUL had to contend with intense Red-baiting. The WUL had members of the Textile Workers Industrial Union in small Ontario towns like Paris, Galt, and Welland. In Welland, the Party reported, an attempt to lead a strike against wage reductions in the mills failed because the local Catholic Church, a powerful force in a small, immigrant town, used the pulpit to denounce the Godless Reds. Intense hostility to the WUL, of course, existed in cities, too. In a bitter strike of IUNTW Winnipeg fur workers, organizer Freda Coodin led picketers from the factory to the owner's comfortable home. The police immediately arrested Coodin, and she received a severe jail sentence. Already susceptible to tuberculosis, she died shortly afterwards, a martyr to the movement.

Finally, the WUL also encouraged women's auxiliary participation in the labour disputes of their menfolk. Though certainly never intended to enhance women's equality, these organizations did help further the party's goal of building a united working-class movement. Sometimes women's auxiliaries were recruited through the language organizations; planning a strike in the Ontario lumber industry in 1934, the WUL leaders confidently reported that all the food for the strikers would be cooked by ULFTA women.[60] Women were used as support picket duty; in a militant WUL strike in a Kitchener tannery, reported the *Toronto Star*, "scabs were mauled by a crowd of irate girls and women, many of whom were wives of the strikers. . . . One woman was arrested for throwing rocks at scabs, a second for biting a policeman."[61] And in a bitterly fought WUL strike of miners in Flin Flon, Manitoba, local women, aided by a young YCL firebrand from Winnipeg, Mabel "Mickey" Marlowe, organized a soup kitchen, anti-scab demonstrations, and picket support. Amidst a virulent anti-Communist campaign, the Hudson's Bay Smelting Company sponsored its own back-to-work vote. Members of the women's auxiliary helped block the entrance to the hall where the vote was being held and pelted scabs with mushy missiles while they sang rounds of "We'll hang the scabs on a Sour Apple Tree." Despite strong family support, however, the miners suffered a crushing defeat at the hands of a powerful company.

In the aftermath of the strike, a women's auxiliary member was charged with assault and Mickey Marlowe received a one-year sentence for unlawful assembly and intimidation, underlining the danger that Third Period militance could easily antagonize an already hostile state and jeopardize the freedom of Communist organizing. The Party was also aware that women's strike support groups remained fleeting organizations fixed at a crisis point, even though women were encouraged after the strike to continue raising funds for the CLDL and the Workers International Relief Fund. Though never entirely successful in sustaining women's activism, women's strike aid was especially crucial during the Third Period, as the WUL's sectarian isolation cut it off from moral and financial support of the internationals.

In assessing the WUL's efforts to organize women, a mixed balance sheet appears. In contrast to the previous decade, the Party now put more effort into the unionization of women, and although WUL efforts sometimes faltered in the face of economic and political realities or as a result of sectarian tactics, a significant group of unorganized women was drawn into the CPC's ambitious aim to build industrial unions in Canada. The Party's intent to give extra attention to the doubly exploited, however, was constantly compromised as such women's demands as equal pay were pushed to the side in labour disputes. The Party put more stock into organizing heavy industrial targets where fewer women worked, and ultimately, many Communist organizers adopted the prevailing assumption that women were secondary or temporary wage-earners. Issues so crucial to modern trade unionists, such as the discriminatory division of labour and women's double burden of home and work, were seldom addressed in the 1930's. The primary goal was simply to organize the unorganized. Using this yardstick, and comparing the WUL to the older TLC, the Communists were certainly successful in organizing women. Measured by their own proclamations and self-criticism, the WUL was much less successful indeed.

### "Pink Tea Pacifists": Labourite and Farm Women

As the Communist Party attempted to tighten its grip over the Women's Labor Leagues, Canadian social democrats remained scattered across Canada, lacking national organizational unity. During the 1920's socialists and labourites had attempted to build a Canadian Labor Party with a loose federal structure and flexible terms of affiliation. By 1927, however, Communists dominated the leadership and most labourites abandoned the CLP, redirecting their energies to the regional and municipal ILPs and labour parties, which had always formed the backbone of the movement. Across Canada, labourite politics were characterized by distinctive city and regional differences.[62] Yet, however varied the labourite tradition, there were still some important common denominators, including the noticeable increase in women's participation in labour parties during the 1920's.[63]

In the aftermath of World War One, more women turned to political action through labour parties as a means of achieving their goals of social and economic justice; in some cities, too, separate women's sections emerged. Women in labourite politics drew on pre-war traditions, such as the Union Label Leagues, incorporated the lessons of their radical wartime activity, then during the 1920's further sharpened their political skills. Though labourite women seldom directly challenged the male hierarchies within their own parties and, like the men, optimistically placed tremendous hope in the ballot box, they were far from being the passive "pink tea pacifists" condemned by Third Period Communists.

In Alberta, as in many provinces, labourite women were often wives of trade unionists, former suffrage and peace activists radicalized by the war and 1919, or sometimes women with roots in a socialist party. In Calgary, a Women's Section emerged out of the Dominion Labour Party (DLP), an alliance of "ethical socialists and craft unionists" drawn together under the charismatic leadership of William Irvine.[64] From the DLP's inception, women formed a sizable proportion of the membership and some eventually joined the party executive, contested elections, and even served as Labour school trustees and aldermen. The Women's Section had a strong constituency in the teaching profession, with single, career teachers like Rachel Coutts and Edith Patterson offering consistent leadership, as did Marion Carson, a married, middle-class member who had been drawn into the Labour camp by her anti-war sympathies and her connection to Irvine's Unitarian Church.[65]

Labourite women in Edmonton also developed their own section of the Labour Party, inspired by Mary Crawford, a high school teacher who was already well known for her militant leadership of the Edmonton Teachers' Alliance in its battle for collective bargaining rights. In order to focus more attention on women's issues and build a community of labour women activists, a women's column was initiated in *The Alberta Labor News*. Edited for many years by Edith Patterson, the column urged women, especially wives of trade unionists, to support such issues as public ownership and, emulating British Labour women, stand unified with working-class men to elect DLP candidates to government. Though Patterson identified with some feminist goals, she often approached contentious gender issues cautiously, rejecting birth control as a "divisive" issue for Labour and calling for traditional solutions, such as domestic training, for women's employment woes.

More outspoken about women's need for economic equality was Amelia Turner Smith, a dynamic representative of the Calgary DLP and one of the first CCF candidates for Alberta. The daughter of an intellectual though by no means wealthy homesteading family, Turner ventured to Calgary as a young woman and carved out her career in the world of journalism, working first for the UFA's *Western Independent*, then later with her husband, the editor of the *Western Farm Producer*. Turner's interest in socialism emerged from her rural roots and faith in co-operation, as well as from the influence of Bill Irvine and her later conversion to Fabian ideas of efficient and ethical socialism. Inspired by a non-conformist and radical family background and

*Amelia Turner Smith.* (Glenbow Archives)

tutored by older women in the Women's Section of the party, Turner overcame her first reticence in politics and became an organizer of considerable note in the Calgary DLP. Like Marion Carson, Turner took a keen interest in educational issues, entering local politics as a candidate for the school board with a platform of radical demands, including free school texts, good medical care in the schools, an end to military training, and equal pay for female teachers. Though she failed in her first election attempt in 1925, the following year she scored a surprising upset victory over the incumbent trustee when the school board was recalled by petitions protesting the abandonment of free school texts. Then, in 1933, Turner became a CCF candidate for a provincial seat in Calgary and narrowly lost, harmed in part by her connection to the discredited UFA but also by an intense anti-Red smear campaign pursued by the local press.

In the decade following the war, labourite women in other Canadian cities also indicated a strong desire to represent women's concerns in the public sphere and to create autonomous women's sections within their parties. In Ontario, one of the most active women's groups was the Hamilton Women's ILP, established in 1917 after women obtained the provincial vote. Scottish names like McNab and Inman headed the leadership of the Hamilton group. Mary McNab, reared in a minister's manse in Ontario, went to work in the garment industry, a radicalizing experience that led to involvement with the Amalgamated Clothing Workers Union and the Hamilton ILP. A more recent Scottish immigrant, Janet Inman was active in a variety of socialist and feminist causes, from the Women's ILP to theosophy and the Workers Educational Association. Besides providing social and financial aid to the ILP, their Women's ILP acted as an educational and lobby group, pressing the Ontario government to improve legislation governing working-class women. The Women's ILP often used maternalist arguments to justify women's participation in the political process and, like the earlier suffragists, trusted in government as a neutral tool to be captured by honest political work. McNab and Inman, for example, sat on the Mothers Allowance Board, a position the more radical Communists would have shunned in the 1920's and certainly condemned by the early 1930's.

Before the advent of Third Period antagonisms some socialist and Communist women co-existed in the WLLs, as they did for a short time in Toronto. Not every local Labour Party boasted a separate women's section, and some women's labourite groups played a more passive, auxiliary role than others. The creation of a distinct women's section may have been related, James Naylor suggests, to the character of the trade union movement in the city and party, with the craft unions favouring their traditional mode of organization – the wives' auxiliary.[66] Lingering feminist sensibilities, however, may also have influenced the creation of women's sections, which usually asserted women's social problems, from equal pay to speaking in public, to be distinct from men's. And in some cities, women's labourite groups seem to have risen and declined, according to the needs and atmosphere in the Labour Party. In 1924, for example, the Vancouver Labour Women's group was heavily involved in grassroots electoral work in the municipal election; shortly after, the local party became critical of women's auxiliaries as "segregationalist"[67] and inappropriate in a working-class party.

Not all women's labourite groups were linked to one specific party. From Manitoba there emerged one of the most innovative experiments in the post-war period: an attempt to establish a non-partisan women's labour support network across the Prairies. This Western Women's Social and Economic Labour Conference was the brainchild of Beatrice Brigden, a woman whose political evolution linked the pre-war Social Gospel movement with post-war socialist politics.[68] Brigden, a product of a religious Manitoba farm family, was employed by the Methodist Church in 1914 to educate young women to the ideals of social purity and warn them of the dangers of the white slave trade. Dedicated to women's "moral uplift," Brigden increasingly found her religious values tested and her work fraught with difficulties, including the opposition of conservative clergy to her ideas, the disinterest of the "fallen" women in her rescue mission, and her own middle-class naiveté and inability to relate to immigrant and working-class Canadians. Her paternalistic attitudes, however, were increasingly challenged by her contact with lower-income Canadians, and then sharply altered by her experience of the Winnipeg General Strike. In the aftermath of 1919 Brigden left the Methodist Church, joined A.E. Smith's radical "Peoples Church" in Brandon, and devoted herself to labour and socialist causes.

In 1924, she organized the first Western Women's Conference in Brandon. About forty women came; the majority were Labour Party supporters, but a minority came from the more radical Communist WLLS. Each year it met, the Women's Conference served as an educational forum, passing resolutions such as protests against military training and war and making calls for more generous mothers' allowances and minimum wages for women. Because the Women's Conference was never strictly allied with one political party, it could wander over the political map from year to year. Finally, in 1930, as the Communists were attempting their left turn, the conference took a "right turn," endorsing a harsh resolution on sterilization of the feeble-minded. Though the Communists now condemned the Women's Conference, it had served an essential purpose for over seven years, providing a valuable forum in which social democratic, and sometimes Communist, women could share ideas and work together to improve the lot of working-class women. For labourite women in particular, the conference created a network of communication that later aided the growth of the CCF and helped to inspire the formation of CCF women's groups across the Canadian West.

Some early CCF women gained their political education from

farm organizations rather than urban labour parties. This was true of Agnes Macphail, Canada's first woman MP, elected in 1921 as a Progressive to represent an Ontario farm community. As the first female federal parliamentarian, Macphail became a symbol for many Canadian feminists and was often called on to address or defend women's equality. Feminism struck an inner chord for Macphail: she understood women to be oppressed, was a strong supporter of the Women's International League for Peace and Freedom, and clearly believed in women's equal capabilities and right to a career and economic independence. Women, she sometimes also argued in the vein of maternalism, had stronger intuition than men, and because of their care for the family they shared a fierce adherence to "human values" and a desire to "elevate national morals."[69] Macphail, however, was often uneasy about declaring herself a feminist; as an object of curiosity in the House of Commons, she felt isolated and suspect, and she was reluctant to dare further alienation by embracing a cause seen in the twenties as unpopular and anti-male. Moreover, like some feminists, she liked to stress her achievements as an individual rather than her feminist association with women's groups.

Macphail was often ambivalent about women's auxiliaries, fearing they kept women isolated on the sidelines of politics, though she did take an interest in the political work of farm women's organizations. In Ontario and the West, farm women carried on with their pre-war organizational work, fund-raising and discussing issues related to rural education, public health, and social welfare. Moderate in their reform view, farm women might collaborate with the Local Councils of Women, sometimes sharing a sympathy for temperance or, in Manitoba, distress about "undesirable,"[70] meaning non-British, immigrants. Feminist issues certainly appealed: the United Farm Women of Alberta lobbied for better property laws for married women, embraced the WIL's campaign for an end to militarism in the schools, and even came in 1934 to advocate the legalization of birth control. But, overall, there was some ambivalence about public ownership and socialism, and a strong Anglo-Saxon Protestant bias in many women's farm groups, a marked contrast to the radical, ethnic Communist Party.

Only a minority of organized farm women, of course, found their way into the CCF. The United Farmers of Ontario had a stormy relationship in the party,[71] and in Alberta and Manitoba a radical minority of the United Farm Women made valiant efforts

to persuade their fellow members to enter the new socialist alliance. In Manitoba, women such as Margaret McClelland had
their early political education in the farm movement. A farm wife
from Letellier, McClelland tried to help organize the short-lived
radical farmers' party, the Independent Farmers Party, in the early
1920's, then threw her energies into the United Farm Women,
acting as president, and later joined the CCF, serving on the provincial council and running as a candidate in the 1940's. Similarly,
in Alberta, CCFers Nellie Peterson and Alice Ness had their roots
in the United Farmers of Alberta and the rural co-operative movement, and they, too, tried to persuade other women to take their
rural concerns into the newly formed socialist party, but only a
small number actually made the transition from the UFA to the
CCF.

From its inception, women in the United Farmers of Canada
(Saskatchewan Section), or UFC for short, displayed more sympathy for radical politics, a fact that perhaps led to Florence
Custance's efforts to draw them into political debate. Conscious
of the need to involve farm wives in politics, the UFC gave women
assured seats on its provincial executive board and, significantly,
such later CCF activists as Sophia Dixon, Elise Hart, and Annie
Hollis were all introduced to politics this way. In Saskatchewan,
too, a strong women's network was created by Violet Mac-
Naughton, the influential women's editor of the *Western Producer*, who used her writing talents and personal contacts to foster
discussion and connections among political women on the Prairies. One of MacNaughton's contacts was Louise Lucas, a farm
wife and charismatic UFC leader, whose vision of a new economic
order was portrayed in millennial terms, equated with the reali-
zation of the Christian Brotherhood of Man. In the early UFC
years, Lucas, tied to a young family, organized and wrote from
her kitchen table; later she became a travelling organizer, covering
the province at a pace unparalleled by many male board members.
As official UFC women's president, Lucas attended Farm Wom-
en's Week, held every summer after 1928 at the University of
Saskatchewan. A woman delegate from each UFC lodge attended
this week-long program of education and discussion, at the end
of which a list of resolutions was prepared for the larger UFC
convention. Attendance was a difficult proposition for farm wives
hard-pressed for time and cash, but solutions were improvised,
even if women had to ''carefully keep back some egg money all

*Louise Lucas.* (Saskatchewan Archives Board)

year'' to allow themselves the treasured respite to ''discuss issues and socialize with other women.''[72]

At the inaugural Farm Women's Week in 1928, the women were addressed by feminists Irene Parlby and Laura Jamieson; then the delegates tackled a number of contentious social problems, including a resolution calling for legal access to birth control. The resolution appeared again in 1929, and in 1930 it was finally sent on to the main convention only to be rejected, even by women such as Louise Lucas, who were afraid of splitting the farm movement on religious grounds. More adamant farm feminists, such as Sophia Dixon, disagreed, arguing that women's rights should not be sacrificed for a vague notion of class unity. The frequency with which Dixon and others defended birth control indicates strong grassroots sympathy for legalization; yet the issue remained marginal and secondary within the larger farm movement. It was a situation all too familiar to women labourites, who also ran up against fears, even their own, that "feminist" concerns would shatter the class unity needed to build a socialist movement.

In 1932, many women from the UFC were drawn into the Farmer-Labour Party, a precursor to the CCF. Within the UFC women had built a reservoir of talent and gained leadership experience, which was later to prove useful in the CCF. As well, Farm Women's Week had inaugurated a women's network and an important practice of separate women's organization, with a sense of common dedication to the improvement of rural women's lives. "We discussed resolutions, and socializing with other women created a comradely situation," remembered one participant. "Every woman was vocal, they felt freer than in mixed groups . . . it gave women confidence and knowledge."[73] Like the women's labour parties, some farm women were paving the way for the creation of a socialist and feminist praxis within the new CCF.

### Conclusion

When an appeal went out in the drought-ridden summer of 1932 for a western conference to discuss a new socialist party, labourite and farm women were ready to answer the call. Far from returning home after the war, they had maintained and sometimes even increased their public profile. The impact of suffrage, women's increasing role in the work force, and the growing desire of farm wives for recognition of their economic contribution to the family all stimulated women's bid to participate in politics. Like the earlier suffragists, labourite and farm women usually came from English-speaking Protestant backgrounds, and they often promoted the maternalist view that women should bring to politics their special concerns relating to the family. Maternal feminism lived on, rooted in persisting patriarchal assumptions about women's role in the family, though the contours of maternalist politics varied greatly from suffragist to labourite politics. The 1920's also witnessed the emergence of a new generation of socialist women. Some, such as Beatrice Brigden, linked the earlier social reform movement to labourite politics in the twenties, while younger women, including Amelia Turner, represented a new wave of socialist-feminist politicians. Their feminist consciousness caused a few waves of tension within the social democratic movement of the twenties, foreshadowing later feminist dilemmas within the CCF, but it in no way measured up to the strong antipathy to feminism evidenced in the rival Communist Party.

In contrast to labour and farm groups, the Communist Party was composed largely of working-class immigrants and lacked an historic link to the feminist movement. Like labourites, Communists saw a close connection between women's domestic and political consciousness, but they put more emphasis on the recruitment of women wage-earners to the revolutionary movement. And in the early 1930's, "Red revolutionaries" were precisely the female recruits the Party was seeking, as the Comintern called for a militant left turn in political organizing. Indeed, the Comintern's influence on the woman question provided a further contrast to the varied local women's labourite groups spread across Canada. Directed by a centralized leadership and inspired by directions from the International, Communist women were organized more efficiently, though more rigidly, than labourite women.

After 1929, the woman question in the CPC became synonymous with a pro-Soviet peace lobby and with direct challenges to capitalist enterprise. Debates on women's inequality were narrowly focused: the Party centred its gaze on the workplace, letting issues like birth control and the family fall by the wayside. The devastating impact of the early depression reinforced this economism, just as state repression heightened the Party's militant rhetoric, for the alarming growth of poverty confirmed leaders' views that all but the key economic issue were peripheral to the movement. The CPC's emphasis on class struggle also appealed to many rank-and-filers, whose consciousness had been shaped largely by their experience of nativism, working-class life, and wage labour. Moreover, members' immersion in Marxist and Leninist education, which had always stressed women's role in social production, further reinforced and solidified the Party line.

During the early thirties, some Communist women did take an equal and courageous part in such dangerous activities as the free-speech fights and union organizing. By and large, though, women with families remained tied to traditional tasks like fund-raising, petitioning, and union support work. To the Party's chagrin, the Women's Labor Leagues remained ethno-centred housewives' organizations, and increasingly they were replaced in Party priorities by the WUL. By 1933, the Workers Unity League had some success organizing women workers, and though it was a welcome contrast to the apathetic TLC, the League could not measure up to its own goal of building mass industrial unions in Canada. Furthermore, the Communist Party's aim to mobilize unemployed and working women faltered not only because of difficult depression conditions but also because women were not considered as important to the revolution as male workers in the steel industry. For some Communist leaders, such as Becky Buhay, the failure to recruit women was a cause of intense frustration. Buhay publicly exhorted her comrades not to look down "sneeringly" on women and privately begged organizers to "read and *follow*"[74] Women's Department directives, rather than assigning them to the dustbin. Wrestling with porcupinism, it appears, was still a Party dilemma.

Finally, the Party's recruitment of women was sometimes marred by Third Period antagonism to the "pink tea pacifist" labourite women. These sectarian barriers, however, were being challenged by 1934, as the Comintern began to turn its sights to an alliance against fascism. Shortly after labourite and farm women joined together in the CCF, they were faced with appeals for unity from Communist women, now emerging recalcitrant and reformed from their Third Period excesses.

# 4

# Militant Mothering: Women in the Early CCF

At the founding convention of the CCF in Regina in 1933, the women delegates were far outnumbered by the men in the conference hall.[1] Despite their small numbers, they were a determined and dedicated group, many of whom, like the men, had to improvise and economize to reach Regina that summer. Dorothy Steeves and Mildred Osterhout Fahrni, from Vancouver, shared a bumpy car ride to Regina with frequent tire blowouts. They had feared that the car would not make it through the mountains. Lorna Cotton-Thomas, an unemployed graduate of the University of Toronto, made illegal use of a friend's CPR pass, despite the disapproval of her boyfriend, who tried to persuade her that in this case the end did not justify the means. Elizabeth Morton, an Ontario SPCer, drove from Toronto, sharing a car with four other delegates and raising money for her expenses with speaking engagements along the way.

These women, along with other female delegates at Regina, symbolized the important presence, although less influential role, that women were to play in this new party. Women who joined the CCF were deeply moved by the economic upheaval of the Great Depression, and they had found their despair with the social system answered in socialist literature by Edward Bellamy, Karl Marx, and the British Fabians. But once active in the party, they were rudely awakened to a less than ideal socialist division of labour. Women were to be found primarily in grassroots work, but rarely in the leadership. Drawing on traditions of earlier labourite groups some women set up their own organizations, which were encouraged by the CCF, though it did not, as a rule, see the woman question as a priority issue. Indeed, only a very small minority of women became involved in the CCF with feminist goals in mind. These early socialist-feminists recognized that despite the egalitarian principles of the CCF, in practice, the party, like the society it strove to change, upheld distinct and sometimes unequal roles for women.

### Who Was the Party?

The CCF was an alliance of socialist, labour, and farm groups united against the economic inequalities of capitalism, which had been greatly magnified by the depression. The precise analysis of capitalism, however, varied among the CCF's constituent groups, as did their remedies for change. Agrarian groups, intellectuals from the LSR, moderate labourites, and Marxists made for an eclectic and sometimes uneasy alliance. At the local level ideological differences often erupted openly in the early years: in Ontario the party's three sections – labour (including SPCers), club, and farm – co-existed uneasily until a major conflict in 1934 was patched over by Woodsworth's forceful intervention from above. Similar differences existed in B.C., where those who came from the LSR were viewed by labour men as middle-class intellectuals remote from the class struggle, and in Manitoba, where the ILP guarded its organizational autonomy fiercely. By the 1940's some of these differences had been resolved, in part because of the national office's insistence on a role in local matters. Indeed, until the increased centralization of later years, it is difficult to speak of a "national" CCF, for each provincial party had its own organizational apparatus and particular political flavour.

Despite all these divisions, the CCF alliance persevered, united by its umbrella statement of principles, the Regina Manifesto. The Manifesto, hammered out at the party's inaugural convention in 1933, provided a critique of capitalism and advocated both short-term reform and fundamental social change to alter a system geared to profit to one based on co-operation and public ownership. Considerable attention was given to the economic needs of small farmers, with demands such as socialized finance, and in compromise to the labourites it was made clear that constitutional means were means for political change. At the same time, Marxists successfully included important statements on public ownership and calls to "eradicate all capitalist property and social relations."[2] Unlike the Communist Party, the CCF did not include a platform on women's rights in its Manifesto, but one resolution called for equal pay, a reform socialists saw as central to women's economic independence.

Many women who immediately joined the CCF had already been active in the LSR, labour parties, or farm groups in the twenties and early thirties. A second generation of CCF women, who grew to maturity in the thirties, often came from highly politicized and progressive families. Hilda Kristiansen, for example, grew up in a prairie farm family well versed in co-operative and socialist ideas. Her father was active in the local co-op, the United Farmers of Canada, and he attended the CCF's Regina Convention, while her mother was "quietly supportive of these causes." Like many young women of this period, Kristiansen took her father's political work in the public sphere as her important role model. After moving to B.C. in 1933 to work, Hilda joined the Young Socialists and eventually became active in the B.C. CCF women's committee.

Still, the commitment of women to the CCF cannot be explained simply by the inheritance of family politics. What, then, were the motivating forces behind women's interest in socialism? Underlying women's activism lay certain common themes: women's experience of working-class or farm life, or their witness of social inequalities, combined with exposure to socialist ideas led them to the CCF. Economic insecurity and arduous working conditions were the lot of most working-class and farm women in the 1920's; the Great Depression only worsened their lot. Single and married women working for wages faced wage reduction, speed-ups, and job loss; women workers were often forced to resort to the only alternative open to them – despised and poorly paid domestic work.

Women were also affected by the depression experience of friends, relatives, or even strangers around them. Irene Biss, for example, a professor at the University of Toronto and LSR activist, investigated and wrote about conditions of Toronto garment workers. Unemployment and relief – either experienced first hand or viewed second hand – were radicalizing forces for many women. In East York, a Toronto municipality hard-hit by unemployment, relief recipients, aided by local socialists, organized collectively into a self-help and action-oriented organization, the East York Workers Association (EYWA). Women in the EYWA organized their own women's Marxist study group and aided the association's anti-eviction lobbying campaigns. Some of these women subsequently joined the CCF.[3]

Nor was the relief experience limited to urban Canada. In the West, particularly in Saskatchewan, depression and drought carved out a path of destruction and poverty: income levels plummeted and some families, if not forced off their land, were reduced to the most meagre subsistence or the "humiliation" of relief. Letters from women to the *Western Producer* and later to the CCF newspapers often included poignant descriptions of their struggles with economic adversity. These years, according to many women who became CCFers, left an indelible mark on their memories. Women were forced to leave school early to support their families; they were faced with the fear – and the reality – of crop failure; they were sometimes uprooted to the city; they were given no alternative but relief; they scrimped and compromised on their family budget; and they saw brothers and friends leave to ride the rods or head to the relief camps. In the midst of such social upheaval, it is hardly surprising that some women began to question the status quo. Although the depression did not "cause" the emergence of the CCF, it did encourage some women to reflect on the social order and it stimulated their search for an alternative system. "It seemed by 1933," recalled Sophia Dixon, "as if the capitalist system was simply crumbling before us and our task was to find and build a new system which could replace the old."[4]

Radical ideas, along with material realities, led women to the CCF. For many, progressive Christian politics and such groups as the Fellowship for a Christian Social Order (FCSO) provided an introduction to socialism. Young CCFers had their early education in the Student Christian Movement, a progressive student organization founded in the 1920's. Avis McCurdy, who came from a middle-class Maritime family, was also schooled in the SCM's Christian politics:

> I came straight to the CCF because I was convinced I had to be my brother's keeper. It was right out of my religious background – CGIT and SCM. I had also worked in business in my summers, and was overcome with the injustice and inequality. But mainly, it was my moral, religious background.[5]

Louise Lucas, Beatrice Brigden, and Mildred Osterhout Fahrni, among others, found the CCF a logical extension of their Christian belief in the brotherhood and equality of humankind. Mildred Fahrni, who grew up in a religious household, found her eyes opened to the inequalities and waste of capitalist society during the depression, particularly when she worked with single unemployed women in Vancouver. At the same time, her intellectual growth as a Christian and pacifist was also integral to her activism. The influences of her university studies, especially at Bryn Mawr and the London School of Economics, of her travels to Russia

*Beatrice Brigden, original in*
Western People. (Reproduced by
Lawrence Stuckey, Brandon,
Manitoba)

*Sophia Dixon, founding member of*
*Saskatchewan* CCF. (Saskatchewan
Archives Board)

and later India, and of her life at Kingsley Hall Settlement House
all shaped her socialism, which was ethical, humanist, and Christian in nature. "We CCFers were evangelists," she remembered,
"out to build a new world order, out to build the Kingdom . . .
and we felt it could be done!"[6] Even CCFers who did not participate in organized Christian groups often described their politics
as "applied Christianity." To many of us, commented Nellie
Peterson, socialism was simply the practical expression of Christian ideas about equality.[7] In a society receptive to the moral
language of Christianity, CCFers culled their metaphors from radical Christian ideals, just as earlier socialists had used these metaphors to plead for social justice.

Mildred Fahrni, for one, found Christian ideals to be inextricably intertwined with pacifist ones, and for many CCF women the
new party appealed because of its commitment to international
peace. Behind Fahrni's pacifism lay both a materialist analysis

of war as a means of economic aggrandizement and, perhaps more predominantly, a Christian belief that under no circumstances was taking a human life justifiable. Although other CCF women subscribed to different variations of anti-war ideals, most saw some connection in their socialism, pacifism, and feminism, and a great number of CCF women found common cause for these ideals in the Women's International League for Peace and Freedom (WILPF), popularly known as the WIL. In the 1920's the WIL had branches in Vancouver, Winnipeg, and Toronto and was affiliated to some women's farm groups; it was led by such women as Violet MacNaughton, editor of the women's column in the popular *Western Producer*, and Laura Jamieson, a suffragist and social reformer who became a CCFer. In the 1920's the WIL's campaign against cadet training in schools was supported by many socialists, and by the early 1930's a list of WIL leadership began to look like a list of well-known CCF women. Although the WIL also included liberal pacifists, it did have an important appeal to socialist women, with its calls for elimination of social, economic, and sexual inequalities, as well as violence, from all societies.[8]

For Rose Henderson, Laura Jamieson, and Lucy Woodsworth, who had been influenced by the maternal feminism of the suffrage era, WIL principles and the CCF's pacifist connection had a special attraction. Not only did the WIL address the economic causes of war, but it also spoke to women's maternal aversion to violence and war. Henderson published a pamphlet in the 1920's titled *Women and War*, which reflected these ideas. The basic causes of war, she argued, were economic: "they are hatched within capitalism." Furthermore, women, as the bearers of life, and the working class, who were inevitably used as "cannon fodder," both had the most to lose from war. Thus, women, in alliance with the working class, must become leaders in the cause for peace. And it was because they experienced motherhood, she emphasized, that women best understood the value of human life:

> Are not all mothers one people? Do not all mothers love their children? Would not all mothers die to save their children from slaughter and suffering?. . . . If humanity is to exist – if peace is to be a reality, the mothers of the world must become the standard bearers, martyrs in the cause. They must be prepared to suffer as much in the cause of peace as they were willing to suffer in the cause of war.[9]

Henderson's pacifism was a blend of socialist and feminist ideas not uncommon to other CCF women. Drawing on both a materialist analysis of imperialism and an idealized view of women's commitment to non-violence, many women came to see peace as a socialist issue *and* a women's issue. Moreover, the close relationship between the WIL and CCF women aided the growth of the CCF, for some women learned of the CCF through the WIL and vice versa.

There were other important ideological traditions, such as Marxism, stimulating women's interest in socialism. Although the CCF did not rely predominantly on Marx and Engels in its educational work, as did the Communists, Marxist books were offered for sale through many provincial literature committees, and where a strong tradition of Marxism existed, as in B.C., Marxists within the party were certain to share their viewpoint with newcomers. George Weaver, for instance, a self-educated Marxist in B.C. who was a regular party speaker and columnist for *The Federationist*, used Engels's *Origin of the Family* as a key text in his columns on women. Though Weaver tended, like the CPC, to stress women's primary class oppression, for that period his writing represented a fairly sophisticated attempt to construct a dialectical understanding of the class and sexual oppression of women.[10]

Women whose radicalization crystallized around Marxist ideas saw the economic devastation of the depression as a sharp reminder of the inherent contradictions of a capitalist economy. Some, however, were less interested than Weaver in the woman question, and they downplayed women's secondary status in the party and stressed the need for class solidarity. As Eve Grey Smith, a British Columbia activist, explained: "My main attitude was that women shouldn't be separated from men. The problem was not a sexual one, but an economic one, and the economic problem makes a sexual one." But Smith's own enthusiasms may have made her seem tactless in some women's eyes:

At the National Convention in Edmonton (1938), the women asked me to speak to them. . . . I said, "Why do you have a women's group? Why do you not have a mixed group?" They said women can more easily attend day meetings, and at mixed meetings, women don't like to talk in front of the men. I said, "Well, you just *have to* get up and talk at mixed meetings!"[11]

Of course, Marxist ideas may have also sensitized women to problems ignored by others: Eve Smith was also active in the

98 DREAMS OF EQUALITY

Single Women's Unemployment Association and in her brief turn as women's columnist for *The Federationist*, she stressed some of the urgent problems of women wage-earners. Furthermore, Marxists within the CCF sometimes differed in their perspectives, and some CCFers contributed selected Marxist ideas to an eclectic socialist philosophy.

Indeed, the socialist development of women did not emerge either from Christian principles or from Marxist ideas, for, as we have seen, the intellectual traditions influencing the CCF crossed the spectrum from Fabianism to Bellamy's co-operative socialism. Moreover, in a young political movement offering discussion in weekly club meetings, educational forums, and summer camps, the intellectual options open to new members were constantly broadened. And the precise way in which women's personal experiences and intellectual development mixed to form a radical view of the world was also an individual process. Sympathy for feminist ideas, for instance, varied, even among women with similar backgrounds. In B.C. Dorothy Steeves was less interested than Laura Jamieson in organizing separate women's groups, yet they both came from middle-class backgrounds, were well educated, and had had some contact with the suffrage movement. Quite naturally, the way in which women entered politics also varied according to region and class: farm women were more likely to come through the co-operative movement, working-class women through relief organizations. The final mixture of middle-class, working-class, and farm women in the CCF contrasted to the Communist Party's predominantly working-class and immigrant membership, and it resulted in the CCF's initial weak links to the union movement. Although many middle-class CCF women were sympathetic to the struggles of wage-earning women, their own lives reflected a different social and economic reality.

Whatever their background, once active in the party the majority of women gravitated toward "female" areas of political work, revealing the existence of a political sexual division of labour within the CCF similar to that in Canadian society. Although a few notable women, including Grace MacInnis and Dorothy Steeves, became party leaders, most women were active at the grassroots level of the party. It is axiomatic that, in political parties, women were called on to "make the coffee and lick the envelopes," yet it is important to remember that this day-to-day support work was essential to the life of the party. As one Saskatchewan CCF woman succinctly put it: "the CCF was made in

the kitchen and you didn't find too many men in the kitchen.''[12]
To some extent, the party encouraged women to fulfil these supportive but less powerful roles. In an article in *Ontario New
Commonwealth*, one writer described ''How to Organize a Successful CCF Unit,'' explaining that the social committee, an essential unit, should be at least two-thirds women because they
were ''perfect jewels'' at raising funds and loved ''playing am-
ateur salesladies at bake sales.''[13] Such exhortations for women
to remain the drones in the movement were not, of course, part
of a conscious design to segregate women in inferior roles, but
they did reflect an unthinking acceptance of prevailing sex roles
and the male-dominated power structure of society.

Election time usually found CCF newspapers discussing the role
women could and should play in politics. Like the more radical
Communist Party, democratic socialists often assumed that women
were predominantly homemakers and that they had little inclination for politics. As a result, CCF articles indicated ways in
which government decisions affected women's domestic labour
and the lives of their children. Politics do not simply involve
abstract principles, they would say, for government decides whether
or not your husband will have work, how much you will pay for
milk, what kind of education your children receive, and whether
your family will get adequate medical care. On the one hand,
these appeals once again promoted the perception that women,
isolated amidst diapers and dishes, were less knowledgeable and
more apathetic than men about politics. But the party's approach
also reflected pragmatic thinking: the CCF put important emphasis
on electoral politics and since most women were homemakers,
the party felt it must convince this large constituency of the need
for socialism by speaking to the immediate, daily concerns of
women in the home. And such appeals to woman's maternal
concern for her family's welfare were often effective, for many
women explained their attraction to socialism in terms of the
humanitarian answers it offered to the problems that comprised
women's daily realities. As one Saskatchewan CCF woman put it:
''the CCF may have had a special appeal to women . . . the appeal
of humanity, of health services, educational opportunities, and
so on . . . because most mothers wanted the best for their
children.''[14]

Women were also asked to take an active role in party work,
and to many CCFers this signified a more egalitarian approach
than those of the Liberals and Conservatives. As one male CCFer

commented (and not in jest), "in clubs, women not only fold and stamp literature, they also go out door to door with male comrades to distribute it . . . whereas under the old parties, women are almost disenfranchised."[15] It does appear that CCF women played a more active role than women in the Liberal and, certainly, the Conservative parties. Many CCF women did their door-to-door work only during election time; others remained actively involved between elections. In Winnipeg, Edith Cove became known as the efficient manager of election victories in Woodsworth's riding of Winnipeg North Centre, while in Saskatchewan, Gertrude Harvey, Florence Baker, Eve Pfeifer, and Elsie Gorius all developed respected reputations as membership and campaign organizers. "Those Saskatchewan women," remembered Grace MacInnis, "they were organizers! . . . many MPs were only in Parliament because of the women's organizing skills."[16]

Such women as Elsie Gorius in Saskatchewan and Nellie Peterson in Alberta were able to work as travelling organizers for the CCF, not only because of their proven organizing talents but also because of the essential aid of supportive families, including someone to care for their children. Many other married women found that long absences from home were not tolerated by their husbands, who shared the community's suspicions of such "wandering wives."[17] Gorius's mother looked after her son; "otherwise," she concluded, "I wouldn't have been able to do political work."[18] Similarly, Nellie Peterson had a sympathetic mother to help look after her son, and a politically supportive husband – an essential to the career of any woman organizer.

Many women who were active at the local level, especially in urban areas – doing constituency work, gathering memberships, and fund-raising – had to combine their domestic work with their political activities. One local publicity organizer in Fort William described her normal day, aptly revealing the kind of work women did and the way married women integrated domestic and political labour:

> Up at 8, feed family of 5, make lunch, send boy to school, do report on meetings, draw up ads, numerous phone calls. 9:00, dress baby, wash dishes, answer phone, make beds, sweep and dust, answer phone. Sell potatoes donated by country CCF units. Write letters and notes for tonight's speech. Dish washing, cleaning, calls, dress baby for outdoors, odd jobs, supper, prepare kids for bed, go to meeting.[19]

At the local and provincial levels, women were also prominently represented in educational work. Within a constituency CCF club, women were often put in charge of local libraries, or they sat on provincial education committees that ordered books, drew up reading lists, and organized discussion groups and summer schools. The high profile of women in educational work may have been partly the consequence of the widely held notion in the CCF that women were eminently suited to such "practical" tasks, as well as the fact that women, who were not encouraged to see themselves as leaders and therefore lacked self-confidence, opted for behind-the-scenes work. Another key factor was the duplication within the party of occupational roles found outside it. In the 1930's one of the only professions truly open to women was teaching; women's educational work was thus perceived as a logical and natural role for women. Because women had experience teaching the young, it was said, they could put these same talents to use in explaining socialist ideas to new members. As Mildred Fahrni, for a time a CCF school board trustee in Vancouver, explained:

> Women teachers worked with youth and this helped them to realize that we had to reach the younger generation. Their mind was turned to the channels of education – how to get ideas across, that is why women were involved in education . . . . [20]

And, of course, many CCF women, especially on the Prairies, had worked as teachers and were probably eager to use their skills in party work. Although women's participation in educational work thus emerged from a narrow and traditional definition of women's "proper sphere," we can't lose sight of the fact that education *did* have a vital role to play in the party. Because the CCF was a new socialist party that opposed the dominant ideals of competition and free enterprise, it desperately needed the committed and well-informed recruits that good educational work might produce.

As part of their mandate to recruit new socialists and re-educate old ones, educational committees established CCF summer camps, and women often worked as camp organizers. This took considerable time, for camps lasted for a week or more and, besides producing educational material, the mundane essentials of accommodation, cooking, and cleaning all had to be attended to. Gertrude Telford, who oversaw the Saskatchewan Crystal Lake Camp from 1937 to 1942, recalls her long list of duties: "we had educational programs, lectures, speakers were brought in; we had discussions on economics, debating and also recreational activities, swimming, games and campfire programs."[21] CCFers recall the camp experience fondly, for, as with the Communist summer camps, learning and discussion took place in an atmosphere of camaraderie and common purpose sustaining a sense of socialists' "counter culture." Women who were homemakers could often integrate political work with family responsibilities, for provisions were made for children's tents and programs. Within camp life, however, women were never limited to domestic tasks: because camps were organized as a microcosm of the communal socialist future, everyone shared in the dishwashing, a fact commented on so emphatically by the women that one suspects it was not the practice outside camp life.

Some women on provincial education committees did eventually get elected to provincial council, or even to the provincial executive. Women's degree of underrepresentation in the leadership varied over time and by region. In the 1930's, in Saskatchewan, women sometimes comprised up to one-third of the provincial leadership, a high percentage that might be explained by established traditions of female participation in the farm movement. And in B.C., three women – Laura Jamieson, Dorothy Steeves, and Grace MacInnis – were elected as members of the legislature and had a high profile in the party; Dorothy Steeves eventually became vice-president of the B.C. party; Grace MacInnis later became a national figure.

No simple generalization can characterize women in leadership positions, for female notables held differing political perspectives and had different styles of pursuing politics. Steeves, for example, was known as a sharp-minded and sometimes sharp-tongued debater, who once said that she was as good as any man. Saskatchewan's Louise Lucas, on the other hand, had a different persona. Not an intellectual but a charismatic, religious-minded woman, Lucas was a never-tiring evangelist for the movement, and her popular title, "Mother of the CCF," indicated a different reputation, which stressed the feminine attributes of her leadership. Although women who became leaders could be as different as Steeves and Lucas were, one wonders if they were assigned stereotypic images, stressing either their maternal and feminine qualities or their similarity to men. One CCF newspaper, for example, had the audacity to publish an article pigeon-holing women into three stereotypes – the "clinging vine," the "aggressive, mannish" woman, and the "normal" woman who was neither superior nor inferior but interested in children, home, and career. Needless to say, similar pseudo-psychological pronouncements on men's character types did not appear in the paper.[22]

Whatever their styles of politics, it was simply more difficult for women to reach the leadership. Women's economic dependence and double burden of work, as well as the influence of prevailing sexist ideas about gender roles, were fundamental causes of women's secondary status in the CCF. Not only did women have less money and work for longer hours than men – leaving them with fewer material resources or even the energy so necessary to political participation – but the dominant ideology of gender presented women as "private" beings whose lives centred on marriage and family, rather than public beings whose interests should be politics and government. Women in politics were considered an oddity: mass magazines, on the rare occasions they addressed the subject, treated women politicians as "freaks,"[23] as Agnes Macphail so frankly put it, and assumed a political career and family were almost incompatible. But also at fault were socialists themselves, who failed to challenge these traditional ideas and inequalities within their own ranks. Unfortunately, many CCF members, including some women, stubbornly held that, as a socialist party, the CCF *was* egalitarian – and they refused to see any evidence to the contrary. Yet, evidence indicates that women were channelled into social committees; that women's feminine character was often described as emotional and sensitive, implying a female inability to cope with the "rational" world of politics; and that women were seen as more apathetic and politically backward than men. Moreover, and perhaps most important of all, because women's primary responsibility for the family was never questioned, an essential barrier to women's wholehearted participation in politics remained unchanged.

Nowhere was women's secondary role in the party more glaring than in the selection of candidates for election. Although the CCF often fared better than its Liberal and Conservative counterparts, women were still placed in unwinnable ridings or given inadequate support in their bids for CCF nominations. After Agnes Macphail's election defeat in 1940, Jean Laing lamented that so few women were seriously considered as candidates by the party:

In Toronto, in all the Parties, the men were doing all the contesting as candidates and the women were doing all the work. . . .

We expect of the old line Parties that they will nominate all men candidates but from the CCF we look for equal recognition of the women. Yet, in Ontario, the only woman CCF candidate was Mrs. Dymond, and she was nominated because one of the man candidates was sick.[24]

In Saskatchewan, shortly after this, Gertrude Telford lost a provincial nomination to a man whose attack on her candidature, she said privately, was "on her *as a woman*."[25] Telford had for years done the hard leg work in the riding and justifiably felt unhappy when an outsider, who assured her he was not going to run, threw in his hat at the last minute.

Despite some unusual circumstances surrounding the nomination meeting, the case was not investigated by the party. Telford was later considered as a potential replacement to Louise Lucas in the federal riding of Melville, but again she was by-passed. Lucas expressed her sympathy to a disappointed Telford, and voiced her anger about men's tight control of the party:

There is no need to tell you how chagrined I am over B's nomination. If it had been Mrs. Baker, Mrs. Strum or you I would have felt reconciled in fact elated, but you know what I think of this. . . . I had written to Mr. J.C. from the conference pleading that he think of Christ and the women's cause in their deliberations. Replied that he agreed we need more women in the Party but said they would have to take a more *prominent* part. These men don't seem to be able to grasp that they are not *allowed* to take these prominent parts. You know what I mean.[26]

Out of loyalty to the party, Lucas's criticisms, like those of Laing and Telford, were voiced privately, rather than in the columns of the CCF newspaper. Dedicated to their party and to an ideal of socialist egalitarianism, they always hoped that women would be accorded the same opportunities as men. Privately, however, they sometimes shared their bitter disappointment as women were held back from nominations and discouraged from advancing into the leadership.

### CCF Women's Organizations

CCF committees emerged, in part, to counteract women's secondary role in the movement, for they were seen as a training ground for female leadership, as well as a medium through which women's special concerns might be addressed. Some provincial newspapers also introduced women's columns, which included everything from sophisticated political editorials to news of local CCF women's groups and even household hints. Within the party there was always a running debate over the desirability of such "special" appeals to women. Even the women's columnist for *Ontario New Commonwealth* revealed ambivalence about her task – well symbolized by her name for the column, "Fairly Feminine" – for she explained that, on one level, she "disapproved of women's pages . . . for women should read all articles in the paper." On the other hand, she added, "women are rather backward about expressing their ideas in print, especially in competition with the masculine point of view."[27] She concluded more positively, urging men to acquaint themselves with the column, but overall, her passing remarks seemed to combine a negative view of "backward" women with an honest desire to help women become more vocal and powerful in the movement. Although the column only ran for a short time, it did contain informative articles on women's history, the activities of CCF women, the peace movement, and women on relief. Its author was sometimes daring enough to challenge some of the staples of "bourgeois" women's pages, such as her "Behind the Paris Gowns – The Dressmakers' Strike,"[28] an exposé of women's bad working conditions in the fashion industry. On other occasions, however, the column itself reverted to fashion tips and recipes.

In *New Commonwealth* and other CCF papers, women were addressed primarily as homemakers and secondarily as wage-earners. Major strikes involving women invariably got substantial and sympathetic coverage, but women's domestic concerns were seen as the meat and potatoes of the women's political existence. The women's columnist in *Saskatchewan Commonwealth*, for example, argued that women, "who were practical and realistic, although perhaps not theoretically inclined," would turn their thoughts from household tasks – "more patching, crimping, planning" – to tidying up the outside world. "So who is in a better position to understand the economic system than the person who is a consumer for the family," she asked, "to whom is the threat of war terrible and the appeal of peace . . . more significant?"[29]

In all the provincial newspapers, women's columns appeared and disappeared throughout the 1930's, taking on a different fla-

*May Day CCF banner, May 1, 1936.* (City of Toronto Archives)

vour according to the CCF paper and who the author was. In British Columbia party activist Mildred Fahrni put together a weekly radio show named "The Woman's View," while *The Federation* featured a column written in the early years by Eve Grey Smith. Smith's writing concentrated on economic issues such as women's role in the class struggle and the situation of unemployed women, but when Elizabeth Kerr, who had a long association with feminist and socialist causes, took over in 1937, the column also began to address more "feminist" concerns, such as women's role in the family, the need for better divorce laws, and the imperative of increasing women's participation in the CCF. In her column written after the 1938 provincial convention, Kerr lamented the small number of female delegates present, blaming "family responsibilities and male prejudice" for their absence, and she objected strenuously to the male paranoia expressed at the convention that three women on the CCF executive would spell "feminist control" of the inner party sanctums. "We have not shown feminist views," she retorted angrily, "but we have examined a broad range of problems from a human perspective, [and] . . . even if we were stay-at-home types, without a broader view, why shouldn't that womanly view be expressed in our movement?" For a movement "boasting no differences in sex, race and creed," she frankly concluded, "some of our Marxian socialists are pitifully mid-Victorian."[30] Not all the women's columnists were as blunt as Kerr, but it was true that women's columns, even if they included recipes and sewing patterns, often enhanced the discussion of women's issues – from rising prices to the need for birth control clinics – in the paper. Moreover, without them, a feminist point of view, like Kerr's, might not have been heard at all.

Like the newspaper columns, women's committees had different political outlooks and activities, ranging from fund-raising to socialist education and feminist social action. Women's organizations existed in many cities in Ontario and across the West; a limited number of examples can illustrate their ideas, work, and problems.

In Saskatchewan, women's organizations sprang from a neighbourhood milieu or were coaxed into existence by the party's provincial office. In 1936-37 there was some debate within the party executive and at the provincial convention over the small female membership in the movement and over the possibility of giving women's "study clubs" voting status at the convention. The party, however, decided to reject this radical proposition, but as a consolation prize for the women it agreed to appoint a part-time provincial organizer, Minerva Cooper, to help establish new CCF women's clubs.

In her short period as organizer, Cooper aided sixteen new clubs into existence, boosting the number of provincial CCF women's groups to forty-two. Her aim was to orient the clubs to women's need for social contact as well as to their political development. Her assumption was that women needed different, indeed "extra," education geared to their isolated lives and less knowledgeable approach to politics. "We can use the time-honoured custom of afternoon tea," she explained, "to have a programme for the tried and true worker and the new rank and filer, combining business study and social time. In the meeting we can start off with slogans and anecdotes . . . [and] we should avoid dull papers on economics."[31]

The problems of organizing women, Cooper soon found, were generated primarily by the vast geographical area she had to cover and by the CCF's limited finances. The central office could not afford to hire a full-time women's organizer, nor could local clubs afford to pay transportation costs to bring Cooper in. Gas shortages prohibited some women from attending regular meetings, and study materials were expensive for the women to buy and for the central office to supply. Despite all these difficulties, local clubs did flourish; indeed, one dynamic activist in northern Saskatchewan, Dorise Nielsen, helped to establish six new clubs in the space of a year. Cooper believed that local organizers, with a feel for the community, often had the best results. Success was also scored, she maintained, when the women's clubs gradually evolved into mixed ones. New people were thus drawn into the movement and the women, already fortified with executive and speaking experience, still tended to "hold executive positions in the mixed setting, not taking a back seat"[32] as they did in other clubs.

Although Cooper was not rehired for a second term, she did edit *Saskatchewan Commonwealth*'s women's column, which was used as an educational tool for CCF women's clubs. One such club had been formed in a Saskatoon neighbourhood where many families were on relief. Women on the street who shared common worries and advice were persuaded by one CCF supporter to form a political discussion group. Margaret Benson, an original member of the group, recalls that their first "political actions" were whist drives and other fund-raising, but the women also found time to study *The Case for Socialism* and *Looking Backward*, analyse newspaper articles, and present their own opinions on political issues. Ridicule from other neighbours about their "red flag" meetings, says Benson, "just made us more determined . . . for we were militant, unlike [other] ladies' auxiliaries."[33] Across the city, the Nutana CCF Women's Club followed the study program prepared by Minerva Cooper and also knitted socks and raised funds for the Mackenzie-Papineau Battalion in Spain, as well as holding social events. These groups met within the bounds of a culturally sanctioned institution – the women's auxiliary – but they did not limit themselves to whist drives, for they also tried to make themselves and their neighbours more conscious of the need for socialism. Their political discussions often centred on family-related issues, but these concerns were located in a political context qualitatively different from the thinking of the earlier suffragists. In the 1930's CCF women addressed social and economic issues only skirted by these earlier reformers: the economic struggles of farm women, women on relief, and wage-earning women were the catalysts for their politicization, and their solution to social ills was the replacement of private with co-operative ownership. Rather than the patchwork reform efforts to improve the morals of society, CCF women proposed to improve family life by effecting an entire reordering of the economic system.

Women's family-centred concerns were also the focus of CCF women's groups in Winnipeg. There, women's ILP groups, already constituted on a neighbourhood basis and since 1932 federated into a city-wide Women's Labor Conference, became the foundation for a women's CCF network. Fund-raising and political education were the main activities in the small neighbourhood clubs; at the monthly meetings of the city-wide Women's Labor Conference, delegates discussed current issues and pooled their resources on various committees, such as one investigating minimum wage regulations and another attending to members' own education in socialist ideas. By the late 1930's some thirty-six groups were affiliated, and the conference was vocal on local and international issues, urging the federal government, for example, to allow a generous immigration policy for Jewish refugees fleeing Germany. The conference saw education as a key to women's conversion, and so small study groups were formed, using books such as *Social Planning for Canada* and *The Cooperative Commonwealth*, and drawing on the guidance of the conference's leaders, Beatrice Brigden, Lucy Woodsworth, and Edith Cove.

Cove, a school teacher from the Maritimes who had moved to Brandon before the First World War and married a railroad worker, had become active in the Brandon Peoples Church after the 1919 strike. There, she met Brigden, who became a close lifelong friend, and Cove embarked on a long political career – largely as a behind-the-scenes worker – for the ILP and CCF. The commitment of Cove, Brigden, and Woodsworth to the separate organization of women emerged from their experience with women's labourite groups in the 1920's and from their shared belief that, within the socialist movement, women's capabilities, needs, and concerns were sometimes different from men's. Brigden, for example, saw women's primary social role as housewife and mother, but her columns in *Manitoba Commonwealth* also emphasized women's right to employment and economic equality. Resolutely decrying the depression-initiated hostility to working women, she labelled efforts to force women back into the kitchen as akin to "feudalism."[34] The hope for women's emancipation, she believed, would come from an alliance of women with the socialist movement. Co-operation and working-class unity would pave the way to the New Jerusalem: "if humanity is to advance," she once wrote, "then all must march together; no lagging behind by one group, no suppression of one sex for the benefit of the other."[35]

Still, in the long march toward socialism, women's groups provided a useful focus and sometimes a comforting retreat for women activists. In 1937, under Brigden's leadership, the Winnipeg women organized a conference to discuss how to organize from a women's viewpoint and how to express the particular needs of homemakers and rural women. Brigden had already carried these concerns to the national convention the year before, making a long report on the Winnipeg Women's Labor Conference and urging a more concerted national policy on enlarging the CCF's female membership. Clearly, not all the delegates took these "ladies' " groups seriously, nor did the party leadership see any pressing need to discuss women's issues. Indeed, when Brigden described how Winnipeg women had established rapidly expanding groups to discuss birth control, her report was greeted with "chortles of amusement"[36] – a fact even considered humorous forty years later by David Lewis.

A small enclave of women delegates listened sympathetically

to Brigden's speech, then spoke in defence of her crusade to integrate women into the party. Saskatchewan's Louise Lucas added that a flexible and moderate program was the best tactic to use. "We must move slowly," she counselled, "through respectable women's groups and [with] common sense . . . just broach the subject of [women's politics] in some districts and you will be boycotted . . . [so] be sensible . . . start a dramatic club or get into the Ladies Aid."[37] Her cautious recommendations seemed to be accepted by Brigden, who also advocated that socialist women do social service work and co-operate with liberal female reformers. More militant were two Toronto delegates, Jean Laing and Rose Henderson, who spoke assertively of the need to politicize women and to make a place for them in the party. There is no such thing as "neutral" or non-political education work, Henderson charged, "we must point out to women that every aspect of their lives is affected by politics . . . we must directly address socialist issues."[38] Despite this discussion, no formal resolution was passed by the Convention, and even the following year, when a resolution asking the national office for a woman organizer came from Fort William, it was quickly put aside.

In Ontario some CCF women's clubs already existed. In Toronto, the CCF Women's Joint Committee (WJC) momentarily thrived in the mid-1930's as one avenue for the socialist and feminist concerns of women within the group. Many of the leading spokespersons for the WJC were seasoned feminist activists. Rose Henderson, who came from a middle-class Irish background, had participated in the British ILP and the Canadian women's suffrage movement. After the First World War Henderson worked as a social worker in the Montreal Juvenile Court, and she became increasingly active in the Canadian Labor Party and the Women's International League for Peace and Freedom. In the twenties and thirties, Henderson combined her commitment to labour with an increasingly radical analysis of women's oppression by male-dominated society. "Women," she lamented bitterly in one article, "have been turned into cringing, timid creatures by the diabolical gospel of their sin and inferiority."[39]

Alice Loeb, another WJC activist, also came from an educated, middle-class background; in the 1920's she became involved in such feminist causes as the WIL and the birth control movement, though her introduction to the CCF may have come through the LSR. Also a part of the WJC leadership were two women of working-class background, Jean Laing and Elizabeth Morton. Jean

Laing entered the labour movement through the Women's Auxiliary of the International Association of Machinists, and she worked as an organizer for the ILGWU and acted as a spokesperson for the Toronto Unemployed Single Women's Association. Morton, a British emigrant who had worked in a factory when she was young, also entered the labour movement through an auxiliary, the Women's Guild of the Carpenters Union. Tutored by the Guild's Communist president, Florence Custance, Morton joined the Women's Labor Leagues, though she rejected Communist Party membership and opted to join the Ontario branch of the Socialist Party of Canada. Also a leading activist in the radical East York Workers Association, Morton had a stormy relationship with the CCF. In 1933, she was among those expelled from the CCF for United Front work with the Communists and she flirted with the CPC long enough to attend the first conference of the League against War and Fascism in 1935. She subsequently returned to the CCF but remained a supporter of a United Front and eventually, in the 1940's, became a Communist Party member.

Laing and Morton were both ardent trade unionists *and* feminists who looked to separate women's groups as a means to politicize working-class women and to pressure the larger labour movement on women's issues. The feminist goals of the WJC were quite forthrightly stated in its opening meeting: its purpose was to address "social problems, particularly those of women and act as a training school for CCF women."[40] To the WJC, addressing women's issues primarily meant confronting domestic and family concerns. As John Manley points out, it is likely that most of the WJC membership were married women, "consequently, the family and its fate during a period of intense socioeconomic crisis became a central preoccupation of the WJC."[41] These women, for instance, aided the establishment of a progressive summer camp for inner-city children, even bringing old pots, dishes, and towels to a meeting as donations, and jokingly referring to this as a "shower for the camp."[42]

Other aspects of female culture, especially women's maternal concerns, were also utilized by the WJC: the women organized a Mothers' Committee to visit youths imprisoned in Mimico Jail after a relief strike; planned a Mothers' Day peace program with the WIL; and sponsored a conference on unemployment, focusing on relief "in relation to the home and children in the home."[43] As well, the WJC wrote letters protesting the plight of the single unemployed woman and expressed some interest in organizing around the birth control issue. Elizabeth Morton brought the director of the East York Parents Clinic to speak to the WJC, and in response to her talk, the committee immediately suggested that Margaret Sanger be brought to Toronto. This plan, however, never materialized, as Brant suggested building more community support for the clinic first, and the CCF women soon found that within their own movement, "the clinic idea was well received by the women . . . but not by the men."[44]

The second purpose of the WJC – to train women for leadership – was a less threatening issue, in part because the WJC feminists could plead that, in increasing women's self-confidence, the party as a whole would benefit. As the WJC secretary explained:

> Women are very diffident about engaging in discussion at a meeting where men are in the majority. As women in the future will play an important role in the building of Socialism and have a real contribution to make, they must be trained and encouraged to take their place.[45]

To give women more expertise and confidence, the WJC rotated its own position of chair, and it made plans to draw in a wider network of CCF women across the city. The WJC, however, did not live long enough to fulfil its hopes – it was debilitated by conflicts with the party leadership over United Front work with Communists and over what WJC women caustically referred to as the party's opportunistic "vote catching policies."[46]

Some WJC women had considered an alliance with other leftists in the 1935 general election and they continued to work with Communists in United Front organization. These CCF women, including Rose Henderson and Jean Laing, were not, however, simply naive pawns of the CPC, for they looked to the United Front as a means of furthering their socialist goals.[47] But acrimonious debate over co-operation with the CPC split the party and resulted in the expulsions of Laing and others in 1936. The WJC's protests over these expulsions may have only exacerbated its tense relationship with the leadership. Although the WJC visited the provincial executive "to explain the WJC's function,"[48] the women's organization disappeared from existence shortly afterwards, and the WJC women probably took their energies elsewhere, perhaps to the WIL or the League against War and Fascism.

The WJC's brief history indicated that a small socialist-feminist current did exist within the party, though it is true that not all party members attached a priority to women's organizations. Indeed, socialist women often harboured ambivalent feelings about women's groups, as all too often they isolated women into auxiliary roles. Caroline Riley of the Edmonton CCF Women's Council, for example, rather diffidently described her group as a ''very definite, but not very separate place in the Party for women.'' Although the Edmonton group started off with political discussions, aims, and activities, including ''permeation'' of the Local Council of Women, a Mothers' Day peace parade, and support for a strike of laundry workers, it soon found itself concentrating on fund-raising and, at the party's request, electioneering. ''Little as we like it,'' Riley concluded rather sadly, ''we shall probably have to put on teas, bridges, raffles, etc. to fill the treasury.'' Because they were committed to ''working with men to change the economic system . . . as it is not women's sex which hampers them, but their sex under capitalism,''[49] the Edmonton women seemingly resigned themselves to these support roles. Perhaps a little more feminism and a little less loyalty to working-class unity would have challenged women's relegation to the tea tables. For these women, however, the solution was simply to do away with separate women's groups – a suggestion Riley made to the Ontario CCF in the 1940's.

Similar dilemmas and questions about separate women's groups troubled CCFers in B.C. There, fund-raising and educational women's groups evolved in Victoria, Saanich, and some of the interior towns, though the largest concentration of women's committees lay in metropolitan Vancouver, where community-based clubs were also eventually affiliated into a city-wide CCF Women's Council. In Vancouver, the necessary bingos, bazaars, and picnics were undertaken by the Ways and Means Committee, while concern for women's issues and women's leadership training was looked after by Women's Lyceum, later to merge into the Vancouver CCF Central Group, still later called the CCF Women's Council. The Women's Lyceum, remembers Hilda Kristiansen, was begun by such party leaders as Elizabeth Kerr, Dorothy Steeves, and Dorothy Cameron, who wished to ''get women more involved in the party.''[50] The Lyceum gave women political skills training – how to make resolutions and to speak in public – and also provided an educational forum, particularly for women's issues. CCF women sometimes made common cause with other women's groups, a controversial tactic that took socialist women to the right and the left of their own party. Dorothy Steeves, for example, dutifully attended Local Council of Women meetings, though she privately bemoaned the Liberal and Conservative politicking within the Council and questioned CCF participation in such a pedestrian and reformist organization.

On the other hand, CCF women might also make common cause with other leftists, including Communists; co-operation during unemployment and relief camp protests in 1935 and 1938 produced some of the most effective United Front coalitions during the depression – without endangering the political autonomy many CCFers so carefully guarded. In the spring of 1935, following the department store protests and arrests of relief camp strikers in Vancouver, CCF women joined with members of the Women's Labor League to form a Mothers' Committee that orchestrated a massive Mothers' Day Rally protesting the relief camps and demanding work and a decent wage for "our boys." Hundreds of women, led by Peggy Harrison of the WLL and well-known CCFer Sarah Colley, nicknamed "Mother Colley," formed a huge heart in Stanley Park, raising placards reading "Mothers Abolish the Relief Camps." Drawing on maternalist rhetoric, Colley's speech stressed that "this was not a political demonstration, but a mothers' protest" and that government should pay attention to the plight of "our Boys."[51] Other CCF activists, including Helena Gutteridge, Elizabeth Kerr, and Mildred Osterhaut Fahrni, were also involved, though some of their addresses were made with appeals to compassion and the need for a "new social order based on freedom and justice,"[52] rather than maternalism. Soon after this demonstration, the Mothers' Committee changed its name to the Mothers Council, now dominated more completely by Communists from the WLLs. But when the 1938 post office sit-in of relief strikers occurred, CCF and CPC women reactivated a United Front; the CCF Women's Emergency Committee on Unemployment, along with many other women's groups, made common cause with the Mothers Council, trying to offer support "by making food by the bushel for the strikers"[53] and by joining militant efforts to lobby every level of government for decent work and wages for the unemployed men.

CCF women involved in these actions were pragmatic organizers, who, like some of the WJC women, were willing to use the United Front as a short-term method of organizing around a pressing issue. And despite their repeated use of maternalist rhetoric, some of these women had strong feminist sympathies. Though some of Kerr's "mid-Victorian" Marxists in the B.C. party saw feminism as a myopic, class-blind ideology, CCF women involved

*Mothers' Committee demonstrating against the relief camps, Stanley Park, Vancouver, 1935.* (Glenbow Archives)

in the Central Group and later the Women's Council staunchly defended their allegiance to socialist *and* feminist ideals. Elizabeth Kerr suggested that women had a unique perspective to offer socialism, ''a spiritual, as well as material quality,''[54] while Kristiansen implied that women might offer a humanizing touch to the party:

> When the provincial office on Robson moved to Hastings Street . . . well, there was some in the party who thought even saying ''thank you'' was too bourgeois! But we, in the Women's Lyceum, thought otherwise. We set up a room with coffee and books to read in the new office . . . and a hospitality room for out-of-town visitors.[55]

Laura Jamieson, among others, argued that women's family and domestic concerns shaped a distinct ''female'' outlook on politics. Significantly, some of the old guard in the CCF Women's Council, including Jamieson herself, had heard and used these arguments in the suffrage movement. Jamieson came from an unmistakably middle-class background: educated at the University of Toronto, she worked as a teacher and social service worker before marrying a B.C. judge. Widowed at the young age of forty-three, Jamieson was offered a judgeship in Juvenile Court in the 1920's, a reward for her long devotion to respectable reform causes. But Jamieson increasingly altered her political allegiances in the 1920's, replacing an interest in liberal reform with a commitment to the women's peace movement and, eventually, to the CCF. Like Rose Henderson, Jamieson had witnessed class inequality and social dislocation first-hand in her work with the court, and her response, unlike conservative Judge Emily Murphy, was to embrace the cause of social democracy. And like fellow peace worker Beatrice Brigden, Jamieson combined her maternalist understanding of women's inherent sympathy for family issues with a strong belief in women's right to equal opportunity and economic self-sufficiency. Jamieson, who represented the reformist rather than revolutionary stream of the B.C. party, also tried to apply her feminist ideas through practical and philanthropic work with women; one of her schemes was the creation of low-cost, communal housing for working women in Vancouver.

Elizabeth Kerr, a Scottish emigrant who had once tried to organize her fellow nurses in support of an eight-hour day, also had feminist roots in the suffrage movement. As an aspiring writer and feminist, she joined the Women's Press Club; as a dedicated socialist, she joined the Socialist Party of Canada. She brought both influences to bear on her work with the CCF. A generous and warm woman, Kerr felt a strong bond with the female membership of the party; her socialist training, however, made her a determined party leader who did not hesitate to speak her mind, even if it meant defending unpopular causes, such as her support in 1940 for the Soviet Union.

Like Kerr and Jamieson, Helena Gutteridge, also an active member of the CCF Women's Council, carried some of her experiences in the suffrage struggle into the CCF. Gutteridge came from a working-class English family. Faced with an edict from her father that girls were not worth educating, she simply packed her bags and left home, determined to educate herself. After obtaining diplomas in teaching, hygiene, and sanitary science, and following a brief involvement in the British suffrage movement, Gutteridge emigrated in 1911. Not surprisingly, she threw herself into feminist and socialist causes in Canada: before World War One, she worked as a trade union organizer and founded the Vancouver Political Equality League, an alternative to the more conservative, middle-class Suffrage League. In the 1920's she married and left for the Fraser Valley, where she and her husband attempted to farm. Neither the farm, nor the marriage, it seems, worked. In the 1930's she returned to Vancouver, divorced, yet silent about the disappointments of her personal life. Politically, she simply picked up where she left off, supporting CCF and trade union causes. On a personal level, Gutteridge found new socialist and feminist friends; through the CCF she met Hilda and Denny Kristiansen and she became a long-term resident in their large boarding house. In 1937, she ran successfully as a CCF aldermanic candidate, though she was defeated two years later, perhaps because, never hesitating to speak her mind, Gutteridge called the 1939 Royal Tour a "circus" and suggested the money might be better applied to the jobless.[56]

Gutteridge combined her strong working-class consciousness with socialist loyalties and an acute feminist awareness of women's second-class citizenship – even within the labour movement. "Why is it," she said angrily, arguing against women's exclusion from skilled jobs, that "women's natural protector, 'man', protects her if it is a question of his own particular welfare or comfort?. . . Thank heaven the women are awakening, and not much longer will they be exploited by employers and kicked under by their 'natural protectors'."[57] Perhaps, however, Gutteridge's

*Helena Gutteridge,* CCF *alderman, addressing crowd, c. 1937.* (Vancouver Public Library, photo no. 13333)

feminism is more apparent to us than it was to her. Despite her involvement in the Women's Council, remembers Hilda Kristiansen, Gutteridge rejected the label "feminist," always preferring to proudly call herself a "trade union woman."

It was not Gutteridge, however, but Dorothy "Gretchen" Steeves who best symbolized the hesitancy of CCFers to embrace feminism and women's self-organization. A Dutch war bride, trained as a lawyer, Steeves had supported the suffrage movement in the Netherlands before emigrating in 1919. In the twenties and early thirties Steeves gradually travelled the road from middle-class snobbery to concerned social activism, though she always maintained a somewhat aloof, intellectual manner. A respected party leader and theoretician, Steeves never hesitated to support reforms designed to ease the burden of women's oppression; she even took

up the controversial issue of birth control, using the B.C. legislature as a platform to demand that the state provide public information on sex education and family planning. Steeves also
attended the Women's Council, but lurking in the back of her
mind was some discomfort with separate women's groups in an
egalitarian movement. Indeed, she later commented unsympa-
thetically on:

> Women who weren't involved and didn't think . . . I don't
> think there was any discrimination against women . . . some
> women just look for it. I'm as good as any man and I've been
> held to be as good as any man.[58]

Steeves, it seems, found it difficult to look beyond her own exceptional talents to identify with other women. Perhaps she also
feared – with some justification – that the question of women's
equality would be relegated to the less prestigious women's committees and ignored by the party as a whole.

Similarly, Grace MacInnis, who represented the younger generation of women in the party, supported the work of the Women's
Council, but her heart was never completely with the cause.
MacInnis recognized that women's groups provided a comfortable
way for women to involve themselves in the party, and as homemakers, women could better attend daytime meetings. But, raised
in a progressive family, MacInnis never felt inhibited by her sex
and she could not really identify with women's groups:

> I was brought up with the idea that there was no difference
> between men and women. . . . I never opposed women's
> groups . . . but I didn't need them. . . . I always felt that when
> women felt more comfortable with [mixed groups] and more
> mature, they'd leave women's groups for larger work.[59]

Though MacInnis's remarks ring with some condescension, she
later became an important advocate on women's issues, and even
in the 1930's she clearly understood some of the problems women
encountered in political life. In one article on women, she praised
a household where the husband shared domestic labour so his
wife could be more politically active. "No need to talk about
equality in their home,"[60] was her pointed conclusion.

The views of Steeves and MacInnis reflected, in part, their own
personal histories, but within the B.C. party there also existed a
Marxist tradition – stemming back to the SPC – of antipathy to feminism. The fact that such a strong socialist-feminist alliance did

emerge in Vancouver was thus a substantial achievement for leaders like Fahrni, Jamieson, Kerr, and Kristiansen. Furthermore,
more than leadership was needed: women's groups clearly appealed to women who wanted to participate in socially acceptable
auxiliary roles, or to those who wished to discuss women's issues
within the comfort of an all-female organization.

In the 1930's, feminist concerns were not a first priority for
the B.C. party, but neither did it ignore women's issues. CCF
members of the legislature tried to expose the exploitation of
wage-earning women and they demanded legislation to improve
women's interests, including access to birth control information.
Within CCF women's groups, women's issues were often defined
in tandem with a woman's domestic and maternal role. Nevertheless, for CCF women who marched against fascism in the Mothers' Day Peace Parade, or who demonstrated in the Mothers
Against the Relief Camps, political mothering had a different
meaning than it did for liberal reformers like those in the Local
Council of Women. To socialist women, their recognition of class
inequality, their fight against fascism, and their version of a co-
operative society made theirs a distinct, "militant mothering."

### Conclusion

Late into the July evenings, delegates to the CCF's inaugural convention in 1933 avidly debated the party's statement of principles:
was reform or revolution, private or public ownership, centralization or local control to characterize this new party? Feminism,
however, was never a significant part of this political terrain. The
CCF's founding document, the Regina Manifesto, paid minimal
attention to the woman question, and throughout the 1930's wom-
en's issues took a secondary place in party strategies. The intellectual traditions behind the new party, of course, had not, as a
rule, stressed gender inequality. Moreover, many CCF women
were drawn to the party because of their experience of economic
and social inequality in general, not because of their concern for
women's inequality in particular. These women, the younger of
whom were newcomers to politics after the intense feminist experience of the suffrage movement, were principally influenced
by the economic upheaval of the depression, and they simply
failed to see women's issues as primary concerns. As one woman
reflected: "The question of women just never came up. Economics and war overshadowed everything else. I never thought about

the woman question . . . except for resenting always being the stenographer of the group.''[61]

Despite this lack of interest in gender inequality, the party firmly held that women had a distinct political outlook shaped by their domestic and maternal roles. Women wage-earners were a subject of concern – the party tried to intervene in strikes and alter labour legislation – but working women figured less prominently than homemakers in the CCF's electoral strategies. Since many women did work in the home, the CCF's appeal was a pragmatic one oriented to women's day-to-day material concerns, but it also remained a barrier to women's full integration into political life. Women had difficulties carrying the double burden of family and political obligations; they probably had difficulties moving from the social committees into which they were channelled to the centres of decision-making; and they may have had difficulties convincing themselves and others that their ''maternal'' qualities really suited them to positions of power in the ''important'' policy-making areas of economics and defence.

Despite women's underrepresentation in the leadership, they comprised an indispensable army of local educators, organizers, and electioneers who created the supporting edifice that allowed the socialist movement to build upwards. And women's secondary position in the party did not go unnoticed; indeed, women's committees were sometimes set up with the distinct purpose of ''training women for leadership.'' CCF women's groups ran the gamut from fund-raising auxiliaries to more militant socialist-feminist action groups. Even committed feminists, however, shared many of the prevailing notions of womanhood and thus agreed that women's issues should focus largely on women's family-related concerns, thereby echoing one of the contradictions that kept women isolated from the mainstream of the socialist movement.

But at the time, neither the women's auxiliaries nor the more vocal women's committees saw their efforts as marginal or limited by a maternal mystique. As Margaret Benson said, CCF women, in their recognition of class and socialist issues, were ''militant.'' Perhaps Beatrice Brigden, who had personally travelled the path from maternal feminism to militant mothering, best articulated this difference:

Yes, the CCF woman does differ from others. Chiefly in this, we think, she has separated herself very largely from the pre-judices and fallacies of the capitalist order. She repudiates the system of competition. . . . She has accepted the cooperative principle, the well-tested recipe for success in her own home-making: each giving according to her ability and each receiving according to [her] need. The CCF woman proposes to apply this same kindly, enduring fundamental to the social order.[62]

# 5

# More Militant Mothering: Communist Women During the Popular Front

By the summer of 1935, Canadian Communists had charted a new course of action: the pink tea pacifists they had earlier opposed now became sought-after allies in the fight against fascism. Less isolated by sectarian Third Period rhetoric, Communists helped to shape a rising tide of protest against social and economic inequality. Though unemployment remained high and employers' anti-union hostility had not abated, significant changes had occurred: the worst of the depression was over and working-class confidence, reflected in increasing union membership, was on the rise. This period of the Popular or Peoples' Front marked a high point for Communist Party membership and influence.

For Communist women, the Popular Front generated new opportunities for activism and inspired innovative organizing techniques. As a result of the tactical emphasis on anti-fascism and community organizing, women came to occupy a more central role in the Party's strategies. Yet, the CPC's primary goal was to draw women into the fight against fascism, not to understand why they were oppressed and how that might be changed. The new interest in women's issues did not signify a different theoretical approach to the woman question as much as a means of garnering support for the Popular Front. As a result, women went two steps forward only to go one back. The Party had some successes in organizing women workers and persuading homemakers to take their militant mothering into the public sphere. Yet, it failed to emancipate women from the political sexual division of labour that still existed in the CPC. This would have necessitated an assault on the family and gender roles that, theoretically and practically, the Party was not yet willing to make.

## The Popular Front

The Popular Front evolved from growing Soviet fears of fascist aggression and new Comintern policies calling for a world-wide alliance with socialist parties against fascism. As it evolved, Communists advocated an even broader alliance of "working class, petit-bourgeois and middle-class people," including Communists, socialists, and even liberals.[1] This meant a partial break with traditional Leninist tactics, which had been interpreted to prescribe alliances only with working-class organizations, though Leninist organizing methods, including democratic centralism, still shaped the internal workings of the Party.

For Canadian Communists, the Popular Front may have come as a welcome relief from Third Period denunciations of other socialists and trade unionists. Indeed, in trade union work, Communists had already tempered their Third Period strategies by 1934, seeking out allies rather than labelling all other unionists enemies of the working class. Even before the Comintern had sanctioned the new strategy, there was evidence of a thaw; an ILGWU strike in Toronto, for example, was neither opposed nor supported by the Communist IUNTW.

Women, said the Comintern, should be ready recruits to the Popular Front because fascism was misogynistic and because it was a war-seeking, aggressive ideology that threatened world peace. However, when the Canadian Party met in 1935 to discuss Popular Front strategies, the Women's Department was weak and disorganized. Like her predecessors, the Women's Director, Alice Cooke, chided her male comrades for underestimating women's political potential and she deplored the low proportion of women in the Party – women were only 12 per cent of the membership and only one-third of those were factory workers. To give the work among women the attention it deserves, she warned, "*once and for all . . .* we must have a women's department in each district, the promotion of women to leadership and educational material specifically for women."[2] The Party responded with a "new" plan to unionize women and organize them against relief cuts and the high cost of living. While this approach was not especially new, the Party's call for a coalition with middle-class women was. Cooke, for example, recommended city conferences on war and fascism to which "middle-class women, intellectuals and church women be invited."[3] Only a few years earlier, the idea of meeting with church women would have been an ana-

*Florence Theodore, party leader in Saskatchewan, 1942-45.* (National Archives of Canada, PA 126376)

thema. CPC women were also encouraged to reach out to home-makers and professional women, "like teachers and nurses . . . thus forging a link between the labour movement and the middle classes."[4] The range of groups considered appropriate for in-volvement now stretched from union auxiliaries to the women's institutes, parent-teacher groups, community clubs, and women from the United Farmers of Canada.

The Party also encouraged more flexibility in organizing tactics. Rather than the unrealistic mass meetings called for during the Third Period, it began to emphasize community and neighbour-hood activities. Florence Theodore, a Saskatchewan activist who later led the provincial party, suggested women join rural, social, and homecraft groups, then gradually introduce political subjects, like peace, to the discussion. Instead of denigrating women's apolitical sewing circles, Communist women were now to adopt them and use them to good political effect.

More support was given to the idea of separate women's organizations, though it was still noted that "capable male comrades should be placed on the Party's women's committees to ensure that the whole Party is drawn into this vital activity"[5] – a suggestion perhaps also meant to ensure that such committees did not veer off onto a "mistaken" feminist course. Special day branches were advocated in the hope of attracting homemakers who could not attend regular evening meetings because of their children. The idea that men care for their children was apparently never considered. In contrast to the acrimonious debate within the Women's Labor Leagues of 1929-30, many women comrades responded favourably to these new tactics, perhaps indicating an underlying sympathy for separate women's organizations. In *Discussion*, an intra-party paper, one woman wrote on "why I have changed my mind about women's branches," explaining that "the superior political knowledge of men sometimes overawes women" but in women's groups "we can carry on elementary education about women in society . . . and eliminate forever this unhealthy inferiority complex which so many of our women possess."[6] Only occasionally was Lenin's advice to set up separate organizations for women cited; links to the revolutionary, international movement were downplayed publicly in favour of an emphasis on radical, indigenous Canadian traditions.

Although the late 1930's saw a narrowing of options for women in the Soviet Union,[7] in Canada this era offered some exciting possibilities for Communists' work among women. CPC women were encouraged to enrol in many different women's organizations, an about-turn from the Party's previous denigration of feminist organizations. In practice, of course, the Communist Party tried hardest to fashion alliances with socialist women in the CCF and in farm and peace groups. And Communists' faith in the Popular Front may have been reinforced by the growing strength of socialist-feminist enclaves in the CCF and WIL. As we have seen, some CCF women were attracted by Communist overtures: rather than Communists "duping" unsuspecting social democrats, there was an element of consent involved, as some CCF women believed they might further their own political goals within a Popular Front of women.[8]

### The Communist Press

The altered direction in the Party's work was soon reflected in the new women's column added to *The Worker* (later the *Daily*

*Clarion*) in the summer of 1935. Edited by Alice Cooke, "With our Women" contained news items and editorials, especially on peace, consumer, and child welfare issues, as well as information on working women and tidbits on housework and child-rearing. The intent was clearly to appeal to women in various degrees of politicization, but particularly targeted was the Party's continual "problem" – the unpoliticized housewife. To this end, the women's editor included material intended to appeal to the average homemaker: in 1936 a weekly feature on food, beauty, and consumer information, written by Julia Price, was added. In her introduction, Price reassured her readers she was not a strong feminist but "a woman's woman," and she stressed her heterosexual and traditional perspective: "it's the menfolk I prefer . . . which I have in common with the rest of womankind . . . . Ergo, I'm qualified to write a column for women!"⁹

The inclusion of household hints met with at least one opponent. An angry reader demanded to know why Communists had "adopted one of the worst features of the capitalist press – the woman's page," thus perpetuating the "segregation" of women from the class struggle. The author may have been one of those members who saw work among women as a detraction from the important class issues, but she also showed considerable sympathy for women in the home. Opposing what she called the "trivialization of household work," she argued that domestic labour required "a higher degree of intelligence than mass production work yet this is not recognized." She also called for a "little Communism in action," that is, husbands doing the dishes, and suggested that a household hints column for men could recommend more nights out for the wives.¹⁰ Her protest letter is interesting in part because it indicates the more open discussion allowed in the paper after the Third Period, but also because of its claim that domestic labour was "productive" – which was categorically rejected in the next decade – and for its militant demands for equality in the family.

Despite this singular protest, the column continued unchanged; in fact, the critic's letter was followed by a recipe for mustard pickles. The women's editor replied that there was a difference between the women's page in the capitalist press, "meant to dull class consciousness," and one in the Communist press, which "does not perpetuate women's regulation in the kitchen, children and church" but understands that "household aids will help women devote more time in the end to outside activities."¹¹ Addressing women as homemakers may have been a practical political starting point, but encouraging women to do their work faster so they might have more time for politics created a difficult double burden for women. Moreover, the *Clarion*'s inclusion of syndicated columns on patterns, recipes, child-rearing, and even beauty hints imitated the stress on personal life, appearance, and the home that characterized bourgeois women's magazines. Even if a *Clarion* writer offered her own critique of the fashion industry, her message might be contradicted a week later by a syndicated beauty column that marvelled at the fun and frivolity of red nail polish. Caught in the Popular Front dilemma of producing a women's column of mass popular appeal, the Party sometimes copied, rather than criticized, the dominant cultural capitalist norms.

These criticisms aside, the *Clarion*'s women's column did provide a widened opportunity to discuss women's issues within the Party, and although women's issues were often placed within the feminine boundaries of children, consumer issues, and peace, the paper did encourage women to involve themselves in the public sphere, indeed, in the world of radical politics. Political commentary and information on working women formed the core of the column's editorials and on occasion a militant women's voice penetrated the moderation of the Popular Front, lambasting an oppressive system that "condemned women to double drudgery in factory and kitchen and [by failing] to provide . . . birth control, compelled women to servitude."[12] Finally, domestic and beauty hints were sometimes served up in a critical framework: *Clarion* writers often criticized the daily press's recipe suggestions, which had no relation to working-class incomes, and urged young women to adopt healthful home remedies rather than buying cosmetics and thus fuelling the profits of big business.

Furthermore, some Communist women did hope that, ultimately, the paper would develop an alternative image for women. In 1936, Beatrice Ferneyhough, a young activist in the Party, shared her vision of a future Communist women's magazine that "would describe, with realism and compassion, the conditions of life for most women – including low wages and unemployment – and could help women to see these problems as social rather than personal." Such a magazine, she continued, would not instruct women "in anti-intellectual and submissive attitudes . . . implying we are mentally inferior, instinctual and emotional" as do bourgeois magazines. Instead, it would "speak to our needs . . . to know about women elsewhere . . . to understand our role in public life, receive guidance and learn from the experience of others.''[13] This was a mandate which *was* different from that of *Chatelaine*.

### Unionizing Women

Ferneyhough's dream of a women's magazine did not materialize, but the *Clarion* devoted considerable space to the concerns of wage-earning women, and the paper consciously singled out women workers' militancy for praise, drawing the conclusion that women workers were not necessarily more conservative than male ones. Much of the *Clarion*'s coverage reiterated themes reminiscent of *The Woman Worker* in the 1920's, such as the ineffective minimum wage laws, simply because these issues represented persistent social problems. For most working women in Canada, the depression still defined their work lives and expectations – or lack of them. Despite a slight upturn in the economy, many women remained unemployed; and even those with jobs feared losing them. In the late 1930's, some women were drawn into revitalized mass production industries like rubber and auto, but even here they were ghettoized into lower-wage jobs.

Within the Communist Party, a few female leaders persisted in their attempts to nudge male comrades out of their complacency in regard to women workers. ''Women in industry,'' Annie Buller reminded her comrades, ''must be seen as a permanent, progressive factor . . . and every effort must be made to close wage differentials.''[14] Organizing women workers did have a certain urgency in Party strategies, since women's integration into social production, it was still believed, would raise women's class consciousness and engage them in the class struggle.

The Party, however, now rarely spoke of women's ''revolutionary'' consciousness, and with the disbanding of the Workers Unity League it turned to the international unions as vehicles for organizing. If this had meant only the TLC, women workers might have been by-passed, as they were in the 1920's. But the formation and popularity of the CIO meant that women were included in Communist organizing attempts. Moreover, some flexibility in the CPC's industrial tactics allowed dedicated local organizers to respond to calls of women whom other trade unionists might have dismissed as ''unorganizable.''

In one women's occupation, the needle trades, the Party had already carved out a sphere of influence. The decision to merge the Communist IUNTW into such unions as the ILGWU and the

Furriers diminished the concentration of Communist influence; mergers thus created the possibility of influencing more women, but also posed the reality of hard work in trying to sway non-Communists to the Communist viewpoint. In the latter case Communists occasionally found factional hostility within the international union as intense as the previous antipathy between the WUL's dual unions and the TLC. In Toronto, for example, social democrats and Communists battled – sometimes physically – for control of Local 40 of the International Fur Workers Union. The conflict engendered epithets as vicious as those used during the Third Period, as Communists denounced the social democrat union president as a "gangster" and he responded by calling Pearl Wedro a "Stalinist fish wife."[15]

The battle for Local 40, which the Communists temporarily won, was not, however, the norm during the late 1930's. More often, Popular Front strategies were beneficial to the CPC, gaining them at least a measure of co-operation with other trade unionists. In Winnipeg, for instance, a 1936 strike of fur workers obtained support from a citizens' solidarity committee composed of both Communists and social democrats. After ten weeks of employer intransigence, a women's solidarity demonstration marched to the legislature and was addressed by Communist MLA Jim Litterick and by CCFers Beatrice Brigden and Gloria Queen-Hughes. The endorsement of the march by a number of organizations, including the Winnipeg Women's Labor Federation, added support to the cause, and by the end of the month the government had ordered an inquiry and charged some employers under the minimum wage laws.

The Party continued to expend some energy on women workers in small workplaces and seasonal employment. In Toronto, for example, picketers were sent to the New Method Laundry strike and to Child's Restaurant on Yonge Street, a popular coffee shop that refused to negotiate with its unionized employees. In Calgary and Vancouver aid was given to waitresses trying to organize, and in 1937 Beatrice Ferneyhough was assigned the task of building an Office and Store Workers Union. The creation of new CIO unions for clericals and the Popular Front emphasis on constructing alliances with middle-class and petit-bourgeois women both led naturally to the Party's increased interest in unionizing white-collar women. Party efforts with women clericals, however, possibly also had a more cynical twist to them. Many Communists believed that the deferential and conservative petit bourgeois in

*Pearl Wedro, a member of the women's delegation to the Soviet Union in 1929, was active in trade union work in the 1930's.* (University of Toronto Rare Books Room, Kenny Collection)

Europe had supported the fascists; thus, North American clericals should be organized to prevent the spread of right-wing ideology and to support the struggles of blue-collar industrial workers. Ironically, says American historian Sharon Strom, the Communists helped to promote new unions for white-collar workers, but the Party's anti-feminist views and inability to take these unions seriously hindered their effectiveness.[16]

Communist organizing also floundered in the face of persisting external obstacles: the hostility of employers, a ready supply of cheap female labour, fears of firings and reprisals, and women's small workplaces. Moreover, every union drive was not part of a centrally administered strategy. The Party did try to colonize key industries and set up factions within the unions, but local conditions might also shape the who, what, and how of union organizing. Similarly, in the Communist Party of the U.S., argues Harvey Levenstein, ''there was no indication that plans drawn up in Moscow and New York determined which unions were heavily CP in orientation.'' In fact, the Party's ''egalitarian impulse led them to expend inordinate energy on . . . the least powerful and . . . tragic cases, such as the migrant workers . . . the infinitely replaceable Macey's salesladies, or hospital workers. These people lay at the very bottom of the union ladder.''[17]

A good example of a local organizing initiative undertaken by Communists in the late 1930's was that of four Vancouver women who attempted to build a union for domestics, workers most definitely at the bottom of the union ladder, if not below it. The Party quite correctly noted that the depression was forcing women into low-paying domestic jobs and in convention resolutions urged that these women not be forgotten.[18] In Vancouver, four Communist Party women, all domestics themselves, took these words to heart and worked through their Party contacts, the YWCA, classified columns, and employment services to locate recruits for the Domestic Workers Federal Union. When they approached the Local Labour Council for help, it rather paternalistically reminded the women that domestics' unions had ''always died,'' but the women proudly countered that ''this is different due to the loyal Communist women involved.''[19] They, too, encountered obstacles that had killed previous unions: most domestics were difficult to locate, were fearful of being fired, and had no experience with unions. In the end, though, their Communist zeal paid off: a small union did emerge and Party ranks were also augmented. The union did not survive as a long-term entity; geographically scattered workplaces and an immense labour reserve posed a Sisyphean task for any union. Nonetheless, the fleeting success of these Party women indicated the possibilities that might accrue from local initiative and a commitment to organizing women.

The Party leadership, however, was most keenly interested in workers in the mass production industries such as steel, auto, and rubber. Few women were found in steel plants, though women machine sewers worked as inside finishers in the auto industry. Female auto workers in the trim room at the Oshawa plant supported their fellow workers in the major strike of 1936, but it is noteworthy that neither the CIO nor Communist organizers challenged women's relegation to lower-paid finishing jobs. Similarly, Communists involved in two major rubber strikes in Kitchener plants did not challenge the industry's unequal division of labour. In one factory, the United Rubber Workers' aim was to augment the male wage of fifty cents an hour and the female wage of thirty-two cents an hour, not to close the gap between the two. And when workers struck Kaufman Rubber later the same year, the union demanded "equal pay for equal work," but added the revealing demand that "men's work be done by men only."[20] Communists, like most trade unionists of the time, understood equal pay to mean equal pay for precisely the same task, and they rarely objected to the division of labour into male and female jobs – despite Annie Buller's exhortations to close wage differentials. As in the early 1930's, Communists probably saw union recognition as the crucial demand, with more utopian demands, such as equalization of wages, much further down the road. A thoroughgoing critique of sexual discrimination in the workplace, as we know it, was simply not a part of the Party's industrial strategies at this time.

Lower wage rates were also the lot of female textile workers, a target group for Communist unionization drives since the 1920's. Pointing to the low wages and unsafe working conditions in textiles, the Party argued that women workers should be class-conscious union material. By the late 1930's, textile workers in Ontario and Quebec gave every indication that they would fulfil the Party expectations as protracted strikes broke out, reflecting workers' "urge to make up for years of wage-cutting, unemployment and deprivation, and the suppression of trade unions in the industry."[21] Late in the summer of 1936 a strike of 1,700 rayon workers, including 700 women, exploded at the Courtaulds Mill in Cornwall. Sparked by a protest of women workers over speedups, the strike became a plant-wide bid for better wages and recognition of the United Textile Workers Union. The union had been organized by two Communists, Alex Welch and Frank Love, who also helped guide the strike to a limited victory, obtaining better wages though not union recognition.[22] Soon after this, a strike at Empire Cottons in Welland earned front-page headlines in the *Clarion*. Communists probably helped to orchestrate this walkout, as they had been trying to organize the mill for a number of years and had recently dispatched Party organizer Ann Walters, a veteran of the Workers Unity League, to finish the job.[23]

A year later, the Party tried to intervene in a bitter strike at Dominion Woolens' Peterborough woollen mills, again organized by Alex Welch. Though the strike was initiated by male weavers at the Auburn Mill, the Bonnerworth spinning and worsted mill, dominated by a female work force, soon joined the picket line. Both men and women wanted improvements in wages and work-

*May Day parade, Silknit strikers, May 1, 1937. (City of Toronto Archives)*

ing conditions and recognition of a union. Although the company tried to make an issue of Welch's role as a Communist and "outside agitator," the workers were much more concerned with the workplace issues of speed-up, piece rates, and distribution of work. Concentrated in different jobs than the men, the women's wage rates were often considerably lower; indeed, the company's use of piece rates and erratic hours of work meant that some women's take home pay was less than the prevailing minimum wage.[24]

When the strike began, support came from a wide cross-section of the community and some local politicians were critical of Dominion Woolens' hard-line approach. Later in the summer, after the workers had rejected one settlement, the city polarized and the strike took on violent overtones. When workers tried to close their picket line against strikebreakers escorted in by city and provincial police, they found tear gas and clubs used against them. The female work force at the Bonnerworth mill reacted most forcefully. The "girls," according to the mainstream press, fought the police by "clawing, screaming and throwing tomatoes": the language used to understand women's actions repeatedly implied irrationality and "hysteria." The radical press, interestingly, deviated from this mode of depicting women, portraying them instead as "militant and courageous."[25] Ultimately, though, the women were no match for Canada's largest woollen company. The strike ended with the intervention of Premier Hepburn and the TLC, but the strikers were left with only a promise of new legislated wage rates in the industry and no certified union.

Both the CCF and CPC took an active part in the strike. The Peterborough CCF provided coffee and sandwiches to the picket line and Lorna Cotton-Thomas spoke at strikers' meetings, while the Communists sent support troops from Toronto, including organizer Harvey Murphy, president of the Unemployed Workers Association. Both parties wanted to support the workers, but they also sought to augment their own credibility; as a result, power struggles broke out within the union. Privately, a local Communist charged that CCFers were trying to bring "[Charlie] Millard [a CCFer] into town to run Welch out of town." Ironically, their battles may have discouraged the very female workers they were trying to reach. "At all the union meetings," complained the local union treasurer privately to lawyer J.S. Cohen, "CPer Townsley [opposed by the CCF] holds the floor twice as long as anyone else until some of the Bonnerworth girls walk out."[26]

The views of this critic cannot, however, be used as a generalization to assess *all* Communist activity on the labour front. As in the early 1930's, Communists were more committed to the organization of women workers than many trade unionists and they did contribute to the building of CIO unions, which held out more hope for women workers than the craft-based TLC. However, the party's union strategies, shaped by a concern for heavy industry and also by an image of the male breadwinner, remained inevitably focused more sharply on the needs of male workers. Aside from such notable exceptions as Ann Walters, one found fewer Communist women organizers and union leaders, and seldom would one have encountered a men's auxiliary offering support to, say, a strike of women white-collar workers. In the final analysis, though, it is difficult to measure Communist influence only by the Party's membership or leadership. Communists may also have had some indirect influence on women workers who respected Communists' militant defence of workers' interests but did not embrace their politics. This may seem true for the young textile worker of 1937: she appreciated Communist support on the picket line, but she was not persuaded to join the Party.

### Organizing Women in the Home

The Popular Front sparked a renewed interest in the organization of homemakers; women were encouraged to join union auxiliaries and strike support committees, and to participate in campaigns around consumer issues, child care and education, health, relief, and unemployment. In 1937 the Women's Department suggested each locality develop its own program, "selecting five or six of the most outstanding needs there, issues that would appeal to women . . . like medical clinics for pre-school children, birth control clinics, nursery schools or better housing."[27] Popular Front tactics were designed to politicize women around their day-to-day experiences as wives and mothers and to maximize Communists' integration into the local community by participation in mainstream women's organizations. Indeed, when Popular Front tactics were stretched to the limit, Party members were told to "offer housewives what they want . . . including bridge, music, movies and bingo."[28]

In Toronto, Communists organized Progressive Women's Associations (PWAs), neighbourhood groups based on the municipal ward system. By 1936, a city-wide coalition of PWAs was effected

and their lobbying around child-care, consumer, and welfare issues earned them support from some CCF women. Organization
based on the ward system had the added advantage of creating
an election machine ready to swing into action during municipal
contests, and by the end of the decade the Party was focusing
more and more on municipal politics as a key avenue for United
Front organizing. As always, the Party feared women's "antipathy to politics," but it hoped that candidates might draw out
the women's vote by addressing such family issues as housing
and prices. Just before the Toronto civic election of 1935, the
*Clarion* editorialized about the apathetic housewife problem:

> Again we are in the midst of an election and many women are
> bewildered to know which Party to listen to. . . . Many have
> an apathetic response. . . . Thus, we must point out how our
> candidates will improve their lot . . . for example, approach
> housewives concretely on their problems such as the high cost
> of living.[29]

The Party claimed some success with this approach, concluding
that, in the 1936 civic contest, it had developed untapped political
skills by using "women for door to door canvassing, and holding
neighbourhood teas." Many women, the report added, combined
domestic and political work, "canvassing with their babies and
bringing [them] to meetings."[30]

Across Ontario and the West, other CPC women attempted to
construct community-based women's associations: in Port Arthur,
a Housewives Association, led by Communist Kate Magnussen
(later Bader), lobbied for extra relief for families on welfare,
while in Edmonton a Mothers Council addressed youth issues. In
some cities women organized under the banner of the Women's
Labor Leagues: led by Annie Stewart and Lil Stoneman, the
Vancouver WLLs continued to lobby governments and sponsor
public demonstrations on a variety of unemployment and relief
issues. In 1936, they sponsored their tenth annual convention,
passing resolutions to obtain better relief for pregnant women and
to sustain a Domestic Workers Union.

By the late 1930's, as prices rose, consumer issues assumed a
more important place in Communist Party strategies. At the 1938
national convention Alice Cooke criticized her comrades for failing to rally women against rising prices, "the most outstanding
opportunity for organizing women in the past year."[31] Consumer
issues, explained Cooke, were synonymous with women's issues

for it was women who had to juggle the dwindling family resources and deal with the emotional and physical toll exacted on
the family by higher rent and food bills. By 1938-39, many Party
women had initiated civic housewives' leagues, whose aim was
to "stand for a living wage . . . a rise in the standard of living
for producers and consumers . . . and to assist organized labour."[32] These groups often centred their sights on campaigns
with limited, specific price objectives. In Vancouver, for example, the Housewives Association protested high meat costs by
boycotting meat retailers for a week. The Toronto Housewives
League organized a successful letter-writing and lobby campaign
against milk price increases in 1937, though in 1939 their attempt
to draw the Local Council of Women into a similar protest against
rising gas prices was not successful. By 1939, potential supporters
were wary of Communist presence; moreover, the whole campaign was cut short by the declaration of war and the Communists'
hasty change of political line.

The essential selling point of the Party's appeal on consumer
issues was its exhortation for women to defend the home because
it was threatened by economic crisis. As the Housewives League's
song so clearly put it:

Every woman should have a house
She can call her own
Decent living for every child
In a decent home
Food and shelter and clothing too
For the family
So she joins in the fight
For a cause that is right
Sharing victory.[33]

In the *Clarion*, Alice Cooke again tried to distinguish between
Communists' "defence of the home" and the design of the bourgeois press to stress "women's place in the home . . . in order
to . . . imply an end to the problem of unemployed women."[34]
The Party did routinely object to sending women back to the
kitchen as a solution for unemployment, but the distinction between the bourgeois and Communist views of the family was
sometimes rather murky. As a result, the CPC's equation of women
with domesticity and its support for the family wage stood dangerously close to the bourgeois message that women belonged
primarily in the home, not the workplace. Occasionally, the Party

did hint at a broader critique of consumerism within a capitalist economy, though usually this was done simply to point out that women could not afford consumer products. Mary Flanigan, for instance, offered an insightful account in the *Clarion* of the advertising industry's attempts to create consumer demands and "sell women a whiter than white wash." This was particularly odious, she concluded, "because most working-class women cannot afford the washing machines advertized."[35]

Defence of one's home also meant defence of one's children. Because women's primary responsibility for child care was usually taken as a given, the *Clarion*'s women's page carried tips on child health and psychology, and women's mothering role was lavished with considerable praise, even sentimentalized as women's "natural urge."[36] Communists saw no contradiction between their portrayal of motherhood as women's natural or normal role and their assertion that women should be able to freely choose motherhood from a number of options. Similarly, many *Clarion* articles on women in the U.S.S.R. outlined the Soviet's strong pro-natalist policies, while simultaneously arguing that women had complete choice about careers and motherhood in the U.S.S.R.

Women were expected to take responsibility for the socialization of Communist youth and for the leadership of organizations to improve children's lives. One Party member admonished women to link together "the women's movement and the children's movement . . . in order to educate children to progressive ideas . . . help children learn to work cooperatively and build new leadership."[37] Many women continued to organize progressive summer camps for children, providing one link in the ethnic leftist culture that knitted Communist friends and family together, while others joined mainstream organizations such as the parent-teacher associations. One *Clarion* correspondent embraced the Popular Front so enthusiastically that she recommended that Communists "involve ourselves and make sure the Boy Scouts is not a reactionary movement,"[38] showing rather cavalier indifference to socialists' long-standing suspicions of imperalist youth groups. Women were also urged to set up *ad hoc* women's groups to fight for children's social and economic improvement. Annie Buller suggested city conferences on maternity and on medical and dental aid for children, "for the health of children is a national problem and we can rally thousands of women on it."[39] Organizations like the PWAs followed these suggestions, holding forums on child welfare and lobbying local governments for better medical care in the schools and playgrounds for the inner city.

Maternalism also supplied one of the rationales used to encourage women's participation in relief protests. Communists urged women to fight for relief sufficient to guarantee their children decent food and clothing. In the *Clarion*, exposés of the inadequate welfare system asked ''What of our children?'' or warned ''Physical Welfare of Children Cause for Concern.'' Despite this emphasis on women's maternal role, feminine passivity was not the byword in many of the local relief protests undertaken by women. In Saskatoon, Communist Anna Pashka organized a women's sit-in at City Hall to protest inadequate relief. When the police came to remove the protesters, they shouted ''that Anna Pashka, right out'' and dragged her down the stairs and out of the building. Pashka, who had at first shouted back in the dark of the night, ''who is there?'', was amused to find the newspaper headlines describing the protesters as ''Screeching Women at City Hall.''[40] In Lakeview a women's relief group also developed its own innovative militant tactics: they held the relief officer and his two assistants hostage until police broke down the door to rescue the beleaguered bureaucrats.

During the famous On-to-Ottawa Trek in 1935, maternalism was used as an organizing motif. In Vancouver, Communist and social democrat women joined together in the Mothers' Committee to organize a large Mothers' Day demonstration protesting the inhumanity and injustice of Canada's relief camps for unemployed men. Then, in Regina, after the riot, a Mothers' Committee, including Communists Florence Theodore and Josephine Gehl, was formed to visit the imprisoned trekkers and lobby for their release. The committee's name, remembered Elsie Gehl Beeching, was less a statement of personnel than an appeal, on an emotional level, to homemakers who were concerned about the future of their children, for ''it was the youth of the land who were the trekkers. These women took it upon themselves to assist and mother them . . . to give them aid, encouragement . . . to adopt them in a sense.''[41] The Mothers' Committee apparently struck a responsive chord, for many left-wing women's groups across the country responded with letters to R.B. Bennett, demanding the trekkers' release and an end to the relief camps.

Although the Trek highlighted the tragedy of young, unemployed men, ten of the marchers on the Ontario section of the

Trek, begun after the Regina riot, were women. The women's contingent marched out of Toronto on a hot July day, led by textile organizer Ann Walters. Lil Himmelfarb, a veteran of the free-speech fights, acted as one of the official speakers on the Trek, for her forte, she admits, "was the street corner or soapbox orating." Women were a minority of the trekkers, she explained, "because there were not many women in the labour force, especially during the depression . . . [or] . . . in the unemployed movement . . . though women helped with unemployment councils and eviction fights." [42] The Ontario trekkers also included Mary Flanigan, an older Communist Party member who acted as cook, and the youngest was Louise Sandler, the fifteen-year-old daughter of a Party member and needle trades worker. Flanigan went ahead on a truck, but all the other women walked, ate, and camped on equal terms with the men. Party organizers asked for the trekkers' exemplary behaviour, and for Louise this included doing her part to dispel any rumours about promiscuous coed living.

> Lil and I were lying on a hillside in Brockville after a long day in our pants and short hair, with our heads covered, and I awoke to hear two women talking, behind us. They were horrified because they thought it was a man and a woman under the same blanket. I poked Lil and said "Sit up!" to make it perfectly clear we were [women]. [43]

This small group of female trekkers symbolized well the plight of the unemployed woman. The object of considerable state and social indifference, the unemployed woman fared only slightly better in Popular Front campaigns. The Party made some efforts to build single unemployed women's associations, but given women's smaller numbers in the work force, most efforts were centred on organizing the unemployed man. Women were considered primarily as wives of the unemployed and were often addressed with a maternal appeal that spoke pragmatically of homemakers' day-to-day worries of family survival but did not question the divisions of labour confining women to the home. Ultimately, this approach channelled women into Party campaigns considered of secondary importance to the revolution. Moreover, the invocation of maternalism had an opportunistic edge to it: it was used not to emancipate women but because homemakers were seen as crucial allies to a successful Popular Front.

## Anti-Fascism

Women were also seen as important recruits for the CPC's anti-war and anti-fascist campaigns. Fascism, warned the Communists, meant the oppression of women "whose small measure of independence and self-respect, won under capitalism, and limited as it is, are totally lost under fascism."[44] The anti-feminist policies of Germany and Italy, including women's loss of jobs and equation with breeding machines, were routinely cited as warnings of fascism's misogyny. Secondly, it was stressed, fascism, an aggressive force, would endanger the lives of women's husbands and sons. In a war initiated by fascists, "there will be no respect for civilian lives," said the *Clarion*, "and are not working women the great sufferers in war?. . . . They see their husbands herded to slaughter and bear babies to manhood only to have them claimed by the capitalist class as bullet targets."[45] Drawing on both maternalist rhetoric and working-class memories of past sacrifices in war, the Party tried to draw women into the anti-war movement. Also, some Party documents frankly added, women had to be recruited to this cause because as potential munitions workers or support troops, they could easily be manipulated by the state and its pro-war propagandists.

In order to build an anti-war movement the Communist Party reversed its complete opposition to such peace groups as the Womens' International League for Peace and Freedom, giving limited though still critical coverage of their activities in the Communist press. The CPC's major initiative, however, was to garner support for the Canadian League against War and Fascism (CLWF), founded in 1934 as a branch of an international organization determined to "build a broadly-based movement against war and fascism."[46] The CPC deliberately took a back seat in the CLWF leadership in order to reassure liberals and socialists of its sincerity, a tactic that did have some success. In 1937, the name was changed to the League for Peace and Democracy, an alteration that reflected the moderate politics of the League and its attempts to draw on a wide membership, as well as the important influence of the Spanish Civil War in turning the League's energies from anti-war work to anti-fascist activities.[47]

By 1937, many League members, including CCF socialist-feminists Jean Laing and Rose Henderson, had moved away from strict pacifist non-violence to support a war for "peace and democracy" in Spain. Women who joined the League believed that one could be anti-war and anti-fascist at the same time, for few were absolute pacifists. Nora Rodd, for instance, began her political life in the Windsor CCF in the 1930's, but she switched to the CLWF and the CPC because she felt "Communists were more committed to anti-fascism."[48] Rodd would later explain that women's life-giving role was a central reason for her interest in peace, but she did not oppose all wars: in Spain, neutrality was not an option because the war was an anti-fascist struggle. This brand of pacifism was very similar to that promoted by the Women's Labor Leagues, which had called for an end to war, but not at the expense of struggles against oppression or class exploitation.

Women were highly visible in the Canadian League against War and Fascism, an indication that fascism was a pressing concern for progressive women. At the CLWF's founding convention, the Communist group included Dorothy Livesay, Julia Collins, and Becky Buhay, while Alice Chown, Ida Siegal, Alice Loeb, and others made up the larger WIL contingent. Women at the convention met separately one evening and formed a National Women's Council that vowed to set up local councils and organize a Dominion conference of women against fascism. It was essential, they argued, that women recognize the dangerous, "enslaving, oppressive" nature of fascist ideology.[49] As CCFer Elizabeth Morton declared in a rousing speech to the delegates: "under fascism, women are relegated to blind unquestioning creatures, even classified for breeding purposes. . . . A thinking woman is a dangerous thing and the ruling class realizes that."[50] At the Second CLWF Congress, speeches by Annie Buller and Rose Henderson decried the fascist tendencies of prevailing discrimination against working and professional women, and the women passed resolutions calling for political rights for Quebec women and an end to all "dogmas" of male superiority.[51] Part of women's attraction to the anti-fascist movement was clearly its association with women's rights. For Communists, however, the rationale was not to embrace feminism entirely but rather to draw large numbers of politically aware women into an anti-fascist alliance with the CPC.

Calls for women to join the Canadian Committee to Aid Spanish Democracy and the Friends of the Mackenzie-Papineau Battalion were not made in such overtly feminist terms. For many left-wing men and women, the anti-fascist war in Spain was a touchstone of their generation and the issue that led them into the CPC's Popular Front. Within the Committee to Aid Spanish Democracy there were also separate women's committees, intended to draw homemakers into the movement with non-threatening programs of humanitarian aid. The CASD's 1937 meeting, for instance, convened a women's committee to reach out to women's social service clubs, plan separate publicity for women, and recommend programs such as "neighbourhood teas, study groups, home-cooking sales or a Christmas drive for a gift of milk to Spanish children, to be called the 'Women's Council for Humanitarian Aid to Spain'."[52]

This committee also suggested another quintessential Popular Front campaign: a national knitting contest, organized through local girls' organizations and the press. Subsequently, Alice Cooke commended those Toronto women who decided to "march in the May Day parade and knit as they walked for Spain." Even the most avid knitter would have had trouble competing with the sterling example of "Mrs. Kisman of Calgary who knitted fifty pairs of socks for the 'boys' in the Mac-Paps." All this knitting, Becky Buhay concluded, was proof positive that "progressive women stand in the forefront of the fight against fascism."[53] Besides knitting socks, many women contributed an important share of the CASD's office and secretarial work, fund-raising, and organizing for tours of speakers, including Norman Bethune. Though most women contributed – as they had in other wars – traditional support work to the Spanish cause, there was one rare exception: Jean "Jim" Watts, a Party activist and theatre worker from Toronto, went to Spain as a *Clarion* reporter and stayed to work as an ambulance driver for the International Brigades.

## Who Was "the Party"?

The success of the Communist Party's Popular Front work can be measured by the Party's expanding membership, of which women, admittedly, were still a minority. Like CCF women, female Communists were drawn into politics as a result of their witness to inequality, their experience of working-class life, and their introduction to socialist theory. Yet, there were crucial differences: more Communist women came from working-class, emigrant backgrounds and most had been re-educated in Marxism and Leninism rather than the eclectic socialism of the CCF. Some of the original members of the Communist Party, affectionately referred to as the "old Bolsheviks," were emigrants from Tsarist Russia and veterans of the European socialist movement who found their politics confirmed by their harsh experiences of working-class life in Canada. To many Jewish immigrants who came to Canada "already fired with hopes for universal social justice," says Erna Paris, "sweating in the Spadina shops only 'proved' Marxist theories of class exploitation."[54]

Many of these immigrants' children, who became the Party's leading cadres in the thirties and forties, shared some of the harsh experiences of their parents: they left school at an early age to pursue wage work at a time when job security was ephemeral, wages were low, and many families needed more than one earner to get by. And in the depths of the depression, those who had jobs saw the inherent insecurity and inequality of the workplace sharpened. Despite strong identification with their emigrant roots, however, this second generation saw itself as Canadian, not European, socialists, and they enthusiastically embraced Popular Front endeavours to make communism an integral part of the Canadian radical tradition.[55]

In the 1930's a large proportion of new female members still came from the Party's three main ethnic groups. Through the left-wing press, theatre, sports associations, or choirs, women gained an entrée to a socialist subculture that had much, in intellectual stimulation and emotional support, to offer immigrants. For Jewish children in Toronto, for example, "there was a special progressive school and during summer vacations, Camp Naivelt. When they were older, the adults sang in their own choir . . . formed their own brass band, had their own modern dance company and produced their own theatre, which was usually about their particular proletarian experience."[56]

The ethnic and class milieu of one's childhood and adolescence could lead the second-generation immigrant quite naturally into party circles. To grow up working-class, Eastern European, and Jewish in Toronto's Spadina district meant a good chance of having a friend, relative, or acquaintance in the movement. If parents were involved, red-diaper children literally grew up on a diet of Young Pioneers and political meetings. Once active in the Party, young Jewish Communists found a subculture "not institutional and religious, but of identity, style, language and social network"[57] to sustain feelings of cultural and political loyalty. Importantly, many Jewish women, like men, were attracted to the egalitarian message of socialism because of their negative experiences of anti-Semitism in Canada. They identified Tsarist Russia with the worst excesses of anti-Semitism and believed, however erroneously, that the Soviet Union was fostering Jewish culture and racial tolerance. Shaska Mandel, an immigrant whose family had escaped violent anti-Semitism in Tsarist Poland, joined the party soon after she began work in the needle trades. "The best solution for Jews was in the Soviet Union," she thought, "and I wanted equality for my people."[58]

Some women moved directly from the ethnic or mass organizations to the Party. Mary Kardash's parents were both active in the Ukrainian Labour-Farmer Temple Association and her father was a Communist labour organizer. Mary became active in ULFTA's youth movement, subsequently worked as a YCL organizer, and later became an important Party worker in Manitoba. Anna Pashka's story also reveals the close connections between the ethnic associations and the Communist Party, as well as the appeal of Communism to emigrant women. Pashka, born in 1897 to illiterate peasants in the Ukraine, recalled that even as a child she questioned social inequality: "I always had a feeling that something was wrong between those who had and those that had not . . . . I was told . . . it was God's will, but within me, I disagreed." When she was fourteen, Pashka's family emigrated; in Canada she was immediately forced to take on arduous domestic, chambermaid, and dishwashing jobs. "I knew I was being exploited, but I didn't understand why," she remembered. At twenty she married, and her husband introduced her to the ULFTA. The education offered immediately appealed to her class consciousness and answered her long-standing questions about social inequality, sparking her determination to join the socialist movement, even though she found it difficult to juggle children and politics. "I had this big carriage," she recalled. "I used to dump [the children] in and go out to meetings . . . . My three children grew up on the benches of the Labour Temple."[59] Pashka's determination and organizational skills were not lost on others; in 1931 she was asked to join the Party and she was soon deeply involved in relief protests and ULFTA organizing across Saskatchewan.

Though Pashka staunchly rejected feminism, she was aware of women's subordination, even within the left. During the 1928 debates, she recalled, "the men told us that we could not decide things for ourselves . . . . I really rebelled against this."[60] Pashka also fought her own personal battle against oppression: her husband, who was opposed to her public life, physically abused her.[61] Pashka's personal and political perseverance sustained her involvement in Party organizing, but her situation was quite unique. Although women's attachment to the ULFTA might lead them to the Party, their Ukrainian background might also help to perpetuate their secondary role within it and obscure their understanding of gender oppression. Ukrainian men, many Party members charged, made little effort to absolve themselves of patriarchal peasant traditions.[62] For Ukrainian women, concludes Helen Potrebenko very critically, this meant women could participate only as second-class citizens, "doing most of the work, without the credit. It wasn't considered nice for women to want positions as paid organizers, or to participate in demonstrations, except by preparing the food for them."[63]

It is true that Ukrainian women were less likely than English or Jewish women to be Party cadres or leaders. This may have been partly due to the Party's penchant for "respectable" Anglo leaders, but it was also the result of inhibitions linked to the background of many Ukrainian women. The Ukrainian women's paper, *Robitnysia*, owed its very existence to the ULFTA's paternalistic belief that women needed extra political coaching, as they were totally ignorant of politics. It was not women's innate ignorance, as some "porcupines" claimed, but rather the material and domestic realities of their lives that prevented their acquaintance with political theory and activity. Most Ukrainian women worked long hours in the home or on isolated farms, with few opportunities to learn how to read and write. As late as 1937, *Robitnysia* admitted that it had been unable to "reduce the level of illiteracy among our female members by one half . . . where our women initiated good work among the unemployed women, they had no success, because almost all the members are illiterate and can't do this work correctly."[64] Furthermore, porcupinism itself, those old-country attitudes that assumed women belonged in the home subject to male authority, may have been assuaged by *Robitnysia*'s persistent campaigns, but it was not eradicated. Ukrainian women were thus caught in a Catch-22: political activity was to be a cure for illiteracy and "backward" attitudes, but without literacy, time, and resources, women's political activity was almost impossible.

Furthermore, though the *Robitnysia* editors tried to combat porcupinism, the desired end was not to allow women to develop their own political agenda but rather to develop the Women's Section into a disciplined, class-conscious extension of the ULFTA. When it appealed to male readers to abandon their porcupine beliefs, *Robitnysia* continually invoked Lenin's dictum that the full participation of women was necessary to the success of the working-class movement. Women were simply described as "workers with an underdeveloped class consciousness." As the paper claimed (admittedly at the height of Third Period antipathy to feminism): "we take the view that working women do not have any interest separate from the interests of the working-class as a whole."[65] When *Robitnysia* folded in 1937, ostensibly due to financial problems, it was still lamenting women's failure to overcome their ethnic isolation and participate in class actions. For some, such as Pashka, the ULFTA had offered unprecedented opportunities for political activity. Even *Robitnysia*'s local reports and letters section revealed increasing attempts by rank-and-file women to express their political views, though always within the appropriate proletarian context. But given the strict political parameters set by the ULFTA, the inhibitions fostered by Ukrainian culture, and women's own material circumstances, Ukrainian women remained on the sidelines of party politics and rarely challenged their own gender oppression.

Jewish women in the Communist Party came from a different European cultural context.[66] Many Eastern European Jewish women brought to North America traditions that encouraged their labour and political militancy.[67] In traditional Yiddish culture, women were secondary in the most "important" sphere, religion, and they were primarily defined in terms of their duties as wives and mothers. Ruth Frager's analysis of the Jewish left, however, establishes that women were not limited to the home and were not seen, as in the Victorian cult of true womanhood, as passive, fragile, or "purer" than men. Women were expected, indeed required, to participate in the economic marketplace. Moreover, in Europe, many women were exposed to the socialist message of The Bund. This political awareness, along with the established assertiveness of women in the marketplace, concludes Frager, encouraged Jewish women's militant role in the Canadian labour movement.

Eastern European culture, like Ukrainian culture, was rewoven in the context of Canadian working-class experiences. For Jewish women, concludes Frager, the separation between home and workplace became more acute in Canada, making it difficult for women with children to do wage work. This important change, combined with persisting notions of women's subordination to male authority within the family, made it difficult for Jewish

women workers, however militant, to challenge the male leadership of the Communist labour movement. Many Jewish women,
like their English comrades, were organized into political groups
closely identified with women's domestic role. In Toronto, Frager
shows, the Yiddishe Arbeiter Froyen Fareyn (or Jewish WLL)
consisted largely of housewives who undertook efforts to defend
their families' standard of living, as in their meat boycott, to
provide education and services for children, as with summer camps,
as well as doing important electoral and strike support work. These
women's political efforts thus emerged from their traditional female roles, though their daring militant and public actions also
widened the boundaries of women's traditional roles. Fareyn
women, Frager concludes, were certainly to be found on the picket
line, but the intent of their protest was to defend the working
class, not to fight women's oppression as women. Given their
class experience, she argues, women "defined themselves in terms
of a working class in opposition to the bosses."[68] Anti-Semitism
and feelings of Jewish solidarity reinforced their ethnic and even
their class consciousness, though not their awareness of gender
oppression. All these factors made Jewish women militant Party
supporters, but not militant feminists in the movement.

Finnish women also brought to the Communist Party established traditions of political activism. Within the pre-World War
One left, Finnish women were noted for their militancy, independence, and political assertiveness. Their outspoken behaviour
was attributed in part to traditions inherited from Finland, where
women, who were largely literate, had exercised the vote since
1906 and had participated in the social democratic upheavals prior
to the First World War.[69] Once in North America, Finnish women
gravitated toward large urban centres where they went out to work,
usually as domestics. Whatever the drawbacks and oppression of
this "serving" role, Finnish women gained internal "community
status . . . and a degree of personal freedom from traditional
family restraints" in recognition of the importance of their wages
to the family and because they were perceived to be in the forefront
of a "modernizing path" in North American society.[70] Even after
the war, argues Varpu Lindstrom-Best, many Finnish women
worked as live-out domestics, often combining marriage with
wage work.[71]

From their earliest days in Canada, Finnish women organized
themselves into autonomous discussion groups or sewing circles
within the socialist movement. A small group of Finns in B.C.

had even attempted a utopian socialist community, Sointula, which emphasized women's liberation from traditional marriage and child-rearing.[72] By 1930, thousands of Canadian Finns subscribed to, promoted, or wrote for *Toveritar*, an American paper that combined socialist-feminist discussion with such popular items as poems, children's stories, and maternal advice from "Aunt Selma." Many of these subscribers had belonged to the Finnish Women's Labor Leagues, which performed an auxiliary role but were nonetheless conscious of the need to address women's subordination, particularly within the marriage relationship. This incipient feminism, however, was often subsumed under a strong class consciousness. It would be wrong to portray Finnish Communists as ardent feminists or as political superwomen whose independence put them on the same level as male comrades. In *Vapaus*, for example, just as in the *Clarion*, women were often relegated to the domestic sphere, strongly identified with maternal and children's concerns. Significantly, argues one historian, there was a contradiction within the discourse of the traditional Finnish folktales that celebrated women's independence: Finnish women were praised for their strength of character *as long as* they did not completely challenge the patriarchal order of the family.[73] This explains why Finnish women, while active party workers, were concentrated in sewing circles rather than the Central Committee. Though more attuned to feminist questions and more vocal about women's subordination in the family than their Ukrainian sisters, Finnish women's experience of work, family, and culture usually led them to stress class and ethnicity over gender consciousness.

In fact, women of all backgrounds in the Party saw class, not gender oppression, as the primary reason for their conversion to communism. "I came from a large immigrant farm family in Saskatchewan, who lost everything in the depression," explained Communist Mickey Murray:

> For us there was no relief . . . . My first job was at fourteen, helping on another farm . . . then I left home for Saskatoon to join my older sister. For single women like me there were only two choices – domestic work or prostitution . . . . I chose the former, but employers took advantage because of the labour pool.[74]

Murray's experiences as a domestic, her sense of social "injustice," and her sister's activism in the Canadian Labor Defence League all combined to lead her into the Party.

Another woman from an immigrant, rural Saskatchewan family, Josephine Gehl, was able by sheer perseverance to work her way through university. She taught school, then in the depression worked in a store, and finally was reduced to relief. Already influenced by her father's radicalism, Gehl was galvanized by the relief experience: "The plight of the unemployed families was terrible . . . and I clearly remember the humiliation when the relief officials snooped through my cupboards to see if I really needed relief." Gehl's most vivid memories, however, were of the Regina riot. Though she joined the Party earlier, it is significant that Gehl rationalized her choice with reference to the trauma of the riot: "I witness the police attacks . . . It was then that I really began to realize to what lengths the power of the government . . . will go . . . . It was not enough to have advanced ideas. I had to act!" Like Anna Pashka, Gehl was aware of women's inequality, but her class consciousness and political training told her that "we should tackle unemployment, jobs, economic issues, first"; she did not believe that the "basic economic issues" could vary drastically for men and women. "Yes," she concluded recently, "old habits [of chauvinism] remain [in the Party], but things don't change overnight and we will move forward."[75]

Many women who joined the Party in the 1930's were also motivated by the CPC's anti-fascist message. As a young student in Montreal, Claire Culhane was instantly drawn to the YCL's analysis of the Spanish Civil War, which she then connected to her own class and ethnic experiences. The daughter of Jewish immigrants, Culhane grew up highly conscious of anti-Semitism and intent-on questioning the social inequality she saw around her. In her training as a nurse, Culhane found she could not leave her social conscience behind: "I was suspended. I'd find myself in the public ward with someone very ill and no linen left, so I went upstairs to the private ward for an armful . . . I was in trouble every week." Radicalized by the struggle for socialism in Spain, Culhane made links with her own life. "I immediately understood what [the YCL] meant by capitalism . . . I had seen it in the hospital . . . . So I was a ready candidate for the Communists . . . . I even tried to go to Spain."[76]

The Popular Front emphasis on anti-fascism also brought more women from English and middle-class backgrounds into the Party. Helen Paulin, for example, came from a Westmount background, but in her student days in the 1930's she encountered Communists in the McGill Student Christian Movement and Social Problems

Club. Her decision to join the YCL, she remembered, came from an activated social conscience and the belief that "I could be a Christian and a Communist . . . and we could work together for peace." The Party, she added in retrospect, offered young people like herself "the sense of belonging to a cause" and even a "touch of revolutionary romance."[77]

When women joined the Party they encountered an education in Marxist and Leninist ideas that confirmed, or shaped anew, an emphasis on class solidarity and fostered the discipline, loyalty, and commitment a revolutionary party demanded. Within these Marxist parameters, criticisms of comrades' chauvinistic behaviour or "male supremacy" and laments for the paucity of women in the leadership were periodically heard. But significantly, these criticisms were not deemed important enough to leave the Party over. Moreover, the laments of some top male leaders about male supremacy or the lack of leadership among women were more ritualistic than heartfelt. Furthermore, some comrades, including women, quite resolutely opposed separate organizations for women, believing that gender inequality would be erased when "women worked alongside the men." Such critics feared women's marginalization in powerless auxiliaries and quite astutely observed that attention to work among women was often tokenistic in any case: "at every convention . . . there would be an agenda . . . and the *last* two items were always women and youth."[78] For a politically talented woman, advancement and responsibility were probably more likely to come through work in trade union or other key organizing areas, not through the less prestigious women's groups.

Save for Becky Buhay and Annie Buller, few Communist women achieved national prominence in the 1930's. After Annie Buller had served her prison sentence in Saskatchewan she went to Nova Scotia to organize J.B. MacLaughlin's election campaign, then later moved to Winnipeg to become business manager for the *Mid-West Clarion*. Buhay worked with the International Relief Aid in Moscow, toured for the Mackenzie-Papineau Battalion, then worked as an organizer in B.C. and for the Canadian Labor Defence League. The directorship of the Women's Department now fell to an older comrade from Owen Sound, Alice Cooke, who inherited all the frustrations of running the Party's programs for women. Cooke was later able to look back on her trying mandate with some nostalgia, in part because of the firm support of fellow sisters-in-arms, such as Becky Buhay. When Cooke gave her first public report on work among women at a CPC plenum, she was "very nervous" given the "general exodus which . . . took place immediately this part of the agenda was reached" – a telling comment on party attitudes. Buhay, however, immediately congratulated her and offered words of encouragement. Their subsequent friendship was important to both women, for to be a female revolutionary was, in Cooke's words, a "difficult and lonely proposition." Aside from her political work, she noted of Becky Buhay, "she was a lonely person . . . I remembered her letting her hair down, as we women will do and I laughingly agreed that I was her wailing wall."[79] Despite the Party's official antipathy to feminism, some women still managed to find female support networks within its ranks. Indeed, many Party activists look back warmly on the supportive sense of "extended family" they experienced in the Party, though like all extended families, this one might also be judgemental and confining for its members.[80]

Alice Cooke also did a large share of the women's page in the *Daily Clarion*, with help from others, including Mary "Ma" Flanigan, who had been a Party member since the 1920's. Flanigan, a colourful personality, assumed notoriety for her maternal social skills: cooking and singing at conventions. Like Mother Ella Reeve Bloor of the American Communist Party, she earned a maternal nickname, an indication of what feminist historians have critically dubbed the "cult of motherhood" in the Communist Party.[81] There were, though, also other styles of female leadership, especially with younger women who worked as local and regional organizers, and in the late 1930's growing numbers of women were moving into these middle leadership positions. After organizing office workers in Toronto, for example, Beatrice Ferneyhough went to work as an organizer in Alberta; Marjorie Cooper, after quitting the CCF, became an educational functionary in B.C.; in Saskatoon, Josie Gehl's roommate, Gladys Macdonald, was co-editor of the Communist farm paper, *Factory and Furrow*; and in the Prairie provinces all three of the remarkable Gehl sisters, Elsie, Ella, and Josie, at one time or another worked for the Party. Theirs was a demanding, exhausting, and sometimes transient life, obviously difficult for women with children, so it is hardly surprising that few women reached Buller and Buhay's positions. Still, this female middle leadership supplied energy, initiative, and labour to the Party's second line of defence, which would prove essential to the Party's existence when the war came.

In Regina, recalled Elsie Beeching, "before the war, women seemed to have a certain recognized place in the movement . . . it seemed as if half of the local leadership were women."[82]

## The Artistic Left

In the 1930's an artistic milieu, composed of both Party members and "free floating" intellectual sympathizers, coalesced around the CPC.[83] These men and women focused their efforts on the Left Theatre movement or on *New Frontier* (the successor to *Masses*), a journal of art, fiction, and intellectual comment generally sympathetic to the CPC. Both projects represented vital new cultural initiatives attempting to join working-class and intellectual discontent with the depression. This was not a protest that primarily emphasized the oppression of women; in fiction and plays the theme of class conflict usually predominated. Some *New Frontier* writers, however, were sensitive to the plight of women unemployed or on relief, or contributed significant articles on the woman question. Moreover, some of the brightest talents in this radical cultural group were women, such as Jean (Jim) Watts and Dorothy Livesay, who were consciously, or unconsciously, carving out new frontiers for women.

Livesay and Watts both came from affluent backgrounds but they rejected, early on, a comfortable bourgeois life for radical politics. In the late 1920's, Livesay's free-thinking father took her and her private school friend, Jim Watts, to hear Emma Goldman speak. "I had already begun to question Christianity and Anglicanism," Livesay recalled, "and I might have joined the Quakers or Unitarians, [but] now I started on the road to dialectical materialism."[84] Livesay was nudged along the way by Jim, already an "anti-family" rebel who would soon renounce all her wealthy parents stood for. Watts, in fact, introduced Livesay to the text on women that helped to revolutionize her thinking: Engels's *Origin of the Family*. Livesay's politicization was completed by her contact with the anti-fascist left during a trip to Paris in 1932. By the time she returned to social work school in Toronto, Communist politics had become her "obsession," despite the heavy cost "in ruptured personal and family relationships."

Livesay joined the Party and participated in various campaigns: in Montreal she organized peace, youth, and cultural events, writing "mass chants and agit-prop plays to be performed in bleak labour halls''; in Toronto she helped with union organizing; and she wrote for *New Frontier*, especially about the moving experience of her tour through the depression-ridden Prairie provinces. In *Left Hand, Right Hand*, Livesay conveys the flavour of these years for herself and her youthful cohorts on the left: their profound disillusionment with bourgeois culture and the poverty of capitalism, their strong feelings of collective dedication to a righteous cause, and also their attempt to challenge the confining boundaries of women's lives. In hindsight, she is critical of her acceptance of Communists' undemocratic tactics, but her actions, she adds, must be understood in the context of the upheaval of the thirties: ''I believe I let myself be duped because no one else except the Communists seemed to be concerned about the plight of our people, nor to be aware of the threat of Hitler.''[85]

Livesay's friend, Jim Watts, also wrote for *New Frontier*, primarily about her experiences in the Spanish Civil War, but she was perhaps best known for her work in the Left Theatre movement in Toronto. An organizer, director, and actress, Watts, says theatre veteran Toby Ryan, was the driving, inspirational force behind the Toronto Workers Theatre, an outgrowth of the larger Toronto Progressive Arts Club. A tall, striking woman with short hair and intense eyes, Watts always had that ''extra humour and vitality to push us on,'' remembered Ryan. First a University of Toronto student in physiology and a participant in the anti-fascist Students League, then a full-time theatre activist, Watts's dynamic presence helped to create Toronto's left-wing cultural milieu of the thirties. Her famous Sunday gatherings, remember friends, drew together ''all the most interesting professors . . . and students and members of the Arts Club . . . there was good talk . . . and important discussions and dreams for the future.''[86] Watts, remember Ryan and Livesay, seemed determined to give away her inheritance from her capitalist grandfather to the movement: she helped fund *New Frontier*, rented the first permanent headquarters for the Workers Theatre, then lent her car to take their repertoire of plays with proletarian messages to the factory gates of southern Ontario.

In 1934 Watts went to study progressive theatre in New York, where she and her future husband, Lon Lawson, found new inspiration in the ''vibrant, bohemian'' artistic subculture of the left.[87] When she returned, Watts directed Clifford Odet's famous play, *Waiting for Lefty*, for Toronto audiences, earning sympathetic reviews even from the mainstream press. By 1936 she was gone again, this time to Spain, where she drove an ambulance for the International Brigades. She escaped near the end of the war and returned to Canada, determined to recount her experiences and raise funds to aid Spanish refugees and orphans. In 1939, her cross-country lecture tour was cut short by the second war, and though the RCMP were carefully tailing Jim, it was her husband, the editor of *New Frontier*, who was arrested in Toronto for anti-war activity.

The *New Frontier* group also included Margaret Gould, an outspoken Toronto social worker. In the 1920's Gould, then Sarah Gold, had worked as an organizer in the needle trades. After earning a university degree, she Anglicized her name and worked as a researcher for the union movement, then joined the Toronto Welfare Bureau. Already known as a radical within her profession, Gould became a regular speaker for the Toronto Progressive Women's Association. Her professional status gave her important access to the media; impressions of her 1937 tour of the U.S.S.R. were published in the *Toronto Star* and later collected in a book, *I Visit the Soviets*. Like many sympathetic visitors, Gould pointed to the improved status of Russian women, contending that the Russian experience proved that "economic freedom is the basis of all freedom." In *New Frontier* she concluded that Canadian women did not need any "special legislation" but rather a "better understanding of the economic conditions which produced women's inequality." Although her analysis seemed primarily to echo well-known Marxist "truths," she also wrote with sensitivity about the problems of working women, defended the right of married women to work and to birth control, and spoke of the need to totally "emancipate women's personality and capabilities"[88] – all indications that she was one of the CPC's more thoughtful exponents on the woman question.

### Relationships, the Family, and Birth Control

Like the *Clarion*, Gould's book on Russia lauded the U.S.S.R.'s attempts to maintain the nuclear family. Her comments may have been partly designed to counter anti-Communist propaganda, which had always warned ominously of the Soviet's destruction of the family and collectivization of women. Still, many Party members did quite honestly support the ideal of a strong family unit. Within the intellectual/artistic left there were some challenges to the traditional, patriarchal family; Livesay, for instance, recalls Communist experimentation with "free love" and their commitment to egalitarian relationships. Lon Lawson and Jean Watts, after living together, decided to marry because they eventually wanted a family. They quickly discovered that within their milieu "marriage was not the thing to do." But Communists' antipathy to marriage, Lawson argues in retrospect, was an anti-establishment gesture that had little to do with "feminism or a concern for the subordination of women."[89]

Moreover, anti-marriage attitudes did not permeate the whole Party; Livesay, in fact, contrasted the "liberal" attitudes of the intellectuals with the more conservative views of the working class: "[working-class] women . . . were unable to play an active role in politics, often because their politicized husbands still regarded them as property – 'I married her to raise my children'."[90] Though some working-class memoirs contradict this characterization, recounting men's and women's refusals either to remain in bad marriages or to legally marry at all, it is true that these couples represented a more radical minority in the Party.

Even the more "liberal" Communists must have found that living non-traditional egalitarian relationships was sometimes a trying and difficult experience; Buhay's relationship with Tom Ewen, for example, ended unhappily as Ewen left Becky for a woman less centrally involved in the Party. Annie Buller, on the other hand, had the difficult task of balancing motherhood with an intense, transient political life. The most difficult problem for women in the Communist Party, said American Peggy Dennis, was to be both a wife-mother and an activist, for "the organizational milieu of the Party [particularly the lack of child care] provided little possibility of both . . . very few women who reached leadership positions had either children, or a permanent personal relationship."[91] This, continues Dennis, demarcates the Old Left of the 1930's from the New Left of the 1960's: Communists' allegiance to a disciplined, structured organization meant that they put the collective cause before a libertarian ideal of personal fulfilment. But this, it should be added emphatically, could have the negative consequences of sustaining traditional and unequal relationships between men and women.[92]

Whatever private experimentation went on, by the late 1930's the Party publicly emphasized the preservation of the family. This reflected prevailing Soviet policies, but it was also a logical consequence of Popular Front strategies. As the Party embraced such issues as child welfare and rising prices, a new accent on organizing housewives emerged. Also, the sanctity of the family was perceived to be at the heart of working-class culture and, above all, the Party wished to make itself palatable to the working class. Women's primary role as mothers was stressed, though clearly women were not to be passive or apolitical women but strong "Ma Joads," defending the working-class family. The *Clarion* would sometimes lament the sad fate of Canadian women, who were denied the husbands and happy homes they dreamed of, then contrast the unfortunate lot of Canadian women with life in the U.S.S.R., where economic security and maternity benefits let women live "a real family life." Capitalism, the argument continued, reduced marriage to an "economic necessity"[93] for women, put the family under stress, and "strained women's mothering abilities."[94] Capitalism is destroying the family, Communism will restore it, was the repeated message, which unfortunately failed to analyse the patriarchal nature of family life that in itself contributed to women's subordination and family discontent.

The view of the family in the Communist Party in the U.S., argues one very critical feminist historian, was barely distinguishable from mainstream women's magazines, for the Party's *Woman Today* and many Popular Front novels "avoided any alienation of the American masses by accommodating themselves to accepted social norms like marriage, heterosexuality and monogamy." Women were usually portrayed as working-class housewives, not as political activists, and if friction occurred within a Communist household, women were simply advised to accommodate themselves to their husbands' politics. Finally, the sterility of middle-class marriage was contrasted to the healthier, robust, and highly romanticized working-class family, although conveniently, in Communist pairings, men "could feel restless with monogamy and pursue affairs, while women could not."[95]

Was the Communist Party, then, simply paying strict obeisance to the patriarchal status quo? The answer, certainly, is more complex. The Party did think and work largely within the parameters of some of the predominant social norms, in this case, the nuclear family. But more than simple political opportunism was involved. Many Communists identified with a working-class culture in which the family appeared to offer comforting personal relationships and an escape from the daily grind of wage work – or, for Communist radicals, a comforting retreat from state and social harassment. Also, the motherhood the Party idealized did signify strength, resourcefulness, and political awareness, not passivity, dependence, and private leisure. In their own accounts of the past, Communists present their relationships as untraditional, pointing to their attempts to establish marriages of "partnership and shared interest" with "some autonomy for women."[96] And when Communists described the ideal socialist future – often projected onto the "ideal" Soviet Union – they again portrayed egalitarian relationships. Margaret Gould claimed that in the Russian family "children receive fathering as well as mothering" and Russian women were "liberated from many of the inhibitions which warp the personalities of women in most countries . . . they are not dependent on men, they stand on their own feet and fight with their comrades for the welfare of all."[97] However illusory her picture of the U.S.S.R., her vision did offer a glimpse of an alternative role for women within the family.

With hindsight, of course, it is easier to see that the CPC's presentation of the family became a more conservative rather than a liberating force for women. Heterosexual,[98] monogamous, and "stable" relationships, along with the nuclear family, were considered the most politically and publicly "respectable" and therefore the acceptable norm. Despite some personal questioning of traditional marriages, the Party's public appeals, not its private visions, came to dominate its discourse on the family, and this discourse accepted prevailing familial values that upheld men's primary power and importance and emphasized women's primary loyalty to one occupation – motherhood. The Party's acceptance of this familial ideology and its economistic analysis of family life were shaped by its antipathy to feminism, its particular Marxist-Leninist ideology, lingering patriarchal prejudices, and its own political pragmatism. Amidst the pressures of constant meetings and intense revolutionary organizing, and in concurrence with class solidarity and Popular Front attempts to integrate into the working class, it was simply easier to wait until after the revolution to transfer personal lives. As James Weinstein points out in his lament for the CPUSA, a "big chill" effect often occurred. Because the struggle against "male supremacy" conflicted with the message to live like "ordinary workers" as well as with the "Victorian moral standards" of many rank-and-file members, "The struggle . . . was taken seriously mostly in the student division of the Party, and . . . as Party members aged, married and went to work their lives became more and more like everyone else's."[99]

Although Canadian Communists reproduced the U.S.S.R.'s emphasis on the family, some Party members were uncomfortable with the Soviet's new policies restricting access to birth control and abortion. In 1936, the *Clarion* received "many letters" objecting to the new Soviet laws, arguing that birth control information was being denied in the Soviet Union and that the state's pronatalist policy was designed to create a "bigger army."[100] Soviet policies were defended in a translated article by Lenin's widow, Krupskaya, indicating that prestigious names were needed to explain an unpopular decision. Krupskaya and other writers claimed that the earlier, liberal laws were made at a time of economic crisis, and popular opinion no longer supported them. Yet, in a frank slip, she admitted the new policies were the state's "encouragement to motherhood."[101] A few months later a Canadian comrade, Sonia Airoff, tried to correct the "many Canadians" who saw the new laws as a "major tragedy." Airoff did her best to argue that the new laws gave women more "freedom," but her logic was convoluted, and her argument was reduced to such homilies as "only one in a million women wouldn't want children."[102]

Did such arguments convince Party members? Some women remained uneasy. Margaret Gould, for instance, avoided voicing direct approval of the new laws and she pointed out that Russian women were themselves divided over the issue. Some members, though, adopted the Soviet explanation uncritically, apparently accepting the militaristic rationale that the U.S.S.R. needed to produce "more babies" for its own army.[103] To many Canadian Communists, too, abortion was still perceived to be a personal, not a political, concern – even if women themselves had endured risky, illegal abortions. Since the decline of the WLLs, birth control, but especially abortion, had been downplayed. Moreover, lobbying for mothers' clinics was seen as quite radical enough; abortion was beyond the pale of accepted political activity.

Despite the new Soviet laws, Canadian Communists remained proponents of birth control in their own country. Indeed, the International Women's Secretariat advised support for this issue, arguing that in capitalist countries conditions still necessitated access to birth control. In Canada, Communist involvement in birth control campaigns increased as the Party encouraged flexibility in local tactics and women's interest in social welfare issues. In 1936-37, the *Clarion* carried a series of articles on the history of the birth control movement and reports of speeches of birth control advocates touring the country. The CPC also supported the Nurse Palmer case, the rallying point for many birth-

controllers in the 1930's. In Toronto, the Party held public meetings featuring speakers such as Margaret Gould, who maintained
that birth control should be available to all classes: "it is not to
solve the economic problem but to give individual women a safe-
guard to their health, and the ability to decide whether or not to
have children."[104] Gould rejected a neo-Malthusian rationale for
birth control, which was becoming very popular in the depression,
and instead stressed the preservation of women's health, the right
of the working class to have information on family planning, and
women's right to decide when to bear children. Her arguments
closely paralleled those of the earlier Women's Labor Leagues,
and in Vancouver the WLL, still alive, initiated a new petition for
birth control in 1936, demanding that the local government provide free birth control information to relieve the "thousands of
suffering women" who required it.[105] By 1939, however, the
discussion of birth control had receded, replaced by an interest
in consumer issues and the anti-fascist movement. Party women
put their energies elsewhere, content to let the birth control issue
fall back into the realm of the personal and private.

### Conclusion

During the Popular Front, Communists' work among women was
moulded primarily by the Party's overall goals of creating a broadly
based, inter-class alliance for socialism and against fascism. Because of the Communist Party's aspiration to mass influence,
women's issues took on more importance and Party women were
offered new opportunities to participate in socialist-feminist causes;
and in the latter case, they were encouraged in their efforts by
the existence of some like-minded allies in the left wing of the
CCF. In the Marx-Engels tradition, the Party still saw women in
the workplace as essential to its cause. In its labour work, Communists could point to achievements in the organization of women
into unions for textile, garment, rubber, and electrical workers,
though the Party's CIO organizing, always more keenly attuned
to the needs of male workers and to the ideal of the family wage,
was never able to draw in the female recruits desired.

At the same time Party efforts were broadened beyond the
workplace. Released from the strict emphasis on organizing "revolutionary" activities for women at the point of production, the
Party now reached out to women in the home, asking them to
mobilize around issues of immediate concern to their community,

whether child welfare, health, consumer, or relief problems. Finally, using maternalist, socialist, and sometimes even feminist arguments, the Party urged all women to remain vigilant on the most pressing international issue of the day, the fight to prevent fascism from initiating a second world war.

For Communist women, then, the Popular Front held out the possibility of constructing alliances with other socialists, addressing new varieties of women's issues, and developing innovative alternatives to bourgeois culture. As the Party allowed more organizational flexibility and community organizing, its female ranks grew. Though still a bare quarter of the official membership, women were finding their way into some positions of local leadership. The Party's growing influence among women, of course, was also the product of persisting evidence of depression conditions. Women were radicalized by their exposure to economic hardship and state repression, by their re-education in Marxist ideas, and through the rich political-cultural life associated with the left's ethnic organizations. Many of these female recruits were aware of women's subordination and envisioned a socialism encompassing gender equality, but their consciousness was primarily shaped by class and ethnic loyalties. They were first drawn to the CPC, not because of a sense of gender oppression, but because in this economic crisis and time of international threat, the Party appeared firm in its defiance of fascism and militant in its opposition to unemployment.

In order to recruit women to the Popular Front the Party sometimes used appeals directed to women's maternal and domestic concern for family survival. This association of women's political consciousness with their roles as homemakers was part of a continuing tradition in the CPC; but, encouraged by the Popular Front intent to integrate into the working-class and middle-class mainstream, the Party used motherhood as a leitmotif more purposefully than before. Indeed, in the late 1930's, the only women who could match CCFers in militant mothering were female comrades from the Communist Party. At the time, Communist women quite justly distinguished their view of motherhood from a mentality that confined women to the private sphere, ignored class issues, and avoided militant action. To Communist women, militant mothering meant a politics shaped by one's feminine preoccupation with the family, but it also meant direct involvement in the class struggle and the transformation of capitalist society.

The language of maternalism and the Popular Front emphasis

on adopting popular forms of culture, however, also presented clear dangers. Excessive accommodation to the dominant social norms, especially the patriarchal family, meant that Communists could imitate the status quo rather than fashion a truly radical alternative for women. Although few activists actually devoted their time to Boy Scouts and bingo, some Communist women did abandon their own organizations for non-partisan women's groups that offered little hope of socialist content. And overall, there were the continuing ideological and organizational constraints of a Party that always saw the woman question as subservient to more pressing international and national concerns. As a consequence, the work among women was moulded to fit Comintern objectives, there were no new theoretical initiatives made on the woman question, and the old political sexual division of labour remained largely intact. The Popular Front, then, held out the possibility of scoring exciting gains for Communist women, but there was also the danger that the woman question would disappear beneath a sentimental meld of motherhood and apple pie. During the next decade, war conditions would provide an excellent opportunity for the Party to either forge ahead on women's issues or fall irrevocably into irrelevance.

# 6

# From Working for War to Prices and Peace: Communist Women During the 1940's

The Communist Party entered the 1940's as an illegal organization, but within two years it was openly tolerated by the government that had declared it illegal. By the end of the decade, it was technically legal again but still subject to anti-Communist harassment by the state. The tumultuous oscillations in the Canadian Party's existence were the product of its loyalty to the U.S.S.R., the policies of the Canadian state, and the responses of the CPC to social and economic conditions in Canada.

The woman question was carried along in these twists and turns in Party fortunes: from 1940 to 1941 women played an important part in the fight against internment, then after 1941 they were urged by the Party to take jobs in war industries. Encouraged by this influx of women into social production, the Communist Party renewed its call for women's unionization, equal pay, and day care; it even maintained that women should have jobs of their choice in the post-war economy. But by the late 1940's the Party was stressing two very different campaigns directed at women: prices and peace. The Party returned to some tried-and-true strategies: maternalism was invoked as a rationale for peace and an "On to Ottawa Trek" was used to protest inflation and rising prices. Their effectiveness was limited, however, partly because anti-Communist feelings hindered the Party's work, but also because these methods had become time-worn and the Communist Party less vital than it had been at the dawn of war. As the Party entered the 1950's, the most difficult decade of its existence, there were signs that its historic claim as defender of women's equality would be challenged and soon found wanting.

## Internment

In August of 1939 Canadian Communists were shocked by the announcement of the U.S.S.R.'s non-aggression pact with Hitler. Horrified, some resigned from the Party, though more remained, eventually rationalizing that the pact "bought time . . . for the U.S.S.R. to prepare its defences [against Germany]."[1] Further confusion reigned when Canada declared war. Initially, the Party accepted the war, but, rebuked by the Comintern, it adopted a new position of "neutrality between two belligerent blocs," which, as Norman Penner argues, really amounted to opposing the war as an imperialist venture.[2] The Party's strong anti-war stance then gave the government an excuse to restrict the whole Communist movement. As RCMP Commissioner S.T. Wood summed it up in 1941, "it is not the Nazi nor the Fascist, but the radical who constitutes our most troublesome problem."[3]

The authorities moved quickly to ban Communist publications and jail some of its leaders. Along with the CPC, its siblings, the Young Communist League, the Canadian Labor Defence League, the Finnish Organization of Canada, and the Ukrainian Labour Temple, were all proscribed and sometimes their property seized. The Defence of Canada Regulations passed by Parliament allowed detention without trial, trial in closed courts, and stiff sentences for anti-war activity. Unable to work openly, the Party reactivated an underground network and illegally published the *Clarion* until a new legal paper, *The Canadian Tribune*, was established by progressives such as Margaret Fairley, previously not identified with the CPC. Pamphlets were distributed clandestinely, in the dark of night, and meetings were held in secret. In Regina, provincial leader Florence Theodore met with fellow Communists for a small "bridge party," which was raided by the police. Unfortunately for Theodore, her host, "a rather lazy comrade," had hidden his undelivered leaflets in the cold-air register, providing enough evidence to jail Theodore for six months.[4] Some comrades were luckier. Josie Gehl remembers her sister Elsie "only narrowly escaped capture," while Becky Buhay managed to "get to Montreal, don a babushka, and get lost in the crowd." Later, she moved to Toronto, but it was a difficult time:

> People were scattered and uprooted, and . . . it was tough financially. For a time, all Becky could do was to stay quietly in her room, her needlework was a source of revenue, but a few comrades who were working also contributed to her upkeep.[5]

Buhay's friend, Annie Buller, was not so fortunate. Arrested on charges relating to an article in the *Mid-West Clarion*, Buller was jailed at Portage La Prairie. She had difficulty winning her release, even after the Party had reversed its position on the war, when she could write to Prime Minister Mackenzie King pleading her "dedication to the common people . . . her opposition to fascism . . . and loyalty to the war effort."[6]

While the government concentrated its sights on first-line Party leadership, second-rank women were not overlooked. Indeed, it appears the government's suppression of the Party was sometimes "haphazard," with some national leaders, like Becky Buhay, able to avoid arrest and eventually become publicly active.[7] On the Prairies, though, many local Party activists, including Ella Gehl, Ida Corley, and Margaret Mills, all spent time in Portage La Prairie, and Gladys Macdonald, a co-editor of the Saskatchewan *Factory and Furrow*, was jailed in Battleford for one year after she was caught secretly mimeoing the paper in the basement of a friend. On her release, she was rearrested and, unrepentant, then interned in Kingston's maximum security prison.

Although not a nationally prominent leader, Macdonald was the kind of local organizer essential to the Party: in the late 1930's she was organizational secretary of the provincial CPC, speaking on public platforms, organizing new units, and recruiting new members. Like Buller, Macdonald chafed under her continued imprisonment after Russia had entered the war. By 1942, a campaign for both Buller's and Macdonald's release was under way. Well-known progressives such as Violet MacNaughton were sent postcards asking for support for these "good, honest progressive" women. Macdonald's postcard biography sounded more like that of Grace Kelly than that of a seasoned revolutionary:

> Right this minute there is a very sweet and charming young girl with a shy and retiring disposition who is sitting behind barred windows. . . . It was the depression which taught Gladys certain lessons. . . . She became interested in the troubles of other people. . . . Now . . . the position of Gladys Macdonald . . . is an insult to every progressive woman in Canada.[8]

While a few Party women were jailed, some Communist women played a very different role during this illegal period: they kept up grassroots political work and contributed to the internees' support and release campaigns. Shortly after an order-in-council made the Party illegal in June, 1940, women were confronted with their husbands' arrests and internment. Mary Prokop remembered well the anxiety, fear, and frustration that followed the police raids. The RCMP broke into the Prokops' Winnipeg apartment in the early morning and within fifteen minutes had searched the premises, taken her husband away, giving no charge, questioned Mary, and confiscated their reading material. For a few days the arrests were surrounded by a wall of silence; slowly, women began to contact one another and collectively deal with the questions about their husbands' whereabouts, financial problems, and family crises. Over the next year, the Winnipeg women met regularly once a month, "sharing letters from their husbands, discussing problems and offering each other moral support."[9] Their domestic problems were exacerbated by continuing police surveillance and government harassment. The government, recalled Prokop, even sent a man "to assess our property . . . the riches we were supposed to have piled up from wages in the hungry thirties. . . . Rose Penner's [response was] to take a broom to the man from the Trust Company."[10]

The immediate problem for most women was how to feed their families. Some picked up old skills and went back to work; others were forced to go on relief. The latter option, remembered Anne Lenihan, wife of a Communist Calgary alderman, was a financial nightmare, but "at least I wasn't discriminated against because Pat was liked . . . and people didn't think he should have been interned . . . even some of his opponents."[11]

Very soon, wives, families, and other CPC members also began to organize a public campaign to speed the release of internees and protect organizational properties seized by the government. A constant stream of letters to Ottawa demanded the internees' freedom, or at least the recognition that Communists were political prisoners who should be separated from fascists. As the remaining CPC leadership in hiding re-established communication lines with the Party, internees' wives were given advice on the release campaigns. Some became active in local politics: in 1940, civic voters in Winnipeg gave very significant support to Rose Penner and Joe Forkin's campaigns endorsing "full democratic rights" for internees, and shortly afterwards elected a well-known Communist, William Kardash, to the provincial legislature.[12] In 1940 a national organization, the National Council for Democratic Rights (NCDR), was created out of the shell of the Canadian Labor Defence League, with A.E. Smith and Becky Buhay at the helm, and it spearheaded the drive for internees' release.

In March of 1941 internees' relatives from Winnipeg, Toronto, Halifax, Thunder Bay, Welland, and Windsor converged on Ottawa to pressure the government to "cease internment without trial . . . stop censorship, allow family visits and provide for family maintenance." The Minister of Justice responded "coolly" to the delegation, but the tide of public opinion had begun to shift.[13] Communists were finding more support from the labour movement, civil libertarians, and even liberal papers like the *Toronto Star*. By the time the NCDR took its case to Ottawa again in 1942, it could add the internees' devoted protestations of support for the war, as Hitler's invasion of the U.S.S.R. in late 1941 completely altered the CPC's position. The war was now presented as a just struggle against fascism, and Communists began to support the war effort so enthusiastically that, ironically, they now tacitly accepted discriminatory policies perpetrated against another Canadian group – the Japanese.[14]

By the spring of 1942 the internees were gradually being freed. Their release came largely because of events in Europe, but the impact on the NCDR should also be noted, particularly women's role in the release campaign. A cursory glance at the NCDR leadership – Kate Magnussen, Jennie Freed, Rose Penner, and others – indicates that many were Party wives, who, one could argue, were simply campaigning out of wifely duty. Yet, these women were often Party supporters and activists in their own right. Although largely by-passed in the arrests, it was these women who had to step into the breach, in a time of censorship, surveillance, and economic adversity, and become the decapitated movement. Communist women were thus offered a temporary opportunity to alter their traditional political roles; unfortunately, the alteration was not permanent.

### The Communist Party and Rosie the Riveter

Reassured by the Communists' new commitment to war, the government released the internees but cautiously maintained the Party's illegal status. The CPC then set up a new electoral party, "with a communist point of view" but supposedly separate from the Comintern. Not coincidentally, Stalin had already disbanded the Comintern in order to aid his wartime partnership with the Allies. The Party's new name – Labor Progressive (LPP) – symbolized separation from Moscow and, the Party hoped, strong ties with the labour movement. Structured publicly as a socialist "educational" organization, the Party had large "club meetings weekly and forums where public figures, including reform liberals, gave lectures."[15]

At the LPP's first convention an unusually high percentage of the 600 delegates (25 per cent) were women, reflecting men's absence in the forces and the important role women had played in the NCDR. Convention resolutions on the woman question were based on two important premises: first, that total war must be pursued, and second, that a "democratic Reconstruction" including "equal pay, childcare, technological training and prenatal and maternity care"[16] for women must follow the war. Women were urged to give unqualified support to the war effort; some Party members may have responded, as Jim Watts Lawson did, by joining the Canadian Women's Army Corps.

More crucial to Communist Party strategies was women's entry into social production: this avenue was promoted in part to spur the industrial war effort, but also because wage labour had long been seen as a key to women's class consciousness. The Party called for an increased proportion of female labour in all war industries, citing many examples of Soviet Rosie the Riveters who had proved their capabilities at hard industrial labour. Women workers, the Party emphasized further, needed special organizing methods, specific promises of equal pay and day nurseries, and a firm guarantee of post-war employment. Some of these ideas were supported by the larger labour movement: at the 1942 and 1944 Canadian Congress of Labour conventions resolutions on equal pay were widely supported, and the 1944 presidential address decreed that post-war work for women was a "crucial" issue for trade unionists.[17]

Communist propaganda may have helped to raise labour's consciousness about women's unequal status in the work force, but how well did the Party live up to its own pledges to organize women and fight for equal pay? Communists did put equal pay on their union agenda during the war and occasionally won their case;[18] but, on the whole, the issue of wage differentials between men and women was left unresolved. When the United Electrical Radio and Machine Workers of America (UE), a left-wing union, organized the Small Arms plant at Long Branch, for example, the union vocally protested women's lower starting rates, arguing these denied women the ability to support themselves decently.[19] When an agreement was finally signed, however, significant wage differentials remained. Obtaining equal pay, argued former UE president Clarence Jackson, was extremely difficult, not only because the companies fiercely resisted it but because the War Labour Board, in setting wage levels, was also unsympathetic. In compromise, therefore, the union might try for an across-the-board increase, which at least narrowed the gap between female and male wages – though these settlements, too, were resisted by employers.[20]

While company and government antipathy to equal pay was certainly difficult to overcome, union strategies must also be scrutinized. To rectify wage discrimination would have meant a labour offensive that unions sympathetic to the Party were simply not willing to pursue because of their total support for the war after 1941. Thus, their tendency was to contain strike action and to look for compromises reached through labour-management committees. The moment of industrial strength, during the war, was the most opportune time to push for equal pay, and that moment was sacrificed for larger Party objectives.

After the war, the Party kept equal pay on its resolution books, but the social and economic climate made it difficult to challenge pay differentials effectively. Many companies, for one thing, were quite determined to return to the previous sexual division of labour favouring male workers within their factories,[21] and while left-wing trade unionists could, and did, take on individual grievances of women doing "men's work" for less pay, the larger and more difficult question of challenging factory-wide wage differentials was often put on a back burner. For many unions in Canada, including those on the left, the needs of male veterans took priority, and the ideal of a family wage reasserted its precedence over the needs of Rosie the Riveter.[22] In 1948, when Becky Buhay presented the party's new statement on organizing women, she criticized continuing indifference to equal pay and prejudice against women in the labour movement, quite possibly a reference to some of the Party's own unionists who were dragging their feet on these issues.[23]

The Party's most concrete legacy for women workers after the war was probably the long-term consequences of its continued CIO organizing. During the war years, the union movement grew by leaps and bounds: the CCL unions tripled during the 1940's in part because of the efforts of CCF and Communist militants. Women workers in rubber, auto, aerospace, textile, and electrical industries were the beneficiaries of these successful union drives, and contemporary observers, as well as historians, believed women's

new union experiences increased their self-confidence and culti-
vated sympathy for the labour movement. By the late 1940's,
only a few unions, such as the UE, remained open and sympathetic
to the Party and also had a sizable female membership. During
the post-war period, the UE was vocal about the specific problems
of working women, including lower pay and discriminatory unemployment benefits, and it hosted conferences for its women
workers on issues such as union participation and health and
safety. Expelled from the CCL during the Cold War, however, the
UE remained somewhat isolated in the trade union movement.

After the war, some Communist women also valiantly tried to
stay active in unions with no Communist sympathies, a difficult
task in the hostile atmosphere of the Cold War. In Vancouver,
for instance, Barbara Stewart remained stubbornly committed to
the Hotel and Restaurant Employees Union, despite attempts to
remove her simply because of her political affiliation. There were
also sporadic efforts to appeal to women in the growing service
sector. Again in B.C., Jean Pritchett and other comrades attempted to organize clerical workers in a trust company, though
their efforts foundered on the shoals of company hostility and
supposedly because of the "middle-class" consciousness of white-
collar women.[24] But Communists had never been as committed
to the white-collar sector as they had to the industrial one. The
Office and Professional Workers Union in B.C., said former Communist Claire Culhane, was a "feeble affair" that never got off
the ground "because even progressive [left-wing] unions didn't
care."[25]

The Party's Women's Commission was well aware that women
workers would face an unsympathetic social climate in the post-
war period. Time and again, in 1945 and 1946, *The Tribune* and
other Party journals warned that "reactionary elements . . . will
try to dismiss women . . . and many will find this desirable . . . .
Reforms have been won – training programs and labour policy –
and these must be retained."[26]

Despite its own predictions, the Party was unable to make
women's right to a job a first priority in its post-war platform.
Given the Communist Party's historic sympathy for the ideal of
a family wage and its past inability to challenge the sexual division
of labour within industries, this is not entirely surprising. And it
is important to concede that the late 1940's did not provide a
hospitable climate for Party trade union work. Post-war prosperity

offered some workers the hope of achieving the "ideal" family wage, and popular culture and government propaganda extolled women's roles as wives and mothers and predicted family problems and juvenile delinquency if married women continued to work. Even more importantly, state and employer offensives and CCF raiding and attacks on Communist unions drained precious time and energy, some of which might have been channelled into the organization of women workers. As the CPC became involved in a life-and-death Cold War struggle with social democrats, new initiatives were difficult; defence was the order of the day.

During the war, the CPC had also pressed for an extension of child-care facilities for working mothers. In Vancouver, the Women's Labor League and the Communist-led Housewives League took the matter into their own hands, organizing a day nursery. Only Ontario and Quebec had received federal funds for new nurseries and as the war neared its end in 1945, the Ontario LPP passed convention resolutions calling for more provincial subsidies to sustain the centres and advocating university training and better pay for early childhood education instructors. When the federal government announced its withdrawal from cost-sharing programs, Communist women joined other Toronto groups in efforts to protect local day nurseries and day-care centres and to press for further government commitments to child care. Communist women were highly visible in the Day Nurseries and Day Care Parents Association, formed in 1946 to lobby for improved child care, while such LPP city councillors as Stewart Smith and school board trustees Edna Ryerson and Hazel Wigdor added their high-profile support to the campaign. Lobbying and demonstrations involving hundreds of parents at Queen's Park helped to save a number of day-care centres, but activists had to face the long-term problem that both municipal and provincial governments were simply uninterested in acknowledging, let alone meeting, the need for day care.[27]

In the immediate post-war period, Susan Prentice argues, Communist women were able to work with other women and social service groups demanding child-care facilities; on the Board of Education, and in deputations to City Hall, CCF and LPP women might even speak unanimously on this crucial issue. Prentice also shows that, like some of their fellow proponents of day care, Communists often utilized conservative arguments of moral regulation to promote their cause, claiming, for example, that day care prevented juvenile delinquency and inculcated good citizenship values in children – though many Communists also implicitly saw child care as an essential service for working-class women.[28]

As the state became more intent on cutting back day-care services in the late forties and early fifties, however, Communist women were increasingly marginalized because of anti-communism, and the campaign for day care was deemed by conservatives to be a ''Red'' plot to produce socialized children. The Communist Party, Prentice also argues, was caught as well in the contradiction of its earlier, conservative rationale for day care, and importantly, after 1949 members were being increasingly urged to turn their sights away from local organizing to national, strategic, and peace concerns. Once again, the important, instrumental work done by Communist women was put second to larger Party objectives.[29] In the wake of all these problems, the day-care movement collapsed in one city where it had become an explosive post-war issue.

### Party Women and the Woman Question

During the war years the Party did garner an important political triumph: the election of a woman, Dorise Nielsen, to Parliament. The product of a Conservative, educated, British family, Nielsen emigrated to Canada in the 1920's and took up a teaching post in northern Saskatchewan. The experience of moving to the backwoods threw her into a profound state of culture shock: ''I was a seedling,'' she later remembered, ''that didn't transplant easily into the rough country and people around me.''[30] Her experience of northern hardship was to deepen over the next years. She married a local farmer and amidst repeated crop failures she had four children, the first of whom died from inadequate medical attention.

Encouraged by her husband's contacts with the Wheat Pool and the CCF, Nielsen became involved in politics, and by 1937 she was on both her Meadow Lake provincial constituency executive and the CCF provincial council. Within a year, though, she was embroiled in a heated inner-party debate over United Front tactics. The Meadow Lake executive felt that the depression necessitated unity with other left-wing parties; the provincial executive felt the opposite and disbanded Meadow Lake's rebel executive. The controversy continued to simmer even after Nielsen won the federal nomination as a Unity candidate in the North

Battleford by-election of 1940. The Saskatchewan CCF remained badly split over Nielsen's candidacy, but she won without its official endorsement, drawing on unofficial CCF support and her own considerable political talents, and by appealing successfully to an impoverished and desperate electorate that had had very little positive representation from their incumbent, absentee Liberal MP. A victorious Nielsen left for Ottawa still sounding like a social democrat, but the truth was that she had recently become a Communist Party member.[31]

Nielsen quickly proved herself a hard-working representative for her rural constituents. In the House of Commons she also tried to present a woman's point of view on the war, women's work, and the welfare of children; and in doing so she introduced important discussion on equal pay, the protection of motherhood, and infant care. In her own prognosis for post-war reconstruction, *New Worlds for Women*, published in 1944, Nielsen argued for women's right to an education and a job, though above all she stressed women's primary desire for a secure home and a healthy, happy family.

Although motherhood was a central theme in her speeches, Nielsen's own family life created a double burden that made her political career emotionally exhausting. Many friends had seen Nielsen's public pursuits as an outlet for the intellectual energy and creativity that had little means of expression in a dreary cabin in northern Saskatchewan. Nielsen's letters to Violet Mac-Naughton, written under a pseudonym in the 1930's, contained poignant indictments of the "prison house" society she felt constricted by. "Poverty, social restrictions and unregulated individualism," she wrote, all constructed prison walls for human beings. Even worse, women were expected to conform to a stultifying Victorian conception of "the nice little woman." Nielsen wanted badly to emancipate herself from "this restricting corset of custom . . . to think, to be a builder of new ideas . . . to shoulder social responsibility and to face the problems of the time."[32] Her election gave her a chance to realize her ideals, but only, she soon discovered, within a society still unreceptive to female politicians.

Her most pressing problems involved child care. Nielsen was separated from her husband, who was unwilling or unable to look after the children. Dorise first took them to Ottawa, then tried leaving them in Saskatoon in CCFer Sophia Dixon's boarding house. This arrangement exploded in unpleasant charges about

*Dorise Nielsen, MP, and her children, from left, Thelma May (Sally),*
*Christine Patricia, and John Kay, on the back porch of CCFer Minerva*
*Cooper's home just before leaving for Ottawa for her first session in*
*Parliament.* (National Archives of Canada, PA 125327)

*Dorise Nielsen giving a public address, Ottawa, c. 1948.* (National
Archives of Canada, PA 125330)

the children's behaviour and, distraught, Nielsen hurried back to remove them. The next year the children boarded in Winnipeg with the Kardash family, and later they moved back to Ottawa. Years later, Nielsen still viewed this period with guilt, lamenting that she "was forced to neglect [her] children." Perhaps these pressures were one reason why Nielsen looked back on her years as an MP as an unplanned, even unpleasant experience:

> I went through years of political life for which I was not really fitted. . . . Never under ordinary circumstances would I have agreed to participate in such a life. But the 1930's were not ordinary, and I was more or less forced . . . to play the role I did.[33]

Nielsen's child-care problems were symptomatic of the stresses placed on women in leadership positions. She had two full-time jobs, both of which demanded excellence: she had to prove herself as a female (and eventually Communist) politician, but also she had to convince the public she was a sound mother. Men, faced with neither the responsibility nor the social expectation of providing the primary parenting, obviously escaped these pressures and often failed to understand the toll they took on women. Unless graced by unusual circumstances, therefore, women were less likely to participate in active Party life when they had young children, precisely the point when many men were forging their political careers.

In any case, Nielsen's defeat in the next election cut short her parliamentary career. Her Communist affiliation and an altered electoral situation (other parties, including the CCF, ran candidates) ensured her defeat. Soon afterward, she moved to Toronto to work for the Party's Educational Department. Though Nielsen often appeared in public for the LPP, she did not occupy the powerful leadership posts one might expect after her experience and prominence in Ottawa. In the 1950's, for personal and political reasons, she left Canada for Communist China, never to return as a permanent resident.

Nielsen's election defeat foreshadowed the Party's increasingly defensive stance in the post-war world. Party optimism still prevailed in 1944, with *Tribune* circulation at 20,000 and membership at an all-time high, some electoral coups in hand, and a lingering public sympathy for the Soviet Union.[34] Within three years that optimism was evaporating as international events and the Gouzenko affair fostered an intensifying anti-communism.

The contrast in Communist fortunes between 1944 and 1950 was illustrated well by the successes, then defeats, of LPP women in civic politics.

Running on a platform that included new housing, free milk for school children, and tax relief for small homeowners, Helen Anderson (later Coulson) was elected as a Hamilton alderman in 1945. Popular with working-class voters after her strong support for the 1946 Stelco strike, she made it to the Board of Control in 1946 but was suddenly defeated the next year.[35] The *Hamilton Spectator* played up Coulson's Communist connections and hinted darkly at Soviet control of the LPP. Despite the exaggerated innuendo behind much of the press's anti-Communist coverage of the LPP, Communists' uncritical ardour for the U.S.S.R. always left them vulnerable to this propaganda.

In Toronto, LPPers Elizabeth Morton, Edna Blois Ryerson, and Hazel Wigdor all ran successfully for the school board, traditionally an electoral focus for political women. These Communist women became known for their advocacy of day-care services, milk and hot lunches for school children, cost-of-living bonuses for teachers, and better care of inner-city schools. On some of these issues – such as child care and free milk – they were able to link up with campaigns promoted by other LPPers in the Day Nurseries Association and the Housewives' Consumers Association. It was not simply support for such reasonable reform causes, however, that led to Communist defeats: it was also their LPP affiliation. By late 1947, conservatives on the school board were damning free milk because it would "result in loss of initiative and entrepreneurship" and were even demanding that city teachers undergo a "political screening" for Communist tendencies.[36] Wigdor didn't run a second time due to the pressures of a young family, but her successor, also an LPPer, was defeated within a few years. Only Ryerson was able to keep her seat on the board into the fifties, a testament to strong constituency support in the face of concerted anti-Communist attacks on her integrity.[37]

In the West, too, there were fleeting municipal victories. In Winnipeg, Margaret Chunn served as a school trustee from 1947 to 1949 and, along with Joe Zuken, lobbied for motherhood issues such as free milk and for the old socialist cause, an end to military training in the schools. But in 1949 she went down to defeat, and the *Winnipeg Free Press* made it quite clear that it welcomed women in civic government – as long as they were not Communists.[38] Josephine Gehl, now working as an LPP organizer in Saskatoon, also secured election to her local school board and she immediately tackled the feminist issue of equal pay for women teachers. Gehl openly questioned the board's prevailing rationale that, because men did "more extracurricular work," they were paid better.[39] The female teachers then demanded a survey of after-hours work, found exactly the opposite to be true, and, encouraged by Gehl, they eventually obtained an equal pay clause in the contract.

LPP women school trustees in Burnaby also supported the rights of women teachers, including the right of married women to work,[40] while in Vancouver Communists savoured, but did not taste, a mayoralty victory when in 1947 LPPer Effie Jones lost by only 5,000 votes in a bid to defeat the incumbent, Charles Jones. An English-born school teacher, Effie had been involved in left-wing politics since she emigrated in 1919. During the thirties, she had participated in the 1938 Relief Strike Mothers' Committee and helped to initiate the Housewives' Consumers Association; by the 1940's she had also made a name for herself in tenants' rights organizations. In the 1947 election Effie characterized herself as "low fare Jones" and her opponent as "high fare Jones," as she completely opposed the B.C. Electric monopoly and its constant rate increases. Effie later recalled that "it was a tremendous fight for a woman to step into the municipal arena," but her politics, more than her gender, disadvantaged her candidacy. She later claimed that when it looked as if she might win, her opposition "rounded up the drunks . . . and told them to vote against me"; a more telling observation was her comment that "I lost the election . . . in the business district, where I had no support."[41]

Not only at the polls, but also in its published documents, the Party exhibited a more defensive stance by the late 1940's. In 1944, Dorise Nielsen's reconstruction program in *New Worlds for Women* included a demand for "equal pay, opportunity for choice of work, scholarships and training for girls." As well as stressing women's "natural" desire for a home, she recommended new social services, nurseries, housing, and even such innovative ideas as co-operative laundries and kitchens.[42] Moreover, Nielsen looked optimistically to a coalition of progressive forces to cement women's wartime gains, especially their right to work.

In 1948, however, Becky Buhay prepared a comprehensive

*Effie Jones,* LPP *mayoralty candidate in
Vancouver, 1947.* (Vancouver Public Library,
photo no. 61453)

new document, "Women's Place in the Struggle for Peace and
Socialism," which displayed a more combative attitude toward
business and government and a more pessimistic appraisal of the
forces opposing women's equality. Intended as a guide to the
Communist Party's past, present, and future programs for women,
the document recognized that post-war reaction had set in: "no
sooner had the war ended," lamented Buhay, "than a drive was
on to send women back to the kitchen." While she took some
heart from the rising employment rate of women, much of Buhay's
document deplored the ghettoization of female labour, massive
wage differentials, and, most reprehensible, "strong prejudices"
against women's right to work and equal pay coming from men
within the labour movement.[43] And although Buhay's list of demands included women's right to employment, it was significant

that she also stressed two new campaigns directed toward women in the home: prices and peace.

Significantly, too, Buhay's document was used primarily in educational work with women (accompanying it was a set of questions and "correct" replies), although at the prestigious national schools, lectures covered everything from historical materialism to imperialism, but not the woman question.[44] Indifference to work among women did not go unchallenged within the Party; indeed, it is wrong to see the Party as a unified monolith when it came to the woman question. In December of 1948, for instance, Hazel Wigdor, in a pre-convention article, called the LPP's proposed resolution on women "undiluted maple syrup" and she argued that the Party desperately needed some "tilling of brain soil" and fresh ideas. Communists, she emphasized, had to demonstrate more effectively Lenin's dictum that women's emancipation was only possible under communism. To do this, the woman question had to be taken seriously, not discarded, "bottled and labelled and put away on the shelf marked 'Women's Commission,' as a housewife does her jars of preserves." "Too often," she courageously pointed out, this question is regarded "with a bored air of tolerance, with perhaps a teasing remark of 'feminism'."[45] Wigdor's comments may have been misconstrued as feminism, but she and other Party women rejected liberal feminist ideas, with their supposed stress on "sexual antagonism"; rather, she was calling for an expanded Marxist analysis of women's inequality and serious organizational attention paid to women.

Yet, discussion on work among women at the 1949 convention revealed the deep-seated problems the Party had in coming to terms with criticisms like Wigdor's. The convention urged comrades to speak about women's issues using "terminology" and language ordinary women understood, to give women electoral work to do, and to provide "responsible" male comrades, better leadership, and special literature for the Women's Commission.[46] These tactics were hardly "fresh ideas" and even they may have been ignored by some local Party functionaries.

Claire Culhane served on the B.C. Women's Commission after the war, and she contended that:

On paper, it was yes, we need a Women's Commission to bring women along, make them more political, but there was never any discussion over *how* they were going to find the time to

study . . . the women's groups were minimal . . . I chaired
the B.C. Commission at one time which was the biggest laugh
because I didn't have a clue about politics, or women.[47]

The Party's inability to take women seriously, Culhane went on,
was directly related to the refusal of Communist men to take
politics into their personal lives and to abandon the traditional
division of labour within the patriarchal family. Here, there existed a double standard:

My husband [a Party leader] . . . was a talented speaker. He
could give a fantastic speech on women's rights while I was
home with the kids! Theoretically, there was no question of
recognizing me as an . . . individual. But in practice? And this
was fairly common.[48]

This personal double standard, combined with a lack of in-
novation and interest in the woman question, underlined the Party's continuing problem confronting gender inequality. At one
public educational meeting in the late 1940's, a panel of prominent
LPPers, all men, passed judgement on the successes and failures
of LPP work among women. Tim Buck succinctly summed up the
consensus of the meeting with his comment that "we've done
better than other parties, but we haven't done enough."[49] The
panelists pointed to the class-conscious efforts of women's trade
union auxiliaries and called for better leadership on the woman
question; these hardly constituted new insights into gender inequality. Concern was expressed that the LPP's membership was
only 19 per cent female, and yet again it was suggested that more
women be promoted into the leadership. Only a few years earlier,
however, Tim Buck, in the privacy of a national executive meeting, reminded his comrades that "we must consider all the boys
who are coming back from the war . . . and see if they can be
integrated into the leadership."[50] No mention was made of promoting the post-war woman, whom Annie Buller publicly lauded
as a woman of new independence and raised consciousness.

### The CPC and Domestic Labour

Despite the call for some fresh ideas on work among women, the
Party did not as a rule welcome challenges to prevailing orthodoxies on the woman question. In the 1940's theoretical discus-

sion on the woman question did not change markedly from the previous three decades, with Marx, Engels, and Lenin still seen as the keys to unlocking the solutions for sexual inequality. There was, however, one significant inner-Party debate on women, and particularly on Engels, that occurred during the early 1940's, sparked by the publication in 1939 of articles and later a book, *Woman Power*, by American Communist Mary Inman. Inman's aim was to explore the class basis of women's oppression, but unlike other Communist writers she delved into uncharted areas, developing a "socialist feminist perspective on the effects of childhood socialization, the process of manufacturing femininity . . . and women's relationship to marriage."[51] Following logically from the latter, Inman tried to develop a Marxist analysis of housework, hoping to find a way to achieve Lenin's call to "organize not thousands but millions of women"[52] for socialism.

Housework had always been a problematic issue for Communists. In the American Communist Party press some debate centred on whether domestic labour was inefficient private "slavery" producing no surplus value, or whether it was socially useful labour. In Canada, similar confusions were evident: in the 1930's some commentators described housework as monotonous, unpaid, isolated work, noting disparagingly that "it is a miracle in such an atmosphere that women develop any talents at all,"[53] or on the other hand, proclaimed the important contribution of women's domestic work to family survival. On both sides of the border, Communists had trouble "distinguishing between the economic value of housework and the human dignity accorded to women as housewives."[54]

Inman came to believe that Marxists, even Engels himself, had underestimated the importance of reproductive or domestic labour in sustaining capitalism. Housework, she concluded, was socially productive and essential to capital accumulation, for women created their husbands' labour power by shopping, cooking, and cleaning; moreover, women as mothers also reproduced new labourers for capitalism. Women, she wrote, definitely worked for capitalism: "the housewife is as indispensable to industry as a man working in a Firestone tire plant."[55] Contemporary Marxist-feminist theorists might take issue with aspects of this argument, but they would applaud Inman's attempt to develop a sophisticated Marxist understanding of domestic labour.[56] In her own time, however, her work was greeted with antipathy by the officialdom of the Communist Party, and in 1943 the Canadian Communist press produced a copy of the book written in rebuttal to Inman, Avram Landy's *Marxism and the Woman Question*.[57]

Landy's book was written just as the Party embraced the war effort and the author admitted that his message had immediate political implications. Since it was feared that Inman's emphasis on the importance of housework would "feed reactionary efforts to keep women out of war production," the Communist Party felt it must counter Inman's "pseudo-Marxism" and offer an encouragement to women's entry into social (war) production.[58] Still, even after the war, Landy's book was seen as a key Marxist document on the woman question, and it remained an important indicator of entrenched Communist thinking on gender inequality and domestic labour. Landy condescendingly queried Inman's grasp of Marxist theory and mocked her idea of housework as labour power. "Of course, the capitalist couldn't exploit the worker if back of him were not his wife, or doctor," he joked, "but the same is true of the sun and the air."[59] Landy's aim was to reinforce the prevailing orthodoxies: that industry tends to separate production from the domestic sphere; that women's housework was "private service"; and that the key to women's emancipation was involvement in social production. "A woman's work in the home," he maintained, "was slavery and drudgery," which, under socialism, would be abolished. Communists should not appeal to housewives, he concluded, by characterizing their work as productive, as this would encourage "pride in capitalism"; instead, they should promise to take women out of their "backward, isolated" existence and to abolish the "miseries connected with the home when the state refuses to provide cheap food, low rent and nurseries."[60]

There were a number of problems with this approach. Not only did Landy tend to caricature Inman to score his theoretical points, but his own attempts to distinguish between Communists' (and his) correct "defence of the family"[61] and Inman's erroneous "defence of housework" were often very clouded. Moreover, his strict construction of housework as private service downplayed Engels's insights on reproductive labour and could potentially be used to ignore the struggles of women in the home. Landy also made few suggestions for women's immediate relief from "household drudgery"; presumably, women were to wait until after the revolution. Finally, and perhaps most significantly, Landy's theory did not necessarily coincide with Party practice. His argument reaffirmed the need to concentrate on women in social production when, after the war, trade union work was hampered by the Cold War and the Women's Department was turning its efforts to a campaign against rising prices. The Communist Party had faced this dilemma of stressing women's wage labour while it organized women in the home before, but it seemed especially acute in the late 1940's as work among housewives became a cornerstone of the Party's work among women.

When reminiscing about this era, Party members immediately point to the Housewives' Consumers Association (HCA) and its anti-inflationary prices campaign. First constituted during the Popular Front, the HCA acted as a consumer watchdog for the Wartime Prices and Trade Board, then after the war advocated a new housing policy, urged the maintenance of price controls, and lobbied for the continuation of day nurseries. By 1947, HCAS existed in Toronto, Winnipeg, Saskatoon, Regina, Edmonton, and Vancouver, and in accordance with directives from the Women's Department to mobilize the "majority of Canadian women" with a "fight against profiteering . . . and to protect the home," they increasingly focused on one key issue: the need to roll back food prices. While this plan was consistent with Landy's admonition to get "women to hate capitalism . . . because it fails to provide cheap food . . . for their families," it stood perilously close to Inman's suggestion that housewives be organized on the basis of their important economic role in the home.

In practice, the Party did not simply promise women delivery from domestic drudgery; it used women's sense of occupational self-worth, commitment to their families, and desire to maintain their families' standard of living to politicize them on consumer issues. The prices campaign thus carried on with Popular Front strategies that had connected women's political world view with their domestic role. Though it did not question women's role in the family, HCA material did offer a radical critique of society's economic institutions. Its pamphlets analysed the excessive profits made by the food industry and outlined the decreasing buying power of workers' real incomes: both issues pointed to the injustice of capitalist social relations. Moreover, the prices campaign was a model of women's self-organization, and valuable political experience led some HCA women into other LPP work.

The HCA program, worked out in local and national meetings, urged a wide-ranging list of reforms, from improved pensions to calls for subsidized housing, but federal lobbying for continued

*Housewives' Consumer League protest, Windsor, c. 1946*, (National Archives of Canada, PA 124366)

*International Woodworkers Women's Auxiliary on union march to Victoria, c. 1946.* (University of Toronto Rare Books Room, Kenny Collection, mss. 179, Box 63)

price controls was the main focus of its efforts. In March of 1947, a western delegation led by Margaret Chunn presented a brief to the federal Minister of Finance requesting price controls. Forewarned about the presence of Communists in the HCA, the Minister met with the women very reluctantly, though some CCF MPs were more welcoming to the delegation. Unsuccessful and disappointed, the HCA listened from the public gallery as the government announced the lifting of price controls. A few months later, eastern women tried their own "On to Ottawa" protest. Replete with thousands of little badges in the shape of rolling-pins, they converged on Ottawa and staged a conference on consumer issues, followed by a parade and delegation to Parliament Hill. Their efforts, however, again earned only a "brush off"[62] by the cabinet.

Trying a different tack, the HCA suggested local buyers' strikes and some small victories were claimed: in Vancouver, for instance, protests over escalating bacon costs brought temporary price reductions. Starting in Vancouver, the Communist youth groups then took up the fight against inflation, holding spirited and well-publicized "Bring Back the Five Cent Chocolate Bar" marches and, in Winnipeg, even announcing they would boycott the mighty Coca-Cola empire when Coke prices went up.[63] Finally, in 1949, the national HCA made one last attempt to lobby Ottawa for price controls with a massive petition protest, the March of a Million Names. Over 500 men and women chartered a train to Ottawa, only to be rebuffed by the Liberal government. The HCA, however, claimed a partial triumph as the government soon after moved to halt price-fixing on flour, thus bringing the prices down. This was small consolation, though, for most of the HCA's demands for price controls were ignored, and the LPP had not succeeded in building a broadly based United Front movement of activist homemakers.

However popular the issue of price controls, the Party was still not able to recruit as many women as it had hoped, and the limited focus of the HCA posed a potential problem of demoralization if no significant victories were secured. Furthermore, the "On to Ottawa" strategy, utilized so successfully during the depression, no longer commanded the same public appeal. Perhaps the Canadian working class was, as Bryan Palmer suggests, becoming integrated into the "atomized mass culture of commercialism"[64] and was simply unmoved by this more affluent protest against rising prices. Finally, once the HCA became closely identified with the LPP, it lost the badly needed support of some trade unions and the CCF. Although some Cape Breton labour social democrats initially supported the campaign and a few Saskatchewan CCF women risked disapproval by participating in the HCA delegation in 1947, by 1949 such support had largely disappeared. CCF women who tried to straddle the social democratic and Communist camps were now forced to make a choice of one or the other. There were to be no more Rose Hendersons allowed in the CCF.

CCFer Rae Lucock faced exactly this dilemma. The daughter of United Farmers of Ontario activist J.J. Morrison, Lucock was radicalized by her early exposure to socialist ideas and by her personal experience of unemployment and relief during the depression. Active in the CCF during the 1930's, Lucock was elected to the Toronto Board of Education and to the Ontario legislature in 1943. In 1945, however, she did not even retain her provincial nomination, presumably because she supported United Front work with the LPP.[65] As Lucock became more active in the HCA, the CCF became alarmed and finally, in 1949, instructed her to either leave the HCA or be expelled from the CCF. Despite continued attempts to negotiate with the CCF, Lucock was forced to give up her membership. She subsequently joined the Canadian Congress of Women and also maintained her activities in the Bathurst Street United Church, which seemed less upset by Lucock's sympathy for the LPP than the CCF had been.

In 1947, Lucock had been involved in a women's support picket for the United Packing House Workers' strike. Trade union auxiliaries were still an important form of women's community labour activism encouraged by the Communist Party. In B.C., for example, Mona Morgan, wife of International Woodworkers president Nigel Morgan, helped organize women into union auxiliaries that formed a women's contingent as part of the Trek to Victoria during the province-wide loggers' strike in 1946. During the strike Morgan had a radio show, "Five Minutes with Mona," which talked about issues like safety in the woods, how the strike affected the family pensioner, and rising prices. "In fact," Morgan remembered, "the prices issue came up in every second broadcast. As controls came off and prices went up it was a ready-made issue."[66]

Though by no means a mass movement, the auxiliaries were able to put on local conferences and collect petitions on consumer issues, thus helping simultaneously to build the Housewives' Consumers Association. As historians of the trade union auxiliary movement had argued, these organizations were shaped by traditional gender ideology assuming women's primary familial role, and as such they represented a meaningful reflection of women's domestic culture. But only in limited circumstances did auxiliaries transform women's gender consciousness and encourage them to assert their independence.[67] Similarly, auxiliaries of unions sympathetic to the LPP were shaped by an emphasis on women's domestic role and also by the agenda of the parent union: the intent was to produce class-conscious women supporters, not independent women socialists. And given the context of the Cold War, auxiliary support was extremely important to such unions as the IWA locals, Mine-Mill, and the Canadian Seaman's Union, for anti-communism was increasingly isolating Communists from the rest of the trade union movement.

### Women's Peace Work

After the prices petition in 1949, some HCA women met to help form a new national federation, the Canadian Congress of Women (CCW). A smaller CCW group had existed as early as 1948, as an affiliate of the Women's International Democratic Federation (WIDF), a post-war international for Communist bloc women's organizations. In 1946 and 1949 Canadian delegates attended the WIDF's first conference in Europe; Dorise Nielsen, Mary Kardash, and Libbie Park, a Toronto nurse with long-standing left-wing sympathies, travelled to Moscow for the 1949 meeting, at which the reigning WIDF council made it clear that a key priority for national women's organizations should be the peace movement. As in the earliest Communist women's peace lobby, absolute pacifism was rejected; rather, Communist women focused on a critique of American atomic power and the need to defend the Soviet Union. Influenced by the Cold War and the needs of Soviet foreign policy, as well as by certain "nationalist" traditions within the CPC, Communists increasingly focused on countering American imperialism in Canada and abroad.[68] Unnerved by escalating international tensions, the formation of NATO, and the atomic bomb, Party women responded positively to calls for a vibrant peace lobby.

Communist women utilized compelling, though sometimes familiar, arguments in their peace work. Massive expenditures on arms, it was pointed out, meant the delay of social reforms that women badly wanted. Rae Lucock, now president of the CCW, reminded a 1951 CCW meeting that without peace the social ser-

vices "needed for healthy families . . . for our children,"[69] will
be given a low priority. The long-established tradition of linking
maternalism with peace activism was integrated into many appeals: in 1949, party women in Vancouver organized a Mothers'
Day "Action for Peace" forum, which intended to "pay tribute
to the working-class mothers who sacrificed their sons . . . in the
last war . . . and to put an end to the arms race."[70] The peace
appeal was also directed more broadly, to all mothers; as *Woman's
Voice*, the CCW's newsletter, quoted from the United Church
Women's Missionary Society: "everything woman creates, home,
family, civilization, is destroyed by war. . . . How can they be
mobilized for peace?"[71] In retrospect, too, Party women describe
their peace work partly in maternalist terms. As one woman recalled, women sought peace

> . . . because women have a built-in nurturing in us . . . it is
> a natural instinct to protect and nurture the young. Women have
> always been the movers and shakers in the peace move-
> ment . . . after all, they give birth to live, they nurture it – and
> when so much of your life is in that child, how could you
> possibly think of the destruction of that child?[72]

On one level, the Communist Party used maternalist arguments
for expedient political advantage. "In the fight for peace," argued
Elsie Beeching, who was in the CCW and the Peace Congress,
"you had to use every weapon you could . . . and the fact that
women were mothers could appeal to women's protectiveness.
Perhaps this is sort of a perversion of an extreme feminist approach, but the struggle for life is primary and if the maternal
appeal . . . works . . . it's legitimate."[73] But on another level,
maternalism reflected earnestly held and deeply entrenched assumptions about women's maternal morality and their desire to
nurture and protect their families. Like the American Women's
Strike for Peace activists, Communist women were products of
post-war cultural thinking about the primacy of women's mothering role. They did, however, reject mothering as a private duty,
stressing instead the connection of mothering to social conscience
and political protest. Maternalist peace crusaders, argues Amy
Swerdlo, tried to use the prevailing ideology of femininity "to
enhance women's political power and dissent from military
politics."[74]

The Canadian Party, however, did not question the military
politics of the U.S.S.R. as much as it criticized American im-

perialism; moreover, its use of maternalism left unquestioned certain patriarchal assumptions about women's nature, particularly a biological determinist equation of women with nurturing. Even as Communists found themselves increasingly isolated in Cold War North America, they were still uncritically adopting values associated with the American "feminine mystique." Furthermore, there were dangers looming on the horizon of the next decade. Maternalism might appeal in the climate of the 1950's, but it would not work for a new generation of leftists in the late sixties, the products of different social conditions who challenged not only women's role in the peace movement but the very association of women with motherhood itself.

## Conclusion

From the "phony" war of 1939 through the "real" war after 1942, Communist women played an important part in Party strategies, first as defenders of the Party in the face of state harassment and internment, and secondly, as industrial workers in the war against Hitler. In the latter case, Communists now emphasized women's unionization, equal pay, and women's right to a job in the post-war world. At a time when government and business were stressing women's temporary stay in the work force and their enduring feminine demeanour rather than equal capabilities, the Communist Party's support for women's right to work and equal pay was a radical initiative. Because of the Party's overwhelming preoccupation with the survival of the U.S.S.R., however, it was difficult to make good on the fight for equal pay, and after war's end it became even more difficult to swim against the tide and demand a job for every woman. The two campaigns that then came to take precedence for women were prices and peace. The first was directed particularly at housewives, despite the Party's recent theoretical reaffirmation that women's wage labour was the key to their involvement in the class struggle. Communists, too, it seems, were influenced by the demographic and economic nature of post-war society: a baby boom, increasing prosperity, and the ideal of achieving a single (male) income family wage.

While bread and peace took centre stage, some women were still active in the few unions that had survived Cold War purges and in Party organizing and educational work. Margaret Fairley edited the new cultural magazine *New Frontier*, and women such as Mary Kardash in Manitoba, Josie Gehl in Saskatchewan, Beatrice Ferneyhough in Alberta, and Minerva Cooper-Miller in B.C. provided organizational continuity at the local level. Yet, there were signs of atrophy even before the disaster of 1956. *New Frontier* lacked the dynamic female writers of the thirties, such as Dorothy Livesay, Jean Watts Lawson, and Margaret Gould; Dorise Nielsen and Minerva Cooper-Miller soon left the Party; and no new young women stepped into the shoes of Becky Buhay and Annie Buller. When the Congress of Canadian Women was formed in 1950, its charter of rights outlined impressive demands for the restructuring of society along egalitarian lines. But this radical platform remained more a showpiece than a call to arms for a mass movement. Despite regular self-criticism for its failure to deal with the woman question, the Party was never able to see gender equality as anything more than a secondary issue. Even those Communist women interested in work among women were still loyal to the CPC's Marxist-Leninist vision of organizing and thus might criticize, but never openly challenge, Party priorities.

Over the past three decades, the Communist Party had prided itself on its progressive platform on women. Its loyalty to the version of socialism found in the U.S.S.R. sometimes inspired, but also limited, its view of the woman question. While highly conscious of women's economic inequality, it had never come to terms with reproductive rights or with the complexities of patriarchal culture, even within its own ranks. The Party grappled with the problems of housewives and in a confused way was sympathetic to their liberation. Yet, familial relationships remained largely unquestioned and intact in the Party, just as they had in the U.S.S.R. By the mid-1950's, Communist women were engaged in some internal soul-searching about their disappointed hopes for the growth of the CCW. This debate within the CCW foreshadowed Communists' ability to come to terms with the feminists of the sixties and seventies. Still crippled by the exodus after 1956, a decimated Communist Party would be confronted by a new socialist challenge to its long claim to leadership on the woman question. A new wave of socialists and feminists would cast a critical eye on the Party's stance on women's issues and, indeed, on the very history of the Party itself.

# The CCF Confronts the Woman Question

During World War Two, CCF women, inspired by the image – and the reality – of Rosie the Riveter, urged their party to develop a truly comprehensive policy on women's rights. The ensuing discussion about the woman question, though never a party priority, did stimulate the construction of new women's committees and encouraged a debate about the two perceived reconstruction options for women: paid employment or work in the home. After the war, women's committees increasingly stressed the latter option and, in the tradition of militant mothering, concentrated on such issues as health care, education, and, especially, rising prices. Their high hopes for a politicized constituency of homemakers, however, were never fulfilled. The 1950's proved to be a decade of retrenchment and reaction, temporarily halting the expansion of socialist and feminist organization. By mid-decade, many women's committees had suffered setbacks, partly because the era of the feminine mystique, with its affluence, high birth rate, and retreat to the home, was a hostile environment for socialist-feminists, but also because the CCF, never convinced of the urgency of women's issues, had failed to defend a radical reconstruction policy on women's rights.

### After the War: Back to Woolworths?

The CCF, once the party of peace, found its popularity increasing during the war. Although a pacifist minority was disturbed by the CCF's support for the war, most CCFers rejected open rebellion in favour of quiet retreat. Feminist-pacifist Mildred Fahrni, for instance, left Vancouver and dedicated herself to work with the Japanese at the Slocan detainment camp. To the larger public, though, the party's policy of critical support for the war and a

# WOMEN

*In Peace As In War*

## PROTECT YOUR HOME

### Your Home Is In Danger

**MILK:** was 10 to 12 cents; is now half as much again.

**BUTTER:** was 44 cents; is now away up.

**MEAT:** even "cheap" cuts are dear today.

**CLOTHING:** you pay as much for children's clothing as you used to for adults; and it is of poorer quality.

**HOUSING:** is expensive and scarce. If you have children just try to find a place!

**MEDICAL CARE:** is scarce too—even if you can afford it.

### Where Will It Stop?

**HERE'S WHAT HAPPENED LAST TIME – AFTER WORLD WAR I:**

Controls Came off

Prices went up

There was a boom

Then a crash

The depression was on

It lasted ten years

Remember?

### Is There Another Way?

### DURING THE WAR

You protected your home. With other women you guarded the consumer front:

You took only your share

You kept watch on quality

You reported breaks in price ceilings

You did with less than you wanted

All this, because you knew that men, money and materials had to go to win the war.

### NOW PEACE IS HERE

Men, money and materials are free from war. But free for what? That's the big question.

### FREE TO MAKE . . .

high-priced goods for the few?  **or**  plenty of what average families need?

Fancy food products?
Costly fashions?
Luxury mansions?
Expensive treatments?  **or**  Milk and butter?
Children's wear?
Low rent homes?
Widespread health care?

## WOMEN KNOW THE RIGHT ANSWERS

We can get what we want.
But only if we guard the home front—in peace as we did in war.

### What We Can Do

Let's get this straight: To protect our homes we must work to elect a government that will put home needs first.

Only the C.C.F. can do that. It is doing it now in Saskatchewan with its health plan, security for farm homes, protection for city workers.

Only the C.C.F. can plan to provide good food for every family, enough clothing, housing, health care—at a price all can afford. Look what the Labour Government is doing in Britain today.

To get a C.C.F. government in Canada YOU MUST HELP. Come to our meetings. See how the C.C.F. works. Meet its members. Study its program. Investigate its record. Then make up your mind. Come and be one of us. Help to elect a C.C.F. government.

Good homemakers today must take political action. For politics is the key to the kitchen cupboard. Only a C.C.F. government can unlock the door to plenty for every family.

### Women It's our Job!

CCF *pamphlet, 1945.* (National Archives of Canada, MG 28, IV, 1, vol. 198) social welfare reconstruction after the war began to appeal. Despite some regional setbacks, the CCF, unhampered as the CPC was by state harassment, made electoral gains, heightening its anticipation of a post-war political breakthrough. Most provinces had expanding memberships, a larger federal treasury produced a more sophisticated operation, and the CCF was making political alliances with some leaders in the labour movement. In the late 1940's, many CCFers felt as Manitoban Margaret Mann did, that "we . . . were going somewhere and that we might even see power one day."[1]

Accompanying the rising hopes of the party was a temporary alteration in the status of Canadian women. Employment prospects brightened, wages climbed, and government propaganda assured women that they could utilize their equal capabilities and talents and "still remain women, after all."[2] This propaganda portrayed women's incursion into non-traditional work as a temporary expedient, but nonetheless, it had a significant effect on women's expectations. Non-traditional jobs, the provision of some day nurseries, and the homage paid to women's capabilities all heightened the feeling of CCF women that change was now *at least* in the realm of the possible. As one commented as early as 1941: "after letting us all see there is nothing a country cannot afford in time of war, men will never again be able to convince women that there is anything peace cannot afford."[3]

The CCF press consciously promoted the concerns of women war workers, encouraging women's participation in war industry and demanding the provision of equal pay and day-care services. While some of these appeals were couched in patriotic terms, the party was also trying to make a forceful case for badly needed labour and social reforms. Even on the Prairies, where few war industries were located, women's hopes for a better life had clearly been raised. The Alberta CCF women's columnist feared that the fortunate "honeymoon for women war workers" would end with the war and that women "would be pushed back to jobs at Woolworths,"[4] while the Saskatchewan paper pleaded for an extension of the wartime tolerance for married women workers. And in the *B.C. Federationist* a lead editorial, a spot rarely assigned to women's issues, called for a reconstruction policy of "planned employment for all men and women, including equal pay for women."[5]

Also in B.C., the three female MPPs – until their defeat in 1945 – particularly Laura Jamieson, focused their attack on continuing sexual discrimination in the workplace. In her reply to

*B.C.* CCF *campaign pamphlet, 1945.* (National Archives of Canada, MG 28, IV, I, vol. 198)

the 1942 budget speech, Jamieson decried the "exploiting society such as ours where the workers never get the full return for their labours . . . [and where women] the weaker group, naturally suffer most." Jamieson specifically criticized war industries that had not provided equal pay and recommended legislation requiring the unionization of all workers and the provision of day nurseries. Government members trotted out familiar excuses for failing to fund child care, claiming there were too few women involved and that such women should not be "neglecting their homes" anyway. Jamieson retorted that criticisms were not made of women "who go to their golf clubs all day" and concluded sardonically that "women who talk most against mothers working in industry seem to feel that it has some connection with the difficulty of getting cheap domestic labour."[6]

Not only did the party show a growing awareness of women's employment issues, but it also encouraged debate over women's role in reconstruction. A sense of optimism was the initial reaction to women's wartime roles. Writers agreed that the war could change women's consciousness, giving them "new confidence and awareness of conditions like wages, so that even those who go back to their homes will carry a broadened interest in affairs outside the home."[7] Like feminists during World War One, the CCF also prophesied that women would take up new political responsibilities. "Women must become a political force in the post-war world," wrote Margaret Williams in the *Saskatchewan Commonwealth*, "they must train themselves for public life, learn about social conditions, become advocates of change and realize that the war is a 'revolution' and bold policies must follow it."[8] Beyond such optimistic generalizations, there was some agreement that the two major choices for women after the war were continued employment or a return to the home.

Those who were concerned with the first option did not always agree on how best to integrate women into the work force. The majority view was that women should be participants in the general reconstruction plan of full employment. Grace MacInnis, for instance, supported this classic socialist emphasis on equal consideration of men and women, though she was sometimes forced to admit that women might be ignored as equal partners in reconstruction. As she observed in a 1943 radio broadcast: "most post-war blueprints ignore the status of women. . . . The post-war world will have to cope with more women wanting work outside the home . . . and for that reason, we need more part-

*CCF MLAS in B.C. From left to right, Laura Jamieson, Dorothy Steeves, Grace MacInnis.* (UBC Archives, B.C. Historical Photo 1917-34)

time work, and social services . . . . Women should be entitled to follow any calling they choose.''[9] A key problem was that women's access to non-traditional work and a direct challenge to the sexual division of labour were not part of the CCF agenda at this time. The party did not, for example, critique government retraining schemes that perpetuated women's relegation to female job ghettos. It promoted the idea of equal participation of men and women in reconstruction, yet women *already* were a disadvantaged economic interest group. Clearly, all the contradictions had not been ironed out of the party's post-war plans for women workers.

While the CCF showed new interest in women wage-earners, the dominant assumption was that, after the war, ''women will continue to find their greatest happiness, and the most important usefulness in the home sphere.''[10] The propaganda showing Rosie the Riveter as a temporary worker must have made its point well, for few voices were raised to oppose women's return to the home or to suggest that women should not have to choose between family and work.[11] One CCF woman in *Ontario New Commonwealth* did advance the radical idea that, until domestic labour was no longer equated with women, sexual equality was impos-

sible, while George Weaver warned of the conservative implications of the well-received British Beveridge Report, which took
for granted that women's primary post-war occupation would be
homemaking. "There is an age-old assumption by both sexes of
male dominance in these plans,"[12] he warned. Weaver's ideas
were insightful, but they were not mainstream ones within the
party.

Of course, now that women's war work had proved their capabilities, housewives could use their new knowledge and confidence to become the "housekeepers" of the post-war world.
"Women can contribute to politics through their roles as mothers
and socializers [of children]," wrote Margaret Williams in the
*Saskatchewan Commonwealth*, "and what kind of world do they
want? . . . one enriched by a true vision of motherhood."[13] In
Ontario a CCF radio broadcast advised women how to make a
wise consumer choice in the approaching elections:

> What *do* women want? A nice home, a job for the breadwinner,
> education for her children, security for old age and sickness,
> and prices at a reasonable level. On these things the old Parties
> have broken their promises, but the answer is not to run away
> from politics.[14]

The answer, of course, was to vote CCF.

Not far under the surface lurked the old bugaboo of housewife
apathy and conservatism. "Some women say politics is for men,"
wrote the women's columnist in a CCF paper, "but Sister, you
should be interested because this is your life being decided . . .
for example, taxes affect the home." In a telling reference to her
maternal feminist foremothers, the author urged, "don't forget
how hard women had to fight for the vote. We must not fail these
trail blazers now!"[15] Indeed, many CCF election drawings used
the suffragists' favourite symbol: the broom. Homemakers, broom
in hand, were shown sweeping away the evils of "disease, delinquency, and poverty" just as an earlier generation of women
reformers had swept away "corruption, graft, and the liquor
interests."[16]

Feminists within the CCF, however, were not satisfied with this
debate on women and reconstruction. In 1944, Harriet Forsey
wrote an article for *Canadian Forum* entitled "Will Women Win
the Peace?" in which she challenged the CCF to formulate a
socialist policy on the equality of women. Any advancement for
women, she contended, would depend on the powers that con-

trolled Canadian economic life. She feared that, with a government controlled by capitalists, women would be pushed out of work, a fact "justified with the appeals to the moral and religious sanctions of the past, articulated through women's magazines, ads, stories and articles."[17] Forsey's article expressed concern for women in the professions, reflecting some of the middle-class emphasis on women's work long present within the CCF. Nonetheless, she made a badly needed and compelling feminist argument for women's right to work and for immediate action by the party.

Forsey was not alone in her views. Across Canada, as the war neared its end, women within the party began to raise their voices, asking for a meaningful statement on women's equality. In Ontario a woman wrote to the *Commonwealth*'s women's page, angrily asking "what is the CCF doing about women and jobs . . . [for] women are losing them and taking wage cuts." Claiming she was "not a feminist on a rampage for women's rights," the author proceeded to make the feminist argument that the party must reject the philosophy of "economic scarcity" being used to exclude women from the work force and publicly proclaim that "no part of society should be confined to dishes, diapers and dusting"[18] as women were. Another correspondent added that women's political apathy might even disappear if the party showed some concern for women, including their equal right to a job. In many provinces these two issues – equal pay and a right to work – were the key demands, though on the Prairies the needs of rural women, such as improved social services and electrification, were also seen as important. In B.C., the party was asked to lay to rest its historic aversion to "distinctions on the basis of sex" and instead recognize that women were a "functional group, needing special attention, like farmers or trade unionists." Even within the movement, a feminist gently reminded her socialist brothers, "women are relegated to auxiliary work and women with families find it hard to be active. [Therefore] . . . outside the movement, even more action is needed to rectify women's inequality, including better educational opportunities and an end to discrimination in the job market."[19]

A concrete resolution was finally presented to the national convention in 1946, asking the federal party to develop a comprehensive policy on women, including:

1. Equal opportunities with men for training for all occupations

2. Equal access with men to all occupations
3. Equal pay for equal work
4. Discontinuance of the present practice of dismissing married women or refusing them jobs
5. Emancipation of the housewife . . .
6. Protection of household workers . . .
7. The setting up of a Women's Bureau . . . .[20]

After the convention, the national council, which "did not have the time to consider the subject," passed the buck to the federal research secretary, Lorne Ingle. Ingle's research produced a draft statement circulated to well-known CCF women. Their critical replies obviously came as a surprise to Ingle. "I personally feel research on women," he grumbled, "is not nearly as useful as research on some other subjects and can better be carried on in the provinces."[21] CCF women, however, had good reason to be critical. Ingle had used a British Commission on Equal Pay that was notoriously pro-employer, and he was decidedly unenthusiastic about maternity leave (a principle of the International Labour Organization since 1919), not to mention schemes like co-operative laundries. Even more damning was his adoption of traditional stereotypes: he spoke of the male breadwinner and "head of the family," and he repeated unproven prejudices about married women workers. These women, he claimed, had higher levels of absenteeism and were less efficient than men, so that no employer "should be forced to retain a married woman if she is incompetent. Married women . . . should not expect special consideration. . . . Neither public nor private enterprise can carry on business with incompetent, lazy or abnormally absent employees."[22] Party women who saw the brief were justifiably horrified. Although the brief contained some good proposals, like better vocational training for women, its weakness on employment issues, as well as its failure to explore section 5 of the resolution – housewife emancipation – ultimately disappointed many women.

Critiques of the Ingle report did not all come from the same ideological perspective. Grace MacInnis recommended federal legislation barring sex discrimination, but she argued that "only in working for *social* equity shall we get *sex* equality." Like many others in the party, she stressed a "society of full employment and opportunities for every human being," an emphasis on "*human* rights, rather than *women's* rights."[23] It was a familiar argument, but once again, it ignored women's structural subordination within the labour force. Moreover, MacInnis was ready to assign a special role to women: as mothers and homemakers, they were well fitted to carve out a "new approach to world problems that is essential if humanity is to survive."[24] MacInnis and others did not see any problem posing this maternalist argument alongside one that women should be treated equally with men.

MacInnis admitted that her perspective might not be acceptable to the "older feminist approach . . . within the party."[25] She was quite correct. Echoes of this "older feminist approach" came from a subcommittee of the Toronto CCF Women's Council, composed of a survivor of the Women's Joint Committee, Alice Loeb, as well as younger women such as Edith Fowke, Barbara Cass-Beggs, and Margot Thompson. This group stressed the economic basis for women's subordination in Canadian society and urged special measures for women workers, including equal pay legislation, vocational training without emphasis on men's or women's jobs, measures to end discrimination against married women workers, and a women's bureau in the Department of Labour. Concerned about married women workers, they also made some innovative suggestions to socialize domestic labour with co-operative laundries and restaurants.

Unfortunately, both practical and innovative suggestions for a federal policy on women went by the wayside. The resolution of 1946 was never enlarged on, partly because many women turned their energies to provincial women's committees but also because of disinterest of the national leadership in this issue. After Gladys Strum was elected to Parliament from Saskatchewan in 1944, an attempt was made to establish a National Women's Committee, which met during conventions and by mail. But without funds for research or organizers, and after 1949 without Strum, it faltered. In 1950, Nellie Peterson wrote to Ingle, trying to discover what had happened to the committee. Anne Peters, the new president of the Alberta Women's Committee, explained Peterson, had undertaken her job enthusiastically, but "the result had been less gratifying than anticipated." "Particularly disappointing," concluded Peterson pointedly, "is the effort at the National level, where there is little indication of life."[26] It was over a decade before new signs of life began to reappear.

## Female Leaders and the Movement

Although a federal policy on women's equality failed to materialize, the 1940's did see more CCF women involved in the trade union movement. In the previous decade, the CCF had often been overshadowed by Communist presence in unions, and save for a few exceptions, such as Mary McNab and Jean Laing, the CCF could claim few female trade union organizers or leaders. A decade later, the situation was altered, but not simply because of an influx of women into unions during the war. The most influential CCF trade union women, Eileen Tallman, Margot Thompson, and Margaret Lazarus, did not rise from the shop floor but came to union work through their CCF politics.

Margot Thompson, a University of Toronto graduate with pacifist leaning, joined the CCYM in the late thirties, and her CCF work led her to staff positions with the United Packing House Workers (UPHW) and later the United Steel Workers (USW). She eventually settled into publicity work, editing the USW paper, *Steel Shots*, a job never before done by a woman. It was not only Thompson's writing and organizing abilities that USW leader Morden Lazarus valued, but precisely her political loyalties, for this was a time when many CCF unionists had resolved to "clear out" Communists from the union movement. Thompson's political loyalty also meant that her work was more than a nine-to-five job. She worked with four other women in an office shared by four unions, and they all felt a sense of camaraderie and dedication to the cause:

> Everyone pitched in . . . if work piled up – whether it was a man or a woman. The esprit de corps was terrific. I could be sent out to leaflet a plant in the morning, or occasionally called at night to help. . . . We were hard-working idealists.[27]

Margaret Lazarus and Eileen Tallman also came to union work through the CCF. Lazarus had been an associate editor of *Ontario New Commonwealth*, while Tallman had served as national secretary for the CCYM. In 1940, Tallman was hired by the Steel Workers to organize bank workers. She helped direct the first Canadian strike of bank employees in Montreal, but when that strike was broken she returned to Toronto to organize – this time successfully – workers at the John Inglis Munitions plant. Subsequently, Tallman was sent to B.C. to do administrative and organizational work and, as she unashamedly states, to rout the Communists from the labour movement. She came back to To-

ronto in 1944 to head up the massive Eaton's organizing campaign. After four years of hard work, Tallman and her staff had
signed up 10,000 Eaton's workers into the Retail Wholesale and
Department Store Union, but her efforts with white-collar employees again met defeat, largely because of the organizer's per-
ennial problems: employee turnover and company intimidation.

During the Eaton drive, Tallman and the union made equal pay
an important issue. Eaton's employees were paid according to
age, sex, and marital status, and as the union pamphlets pointed
out, that meant discrimination for women. "Does a landlord charge
less rent to a woman," asked the union rhetorically, "does the
butcher charge less for a pound of beef to a female customer?"[28]
Thompson, too, was active on the equal pay question. Along with
Margaret Lazarus, she did much of the background research for
the Ontario CCF's equal pay bill.

At the same time, Thompson and Tallman would not have
identified the promotion of women or women's issues as their
primary concern. Discussing the post-war dismissals of women,
for instance, Thompson recalls that "some women did resent their
layoff from unionized plants, but there were no organized protests . . . because it wasn't just women's jobs that were lost, it
was jobs *period* which were endangered . . . and *that's* what is
important."[29] They saw their own staff positions as testament to
the growing acceptance of women within the labour movement;
or, at least, they were willing to put aside evidence to the contrary,
due to their fierce trade union loyalty.

Thompson maintained that she could "do a man's job,"[30] but
her lack of feminist sympathies perhaps involved more than personal disinclination. Like Tallman, Thompson's experience of the
depression and her daily involvement in the union movement
reinforced an emphasis on class rather than sexual inequality. At
that time, the only women's groups associated with unions were
auxiliaries, which these career unionists obviously did not identify
with. Moreover, the overwhelming male ethos and class consciousness of the labour movement could only reaffirm a lack of
sympathy for feminism. CCF trade union women were immersed
in the struggles of a (largely male) working-class movement for
safe working conditions, basic bargaining rights, and decent wages:
to them, these questions appeared sex-blind. And the union movement of the late 1940's was not always a fertile ground for the
discussion of the woman question.

Although some interest was shown during the war for questions
such as equal pay, many male trade union leaders did not question
women's relegation to unskilled jobs and were especially unsympathetic to married women workers. Even a few CCF unionists,
remembered Barbara Cass-Beggs, were lukewarm about the equal
pay issue; one leader was "less than enthusiastic because he had
the idea that if women got equal pay they would end up displacing
men who needed jobs."[31] Given these circumstances, it is not
surprising that these CCF trade union women were primarily concerned with class rather than gender issues. Their presence in the
labour movement in a small way altered the male-dominated union
leadership and offered a needed and important "feminist" concern for such issues as equal pay, but ultimately they represented
leadership appointments rather than a rank-and-file upsurge of
socialist trade union women.

Trade union women were not alone in becoming more visible
in the CCF during the 1940's. The number of women who held
leadership and organizational positions or who ran in elections
slightly increased, a reflection of men's absence in the forces,
women's increasing activism, and the positive effect of women's
altered wartime roles. Yet, women still constituted less than half
of party membership – one estimate in Ontario stood as low as
15-30 per cent – and women remained a distinct minority of the
leadership. Within the movement a sexual division of labour still
persisted, with women more active in traditional roles such as
constituency secretaries, or in publicity and educational work.
And in the latter case, some dissatisfied CCFers argued, education
was becoming a routinized activity with a lower priority for the
party.

Fund-raising remained an important part of women's political
work, and their supportive efforts were not insubstantial. A national CCF cookbook project, organized by Marian Nicholson and
other Ottawa-based women, netted a substantial $5,000 for the
federal treasury, as well as funds for local clubs. Election candidates sometimes sent urgent "SOS's" to women's auxiliaries,
asking for donations, and some constituency associations even
argued over who could control the monetary products of women's
bake sales and teas.[32] In Port Arthur, for instance, the largely
male constituency executive tried to block the auxiliary's attempt
to have a separate bank account. The women defended their financial independence and a heated debate followed: "Our meeting

almost split in two," remembered one participant, "and we the women only won by one vote . . . it was husbands against wives that night!"[33]

A very small group of women continued to work as party organizers, but they could encounter adverse reactions if they tried to assume more powerful leadership roles. Nellie Peterson, a skilled organizer who had paid her political dues, took over Bill Irvine's job as provincial organizer in Alberta in the 1940's. Yet, when she ran for provincial vice-president in 1949, she suddenly found a movement from the convention floor to establish a second vice-presidency. "They didn't say it," she remembered, "but it was the first time a woman had got that far. We stopped it when we faced it head-on, and asked 'are you doing this because a woman was elected?' . . . but we were fairly certain it was."[34]

Not only did women need personal determination and family support to be able to face down such political obstacles, but it was essential that they also have economic resources and, if they were married, some help caring for the family so they could leave home for the public sphere. When Beatrice Trew was elected to the provincial legislature in Saskatchewan, she found her new political role created a serious burden on her family. A man with a family, she said, "has a wife to run the home" while he's away, but

> a woman's place in the home is hard to fill. My teenage daughter had to look after her ill grandmother, help her dad with house-work, and attend school . . . before I could find anybody to help. . . . Finally, a woman came. . . . Without her, I might have had to resign.[35]

Surely few, if any, men would have considered resigning their seats in order to go home and take care of their families.

Gladys Strum, who sat in both the federal and provincial houses, had immense difficulties juggling family and politics, and she encountered little empathy from her CCF brothers, whom she later concluded were unable to accept her assertive feminist style.[36] When she travelled as an organizer, she worried constantly about her teenage daughter, her husband, who had tuberculosis, and the state of their farm. On one occasion, as she hurried home to tend to her ill husband, she referred to the social disapproval of her lifestyle: "I hope the voters believe that Mrs. Strum's husband would probably have contracted the illness anyway, even if she had not been out CCFing,"[37] she confided to the party's office

*Gladys Strum*, MP *from 1945 to 1950. (Saskatoon*
*Star Phoenix* and Saskatchewan Archives Board)

secretary. Later, she pleaded with the executive to make her a
paid organizer, as managing her role as farm wife without paid
domestic help was almost impossible. "Does the CCF contest
divorce cases as a correspondent?" she asked the executive, add-
ing that "perhaps she should warn women in her next speaking
engagement to stay out of politics."[38]

Even women who did volunteer work for the party found it
easier if they had a level of economic security and, if they had
children, a supportive family. It is instructive that Marjorie Mann,
an activist in Ottawa, saw her husband's support for her political
activity as "exceptional": "my husband looked after the kids . . .
but many other women didn't share this situation."[39] Barbara
Cass-Beggs was blunter when describing the dichotomy between
socialists' public lives and their reluctance to abandon traditional
private lives: "there, well, sexism was just not combatted."[40]
Both professionals, Barbara and her husband had a well-under-

stood agreement that she would have a career, and they could afford to hire someone to look after their children. Others were not so lucky, but when Cass-Beggs and her husband together suggested a socialist discussion group on "personal living"[41] to consider egalitarian relationships, they were not particularly surprised to find the idea was received better by CCF women than by the men.

More CCF women did run for office in the 1940's, and the CCF often fared better in its sponsorship of female candidates than did other parties. The negative side, however, was that many women still ran in unwinnable ridings. Alice Loeb charged that the party accepted "comparative strangers as candidates, while prominent CCF women were ignored." Constituency associations feared that, somehow, women just were not "winners," a fear that, according to some CCF women, did mirror social attitudes. When Nancy Zaseybida ran in a northern Alberta riding, local residents told her husband in no uncertain – and even lurid – terms what they thought of women politicians:

> Some of them said openly, "We are not going to have a woman represent us." In fact, some said, "If she gets elected, she will not treat us to drinks." The worse reaction was in Vegreville. One man said . . . "If your wife gets elected she will be in Ottawa only to service the male MPs."[42]

There were female candidates, such as Margaret Mann in Portage La Prairie, who maintained that "they were not discriminated against: if people were going to vote CCF, they did so anyway." Mann admitted, however, that she was a "sacrificial lamb"[43] in an impossible riding, a fact that, as a staunch party loyalist, she simply took in stride.

There were also success stories. Laura Jamieson moved from provincial to Vancouver municipal politics; some CCF women gained election to school boards; Beatrice Trew became the first CCF woman to sit in the Saskatchewan legislature; Rae Lucock and Agnes Macphail were elected in Ontario in 1945; and Gladys Strum was returned in a by-election to Parliament in 1945. Strum made a point of speaking out on women's behalf. Like many CCF women of this period, she saw women's first interest as home and children, but she was also concerned that women be given choices about education, training, and employment. In her response to the Speech from the Throne in 1942, she criticized the government for badly neglecting women's domestic field and thus

*Agnes Macphail, elected to the Ontario legislature
in 1943.* (Provincial Archives of Ontario)

the ''very heart of the Nation'': the home. She called for better
widows' pensions, housing initiatives to protect families against
eviction, prenatal allowances to decrease infant mortality, and
the right of female veterans to employment in the civil service.
In 1949, however, Strum's defeat at the polls meant that women
in the CCF lost their spokesperson in the House of Commons; the
next female CCF MP, Grace MacInnis, was elected sixteen years
later.

## CCF Women Organize Themselves

As in the 1930's, women's columns in the CCF newspapers and
local women's committees were used to stimulate women's interest in socialism and encourage their participation in the party.
Women's groups continued to lobby on women's issues, do educational work, and sometimes raise funds. The mere existence of

such semi-autonomous women's committees remained an issue of contention. Some men argued that women's groups threatened socialist unity with feminist false consciousness, while women, too, could be critical, fearing either that women would be reduced to making coffee or that discussion of women's rights would be ghettoized into one small section of the party. Women such as Nellie Peterson participated in separate women's committees but harboured ambiguous feelings about them. Peterson sympathized with the problems women encountered in becoming politically active, and she also believed women had a distinct perspective to bring to socialism. But she did not want women relegated to traditional auxiliary roles, even though she also rejected any form of assured representation for women in the leadership as "tokenism, for women *had* the abilities . . . and we could and should have earned this ourselves."[44]

These dilemmas were not new to B.C. socialists. The central focus for women's organization in B.C. in the 1940's was the Vancouver CCF Women's Council, now given new leadership by such younger recruits as Hilda Kristiansen, May Campbell, and Claire MacAllister. A school teacher, MacAllister had "her eyes opened" by her witness to the impoverished social conditions in the mining towns of Cape Breton. She returned home to B.C. and devoted her time to the co-operative movement and CCF work.[45] Campbell, too, was a co-operator, a leader in the credit union movement. Both she and Hilda Kristiansen had come from Saskatchewan, where they had already tested the socialist politics of the United Farmers of Canada and the CCF. When Kristiansen moved to Vancouver to work with Francis Telford, she joined the Young Socialist League, then later the CCF and the Vancouver Women's Council, as well as devoting time to such reform and educational causes as the play schools movement. Hilda married a fellow socialist, Denny, who was active in the Left Theatre, and together they bought a boarding house, which Hilda ran while she raised her family and worked at politics.

In 1943 the Vancouver Women's Council decided to expand across the province and become a standing committee of the Provincial Council. Working for six months with a paid organizer, then by mail, they increased the number of women's committees from ten to twenty-two over the next three years. The Vancouver group sent out a newsletter to the hinterland, as well as CCF pamphlets with titles such as "Consumer versus Profiteer" to stimulate women's group discussions. In the smaller towns, women were more easily channelled into their traditional fund-raising roles, but political education always remained an important activity. Some women's committees, especially the Vancouver one, were able successfully to channel resolutions on various issues, including government aid to nursery schools, widows' pensions, and a women's bureau, through their constituencies to provincial conventions. The Vancouver women concentrated on a few key women's issues, especially those relating to the family, offered training in political skills, and tried to reach out to new women through their own radio show and the women's column in the *B.C. Federationist*.

Edited after 1944 by Claire MacAllister, the women's column offered up-to-date information on the Women's Council activities, as well as political news ranging from co-operatives and education to mothers' allowances and rising prices. More keenly concerned with women in the home than women in the work force, the column's emphasis was heartily endorsed by one reader, who also echoed the anti-war sentiments of the militant mothers of the 1930's, though now in the context of the atomic age:

> We must move beyond our little homes. We have to make a choice . . . knit a sweater for our boy today or prevent him from going to war tomorrow. We are paying the price for being absorbed in our own little world; the fate of our sons hangs in the balance.[46]

Older party feminists, such as Laura Jamieson and Elizabeth Kerr, also endorsed all these efforts at women's self-organization, in part because they believed women brought a distinct "humane awareness"[47] to socialism, but also because they hoped women would use their organizations as stepping stones to larger party involvement.

Despite high hopes for this expanding women's network, by the mid-1950's its growth was halted. A lack of funds and resources, the difficulties in keeping in touch with groups outside Vancouver, and party neglect all hampered the organization. While it was ready to accept the view that women's maternal consciousness was distinct from men's, the party was always distrustful of a distinct feminist consciousness within the movement. MacAllister constantly had to reassure the party that women's groups did not detract from socialist priorities, and the secretary of the Women's Council referred openly to the "indifference and skepticism of many women members over the Council's useful-

ness.''[48] The party secretary, who watched the Women's Council
grow and decline, remembered that the ''Council was never considered important . . . it was the wrong time to discuss women's
rights . . . it was simply ahead of its time.''[49] As heated debates
raged in the B.C. party over moderate social democracy versus
Marxist socialism, the question of women's rights was seen as
superfluous. Key female players in that debate, Grace MacInnis
and Dorothy Steeves, though they disagreed on the question of
Marxism as opposed to reformism, would have agreed that gender
equality was not the first priority. Socialists first and feminists
second, they had never placed their hopes and interest in the
supportive network of women's groups, as had Laura Jamieson.[50]

On the Prairies, CCF women's groups also grew during the war
years, though prairie feminists faced some of the same obstacles
as their B.C. sisters. In Alberta, the CCF Women's Auxiliary and
the old Women's Section of the Labor Party merged in 1940 to
form the Women's Council, while in Manitoba women consoli-
dated a provincial women's organization in 1943 under the leadership of long-time activist Edith Cove. The organization of prairie
women was always complicated by the weaker rural base of the
Manitoba and Alberta parties, as well as by women's inability to
leave their farm responsibilities, so that provincial organizations
were easily dominated by the urban CCF women's groups.[51] Nonetheless, both Manitoban and Albertan women made progress in
the mid-1940's, extending their organizations to such outlying
towns as Flin Flon, Red Deer, and Lethbridge. Both groups tried
to gain legitimacy and a higher profile by becoming standing
committees (with voice but no vote) attached to the provincial
councils. This peculiar status had both positive and negative consequences: on one hand, the Women's Council might be kept
alive with appointments made by Provincial Council, but ironically, there was a danger that appointed women would not be
feminists, as was temporarily the case in Ontario in the forties.
Moreover, because the women's organization was not democrat-
ically elected from the convention floor and had no vote on the
Provincial Council it lacked a measure of power and prestige –
if only token prestige – that might have helped it move beyond
an auxiliary role.

Western women's committees did *try* to move beyond fund-
raising. In Alberta, CCF women conducted a radio program, sustained a column in *The People's Weekly* dealing especially with
consumer and family issues, and sponsored political speakers.

Conscious of the need to decentralize and recruit beyond their middle-class and professional membership, they also tried to recruit "wives of trade unionists."[52] Women in Manitoba also did educational work and debated contemporary political problems: in Winnipeg, the council held educational meetings on civil liberties and labour laws, sponsored forums on the need for improved family courts, and lobbied for better old age pensions and the right of women to do jury duty. Ultimately, though, women found it hard to escape their traditional roles: social convening, electioneering, and money-making. In Alberta, veteran socialist Mary Crawford seemed to recognize this age-old problem as she gently counselled the new women's committee to "sit back and quietly study . . . leaving money raising for awhile."[53] And in Manitoba, despite a more extensive provincial network, one senses a less militant organization than the Winnipeg Women's Labour Federation of the 1930's: CCF women now seemed content to support their party rather than carve out new frontiers for women.

In Saskatchewan, the debate over separate women's organizations took a different course; at a 1948 conference, women consciously "rejected the idea of a separate [provincial] women's group and opted instead for the flexible alternative of clubs of either mixed, or women members."[54] Their decision, suggests Georgina Taylor, may have been shaped by women's experience with direct participation in earlier farm organizations.[55] This tradition, along with respect for women's crucial economic role on the farm, she implies, led to a relatively high participation rate of Saskatchewan women in the party. Some party activists did hope that this strategy would encourage women to enter the mainstream of party life, but CCF women could and sometimes did continue to act as a distinct interest group. Women set up their own clubs to raise funds and do educational work, and the *Saskatchewan Commonwealth* sponsored a column on women's concerns that was the longest-running and liveliest women's column in all three prairie CCF papers. Themes relating to women's work as farm wives and homemakers predominated over the theme of woman as wage-earner in the column, but when the Saskatchewan CCF came to power it had to grapple with issues relating to working women, particularly equal pay and the right of married women to equal opportunity. In the latter case, the newly elected government found its commitment to gender equality on trial and, ultimately, wanting.

In 1946, when the Public Service Act was amended, Beatrice

Trew tried to include a proviso disallowing discrimination based on sex, race, or religion. Her efforts were disappointed by the government's addition of a qualification stating that, in an "emergency," married women could be dismissed, unless there was evidence of "special need, circumstances or particular skills." CCF women were extremely disturbed that the government had bowed to public hostility to married working women, and Trew, along with Gertrude Telford, quickly organized an opposition. They circulated two resolutions on women's work to local constituencies, criticizing the government's acceptance of the "specious argument that married women aid unemployment." Telford privately worried that the government intended to "dismiss married women from the civil service" and publicly reminded her fellow CCFers that "Socialism will not be built on discrimination."[56]

Trew and Telford organized well, for the next provincial convention asked the government to review legislation that "fails to provide equal status . . . based on sex or marital status."[57] This victory was short-lived, for a year later CCF women faced a worse disappointment: the government's Bill of Rights purposely omitted discrimination based on sex. Now, CCF women across Canada joined in the protest. The Saskatchewan government was always held up as a shining example of socialism in action. How could socialist-feminists explain this blatant disregard for women's rights? Presumably, the Saskatchewan government was concerned about maintaining protective labour legislation for women, but their "protective" attitude went further, taking on a paternalistic tone. When Margaret Mann protested to the Saskatchewan minister in question, she was informed that "there were some rights, such as jury duty, which women do not want."[58] She immediately started a campaign to get women that right in Manitoba. Ontario women, too, were disappointed. Barbara Cass-Beggs, on a visit to Saskatchewan, expressed her dismay in a letter to Marjorie Mann:

> The thinking women here are heartbroken by the omission of "discrimination on sex grounds" . . . if we really stand for equality in the CCF this should go in . . . although it obviously creates difficulties, it also gains respect amongst just the group which can be most helpful to us: the thinking group.[59]

CCF women were not successful in changing the government's mind. Perhaps this was an instance where a well-organized pro-

*Ontario CCF Women's Committee. Front row, from left: Norma Brown, Marjorie Mann, Barbara Cass-Beggs, Mary Morrison.* (National Archives of Canada, PA 125808)

vincial women's committee might have unified feminist opinion and successfully lobbied for an alternative government policy.

### The Ontario CCF Women's Committee

When Barbara Cass-Beggs penned her letter to Mann, they were both deeply involved in the Ontario Women's Committee. By 1940, a Toronto CCF Women's Council had replaced the disbanded Women's Joint Committee, and within two years it was expanding into a provincial organization. Inspired by the CCF's high electoral hopes, and especially by women's wartime roles, a small cadre of CCF feminists, many of them well-educated Torontonians, began to push for a higher profile for women's issues in the party. At the same time, the CCF leadership was contemplating how the party might capitalize on the war work of women in order to attract positive publicity for the party. The result was the appointment of a women's committee to investigate women's role in the CCF. The leadership's motives, however, seemed more opportunist than feminist, for the first women selected to head the committee were less than enthusiastic about women's self-organization, and it was unlikely they would question reigning party priorities. Caroline Riley, the first president, was a veteran of the Edmonton CCF Women's Council and therefore a respectable candidate. Riley, however, now believed women's committees too often became women's auxiliaries, so she suggested an alternative committee composed of women and men. She was outvoted and, ironically, appointed president despite her ideological objections to the project. Her disapproval of women's groups was quite apparent when she reported that, on a trip west, Laura Jamieson, Beatrice Brigden, Mary Crawford, and Louise Lucas had all told her of ''the importance'. . . of avoiding separate sections for the sexes.''[60] One wonders at Riley's interpretation of their ideas, as all these women were sympathetic to women's groups.

By 1944, the committee had been given an official mandate to ''develop and extend opportunities for women to make their full and distinctive contribution to the building of the Cooperative Commonwealth,''[61] and it had a newly appointed president, Alice Katool. An efficient organizer, Katool quickly realized the need for a province-wide convention of women to elect its own executive if the committee was to thrive. Her recommendation was acted on in 1947, though ironically, Katool, too, had been picked by the party leadership precisely because she could be trusted to be wary of separate women's groups. As she later admitted:

> The provincial executive decided we should set up a women's organization. Well, I was the . . . president. I only did it because I was impartial. I wasn't selective, and I wouldn't make it a separate entity.[62]

Katool was not alone in her views. Avis McCurdy objected to the committee and suggested the party have a women's convener, either male *or* female, to study the problems of women. In her mind, a committee might as well have been an auxiliary, and its chances of being heard on serious issues of inequality would be nil. ''I was opposed to women's committees from the beginning,'' she said adamantly.

> I wouldn't join a women's group like the Liberal and Conservative women's auxiliaries, who did the tea and sandwiches, thank you very much. I was determined this wasn't going to happen in the CCF. . . . It was a matter of principle, to do things

together [with the men], including issues like decent wages [for women].[63]

A well-educated, confident political activist, McCurdy found it difficult to comprehend the psychological and political support to be gained from a women's organization. And significantly, she thought such a committee would not have the prestige to be heard on women's rights, which she did see as important issues. At the 1945 provincial convention, for instance, the question of women's layoffs from war industry was pushed to the bottom of the agenda, and McCurdy reacted quickly, and angrily, in a letter to council:

> To put it mildly, we were appalled that the convention . . . would so willingly ignore what ought to be one of our major concerns. Today, the pressures are increasing to drive women from industry and other public work, to keep pay for women at a low level, to keep women in their homes. . . . the attitudes of men and women in . . . our movement are indifferent and wrong.[64]

One positive outcome of McCurdy's letter was the Ontario council's resolution calling for a policy on women's rights, which was presented to the 1946 federal convention.

While the federal policy never materialized, at the provincial level a small core of women intently concerned with employment issues continued to meet. A Status of Women subcommittee[65] had emerged from a debate between some CCF women and the party leaders over the question of excluding sex from the proposed Ontario Bill of Rights. Though party leaders convinced the women that inclusion would lead to a loss of protective legislation, the women resolved to compensate with an extensive study of the legal and economic discrimination in the work force, as well as concrete recommendations for change. Covering teaching, white-collar, and industrial work, their report was a convincing indictment of systematic discrimination based on sex, and it recommended legislation covering equal pay, a women's bureau in the Department of Labour, and, as the women were unconvinced by previous arguments, a Bill of Rights including no discrimination based on sex. After this major report and some follow-up work on equal pay, the subcommittee gradually faded from sight.

The larger Ontario Women's Committee concerned itself primarily with politicizing the homemaker. After an inaugural conference in 1947, CCF women marked their autonomy from Provincial

Council by electing their own executive. Aside from some veterans of the 1930's, including Alice Loeb and Jean Laing, the committee included a new generation of women activists. They were often middle-class, well-educated, and active in other party work: Marjorie Mann, the first president, was an Ottawa homemaker who had first joined the CCF while working as a teacher in Windsor; the vice-president, Barbara Cass-Beggs, was an Oxford-educated musician and teacher. Conscious, like the Alberta Council, of its poor working-class representation, it even made some efforts to recruit the wives of "prominent trade unionists" – but the committee did not seem overly concerned with the class bias of its membership. Indeed, one member, Peggy Stewart, applauded its mixed membership: "what types of women do we want? . . . from the well-known to the obscure, business women, homemakers – in short, anyone."[66] This was a far cry from the attempt of the Communist Party to recruit the working class into its ranks. The CCF women's political models, of course, were Fabian and labourite; leaders of the British Labour Party such as Mary Sutherland were always given an enthusiastic welcome, and the committee much admired the British party's publication, *Labour Woman*.

At the first provincial women's conference in 1947, delegates attacked a well-worn question: how to recruit more women to the party. The conference made a number of proposals, including use of a woman organizer, radio broadcasts, and "boring from within" other women's groups, and to overcome women's traditional "alienation" from politics, they agreed on the necessity of having such non-threatening activities as socials and fund-raising. At a later women's conference, lessons in basic electoral tasks, for example, scrutineering and silkscreening, were offered. As one historian has pointed out,[67] these educational methods tended to perpetuate women's behind-the-scenes roles, but it is important to remember that the rationale was not to *keep* women in these jobs forever, but gradually to promote women, through their diligent constituency work, into more responsible party positions.

Some Women's Committee members were quite aware of the dilemmas of utilizing, while also trying to change, women's traditional roles. On principle, they wanted to "ask the CCF . . . to accept financial responsibility" for their work; in practice, they realistically recognized that "selling Christmas cards and cookbooks" might be the only way to fund their activities.[68] Writing of an organized visit to a local bakery, Marjorie Mann made it clear that she did not see anything wrong with using women's traditional roles, if it meant gains for the CCF:

> It was the best attended thing the women have had. . . . The whole show proved once again that we have to have an infinite variety (including the illegitimate) of activities if we are going to catch the interest of all the people we have on our lists.[69]

The Women's Committee did make some concerted attempts to promote women into more prominent party positions. It suggested women use a rotating chair to gain leadership skills, and it urged the party to select more women for provincial delegations and conventions. Katool even asked the Provincial Council to place at least one woman on each provincial committee "to give women needed political experience."[70] By the end of the 1940's Women's Committee president Marjorie Mann was pointing to successes: women from her own constituency, she remarked, were "taking on new jobs and doing them well," while Peggy Stewart, who had come into the party through the Women's Committee, "is now riding President and is being considered for an organizer's job."[71]

Given the problems of organizing by mail over great distances, and with few financial resources, the committee's efforts were substantial. By 1950, there were twelve local women's committees and contacts in at least one-third of the province. The executive kept up a voluminous correspondence – mimeographed in the national office at night – with its members, suggesting programs and issues to discuss, even circulating a kit of socialist novels, put together by Adeline Haddow, a Hamilton social worker. Despite its semi-autonomous organization, the committee's loyalty to the party was never in question, and so fears of its dangerous "feminist" tendencies, occasionally muttered within the CCF, seem paranoid in retrospect. Indeed, the committee was less vocal about the need to promote women than it was about its intent to augment the party membership rolls, and its major campaigns used woman's traditional role as homemaker to arouse her interest in politics. The Women's Committee set up sub-groups to study housing, child welfare, price controls, and nursery schools, worked on a questionnaire on mothers' allowances for the provincial caucus, and promoted the respectable causes of socialized health care and lower consumer prices.

As the committee came to concentrate on the latter issue it was confronted with a thorny political problem: the existence of another left-wing women's consumer group, the Housewives' Consumers Association. Influenced by an intense anti-communism shared by many CCF trade unionists and party leaders, as well as experience and disillusionment with power struggles within past so-called United Front organizations, the Ontario Women's Committee completely rejected co-operation with the HCA, though some Sudbury and Toronto CCF women still joined, and a few CCF trade unionists looked longingly at the HCA's "proletarian constituency," lamenting the loss of recruits to the LPP. These unionists suggested that the Women's Committee join the HCA "to present their views to the non-political women involved."[72] Presumably, they were to recruit women to the social democratic point of view, just as Communists were being berated for trying to recruit women to the LPP. Mann, strongly anti-Communist, disagreed, and wanted the HCA publicly exposed as a Communist front group:

> The struggle against the housewives is part of a test against Communism. The LPP find their way blocked in the unions because the men of the unions recognize the signs of the communists when they appear in men's clothes. The LPPers realize that the sign of a communist is more difficult to detect when it comes in women's clothing.[73]

As an alternative, the Women's Committee urged its supporters to join the Consumers Association of Canada (CAC), established in 1947 with a government subsidy. Given the CAC's government connections and moderate outlook, it was a dubious strategy. CCFer Marion Harrington protested from the start that "support for the CAC will drive consumers' protests into a blind alley as [its] message is to teach Canadians to live with austerity."[74] And when Vida Knowles was advised by the party to urge Winnipeg women to join the CAC, she simply refused, asking why she should urge "her organization to join a small 'c' conservative organization, after having kept them out of a left-wing [HCA] one."[75]

Doubts about the CAC proved realistic. Within the CAC, CCF women were isolated and labelled "partisan" in their efforts to put the Consumers Association on a progressive course; by mid-decade, leading committee members had given up on the CAC, considering it a "liberal and CMA [Canadian Manufacturers' Association] dominated diversion for . . . consumer protests."[76] In the end, CCF women were left with no interest group with which to form a coalition on one of its chosen political priorities, and the party had no choice but to advise its members to conduct their own price surveys and lobbying, a decentralized and ultimately less effective political course of action.

Despite the problems it encountered with the CAC, the Women's Committee did not abandon its advice to have women "get into other women's organizations, and put forward CCF priorities." The 1950 conference also decided to decentralize its operation and devote more time to rural areas, and it announced it had been "given" a page in *The Commonwealth* on the rather strict, even paternalistic proviso that the women "write it, advertise it, promote it, and demonstrate a proven interest by other women in the page."[77] Privately, Mann pronounced the conference "our best yet," and for a number of years the Women's Committee continued to thrive.

By the mid-1950's, however, the committee was faltering. Numbers faded, the women's page in the paper could not be sustained, and many women's groups had not moved beyond auxiliary work. Part of the problem was leadership exhaustion; Mann confided that her return to full-time work in 1950 meant less "nervous and emotional exhaustion" than her unpaid political organizing.[78] Secondly, as the party faced electoral decline, especially after 1951, women's committees were seen as superfluous. Party leaders said they drew competent women away from more "important" tasks, and even such women as Peggy Stewart and Margaret Mann remarked that "with the movement in such a bad way, we can't think of *extra* appeals."[79]

Furthermore, Stewart was discouraged that women's role within the movement had not altered in any meaningful way. On top of the party's disinterest in women's issues and women's own material and familial problems in becoming involved in politics, the social and political context was not propitious for socialist-feminist organizing. In the labour force, a persisting "conception of maternalism" channelled women into low-paying "feminine" occupations and portrayed women's wage labour – especially that of married women – as secondary, unimportant, or even undesirable. A baby boom, affluence, and a "drift towards an insular, family-centred culture of consumption"[80] all discouraged feminist organizing. Canadian society had not yet produced the massive conflicts and contradictions that generated the later wave of feminism in the 1960's: increasing work outside the home for married women, rising social expectations, and the influence of the civil rights and student movements.

222 DREAMS OF EQUALITY

The Ontario Women's Committee had tried to integrate itself into the post-war culture of consumerism, family, and domesticity, but this fixation with the preservation of the family ultimately mitigated against a critical analysis of women's privatization in the family and their oppression in the workplace. The party's indifference to women's equality and its denigration of the Women's Committee as an "auxiliary" further dampened the possibility of women's militancy. One historian has charged that "as the Women's Committee developed into a separate organization . . . it prolonged . . . sexual segregation in the CCF."[81] This view simplistically sees the committee doomed to renege on its feminist intentions because of its autonomy. On the contrary, the prevailing social climate, the attitude of the party to feminism, and the women's utter *loyalty* to the party, not their *method* of organization, were to blame. Lacking a well-developed feminist analysis of women's powerlessness, CCF women failed to challenge the attitudes and structures of male privilege, especially the idea that women were primarily responsible for domestic labour, which prevented women from voicing their demands. Loyal first and foremost to socialist ideals and to the party, CCF women tempered and subdued their feminism. A small core of women clearly perceived this problem, but they did not feel the time was ripe for its exposure. They left that to the next generation of feminists within the party.

### Conclusion

Altered roles and raised expectations in wartime Canada prompted the CCF to consider, for the first time, a comprehensive platform on women's equality. In part, opportunistic hopes of electoral victories led the party to court the women's vote, but more importantly, CCF women pushed and prodded their socialist brothers to develop a socialist reconstruction policy embracing gender equality. Unfortunately, the ensuing debate within the CCF on women's issues never became a priority for the whole party, and by 1950 there was no detailed policy on women's rights in sight, or even in mind. In the post-war years, a small group of CCF women did continue to press for reforms for working women; their efforts, however, concentrated on the equal pay issue and placed rather inordinate hope in social democratic solutions of legislation and state regulation. A few women became influential union organizers and staffers, but there was not yet equal success in politicizing women workers at a grassroots level.

In the wake of the war, CCF women also showed new enthusiasm in provincial women's committees; never before had CCF
women been so well and widely organized as they were in the
1940's. The explicit goal of these enlarged women's networks
was to augment the number of women in the party; implicit was
the desire to rectify the imbalance of the party's male-dominated
leadership and to raise the party's profile on women's issues. In
the war years considerable attention was given to the concerns of
wage-earning women, but in the post-war world women's issues
were increasingly related to the domestic sphere. Feminist ideas
took shape ''within the bounds of dominant notions of femininity,'' and central to that notion was ''the idea that women as
mothers brought feminine qualities to society which men could
not provide.''[82] Such a definition also reflected many CCF wom-
en's occupational status and followed the party's historic understanding that women's political consciousness was shaped in an
important way by their role in the family. Such a one-dimensional
characterization of women's calling in life always had potentially
dangerous implications: it could also be used to excuse the sexual
division of labour within the party, relegating women to secondary
roles, just as they were streamlined into lower-paying jobs in the
marketplace. Moreover, a crucial deterrent to woman's political
involvement – her meagre economic resources and responsibility
for child care – was never questioned within this framework.

As the Cold War grew colder after World War Two, many CCF
women adamantly opposed Communists' attempts to mobilize
women. Yet, there were similarities in socialists' and Communists' treatment of the woman question, though CCFers would have
been loath ever to admit it. Women in both parties were a minority
of the party leadership, but still they composed a reservoir of
local supporters, organizers, and educators. Both parties focused
on the economic basis of women's oppression – tackling issues
from low wages to rising prices – and both increasingly emphasized the mobilization of women around consumer issues. And
finally, both parties suffered declining vitality in their work during
the mid-1950's, in part because anti-socialist ideas and prevailing
notions of femininity (not to mention the material realities of most
women's lives) proscribed the possibilities of militancy, but also
because women in both parties, loyal to a socialist vision of unity
in the face of adversity, were not able forcefully to overcome
patriarchal attitudes within their own movements.

# 8

# Conclusion: Women and the Party Question

In 1962 the NDP hired a national women's director to design new programs to draw women into the party; making her first report, the director noted that she had begun her tenure "without records, files, precedent or pattern."[1] Her statement revealed the doldrums that CCF women's groups had fallen into in the late 1950's, but it was also a sad indication of the party's amnesia about three decades of a rich and diverse history of women's organizations within the CCF. Just over a decade later, Canadian feminists resurrected the practice of holding large International Women's Day celebrations and pointed to their demonstrations as "new-found" tactics for the women's movement. A bewildered generation of older Communist women asked how their annual attention to International Women's Day since the 1920's had been forgotten. A rupture in historical memory divided women of the Old Left from younger women of the New Left of the 1960's; while some family and organizational connections hinted at a continuing relationship, in general, the more recent women's movement was unaware of the history of socialist-feminism in Canada.[2] Women had been virtually excluded from the written history of the Canadian left, in part because of the secondary role women and women's issues played in the CCF and CPC, but also as a result of the limitations of traditional political history and its subsequent devaluation of women's political life.

Women's role in the making of Canadian socialism was marked not only by women's secondary status within the left, but also by women's essential – and unique – contribution to the socialist movement. Although often concentrated in the lower echelons of party organization or channelled into "feminine" occupational spheres, women were the indispensable foot soldiers in the battle for socialism. Moreover, issues pertaining to women's economic and social equality were at different times and to different degrees a concern for socialists and Communists. Women's contribution to socialist parties and the left's treatment of the woman question changed considerably over time, as well as within and between the two parties. The CPC and CCF emerged from different ideological traditions and lived out distinct political lives, although sometimes overlapping in causes, converts, ideas, and, increasingly in the 1940's, in competition and hostility. Even within each party, ideology (in the case of the CCF), region, and ethnicity produced variations in political culture, which in turn shaped perspectives on gender equality and women's role in political life.

Ideological variations were particularly evident in the CCF, born as an eclectic coalition of labourites, radical farmers, Christian socialists, and Marxists. Although only the party's Marxist contingent boasted a clear-cut theory of women's oppression, other founding groups had utopian ideals, pragmatic solutions, and well-established practices of women's separate organization to contribute to the new party. The Women's Section of the United Farmers of Canada, the Women's ILP, and Beatrice Brigden's Western Labor Conference all provided models and socialist-feminist networks of communication for later CCF women. After the 1933 Regina convention, women's auxiliaries and committees flourished within the young party; some were largely tea and bazaar fund-raisers, some combined socialist education with fund-raising, while others concentrated on leadership training, socialist-feminist education, and social action. Neither urban nor rural CCF women's groups experienced a linear evolution toward greater and greater strength; they grew, declined, then grew again, the ebb and flow of their existence conditioned by the enthusiasm of local female leadership, the current attitude of the party toward women's organizations, and the wider social and economic climate of the time.

Auxiliaries supplied a secure niche for socialist women uncomfortable in the male-dominated mainstream of the party, but who nonetheless wished to offer support based on traditional female roles. And their dances and picnics, euchres and dinners did contribute meaningfully, in a financial and social sense, to the growth of the CCF. Yet, women's auxiliaries were also places where women were channelled and forgotten by party leaders unconscious and uncaring of the need to break down the sexual division of labour in the party and offer women more challenging political roles. The more politically aware women's committees played an even more essential role in the party, acting as the CCF's feminist conscience by urging the promotion of women into the leadership and the discussion of current women's issues. In light of the party's tendency to skirt these issues or ignore the glaring power imbalance between men and women within its ranks, these women's committees were extremely valuable pressure groups. Without them, the party's discussion about women's emancipation would have been meagre indeed.

In its publications and election appeals the CCF often portrayed women as an occupational interest group, influenced largely by their maternal and domestic roles, and most CCF women's committees would have concurred with this view. Like the Communists, CCFers often feared that housewives, isolated in the private sphere, were politically apathetic or, worse, conservative, and thus socialists stressed maternal and family-related issues like health care, prices, and education in order to awaken women's political consciousness. Even during the unemployment crisis of the depression, the economic concerns of women wage-earners often took second place to those of homemakers, reflecting both the minority status of women within the work force and the prevailing dominance of ideals of female domesticity. In the 1940's, however, such issues as equal pay were raised and demands for a charter of women's rights were voiced as a result of women's expanded wartime role in the labour force, the activity of some CCF trade union women, and the emergence of a new generation of socialist-feminists within the party.

CCF members, however, did not always agree on the necessity of establishing separate women's groups to address these women's demands or to recruit female members. Male fears of feminist control, the old cries of socialist egalitarianism and solidarity in the face of opposition, and women's own apprehensions that women's committees would become tea-making auxiliaries all produced antipathy to women's self-organization – even though the party already consciously addressed women as a distinct interest group. Nor could opponents of women's committees have produced convincing evidence that women and men shared equal roles in the party. Although the 1940's saw more women advancing into local organizing and leadership positions, they still tended to be concentrated in grassroots work and were largely absent from policy-making roles or as electoral candidates. Their underrepresentation in the seats of power indicated persisting, resilient social barriers to women's participation in party politics, not the least of which was women's responsibility for child-rearing.

In contrast to the CCF, the Communist Party attempted a more centralized, directed, and uniform approach to the woman question. Communists' understanding of women's inequality came from Marx, Engels, and Lenin, and their strategies from respected mentors in the Comintern, though local needs and conditions also shared CPC goals and tactics. Communists believed that women's inequality was endemic to capitalism but that women had to be mobilized to further the class revolution, and that through working-class struggle women would emancipate themselves. Unlike the CCF, the Communist Party immediately established a set of women's demands in its platform, as well as a Women's Department to conduct organizational work. The CPC gave more time and thought to the woman question than had previous Marxist parties in Canada, and in its unionization of women workers, its organization of women on relief, of housewives against rising prices, of women against fascism and the atomic bomb, and in other campaigns, the Party set out impressive precedents for Canadian socialism.

From its founding in 1921 to its decline in the 1950's the CPC's work among women and the role of women in the Party changed, largely due to international influences. In the 1920's the Federation of Women's Labor Leagues flourished as a result of a dynamic debate on women's equality in Russia, a dedicated Canadian organizer, Florence Custance, and a measure of organizational flexibility. Unable to oppose the Communist Party's directives to submerge themselves in the Workers Unity League in the early 1930's, the WLLS found their role in the Party criticized and circumscribed. The militant but sometimes dogmatic and economistic treatment of gender equality during this Third Period led to some dramatic initiatives to organize wage-earning women but, overall, narrowed the whole Communist debate about women's equality.

As a result of depression conditions, better internal organization, and pragmatic tactics, CPC ranks began to swell in the mid-1930's; with new Popular Front strategies emanating from the Comintern, the CPC's work among women was strengthened and became more creative as Communists turned their sights to a wide variety of community issues, as well as union organizing and anti-fascist work. Sometimes working alongside socialist-feminists from the CCF, Communist women were beginning to build a move-ment of protest predicated on innovative responses to the growing popular desire to challenge the social dislocation caused by the depression. During the Second World War, the Communist Par-ty's theoretical emphasis on women in social production as the harbingers of class struggle found balance in the Party's attempts to integrate women into war production. But in the aftermath of war, and amidst intensifying anti-Communist feeling, the Party was ill-equipped to extend this work and returned to "bread and peace" as the rallying cries for women's organization.

By the late 1940's the number of women in regional Party leadership had increased since the days of Custance; yet, the CPC evidenced a sexual division of labour similar to that of its social democratic rival, the CCF. Women made inordinate contributions to electioneering, fund-raising, and social convening and were sometimes visible in educational and cultural work. But they were rarely represented as theoreticians, union organizers, or national policy-makers. Also like the CCF, the CPC tended to see women as a distinct interest group shaped by their role as care-givers in the family. While the organization and recruitment of wage-earn-ing women always had a stated priority – and was more important to the CPC than to the CCF – the mobilization of working-class housewives consumed a large amount of the time of the Women's Department.

This emphasis on women's domestic labour revealed an un-derstanding of the important material and emotional role that women played in the working-class family and an astute reading of prevailing ideals of domesticity for married women. Yet, Party strategies to mobilize housewives raised some important prob-lems. For one thing, these women's organizations never com-manded high prestige and importance in the CPC; thus, housewives were more likely to be relegated to supportive rather than influ-ential roles. Even more fundamentally, by the late 1930's, the CPC claimed it wished to defend and preserve the family; at the same time, it also called for an end to the domestic drudgery of women's work in the home. Was it so easy to separate the two?

Concerned that household work was isolating and led to wom-en's apathy or "backward" political views, the CPC tried to in-volve women in political issues, such as rising prices. But it was clear that domestic labour was something to organize around, not something to change altogether. Aside from a few brave calls from Communists for shared work in the households, consistent stress was not placed either on the collectivization of domestic work or on sharing it equally with men. The transformation of family life, an end to women's unpaid labour in the home, challenges to the sexual division of labour, and women's reproductive freedom were either largely ignored by CCFers or assigned to the never-never land of "after the revolution" by Communists.

Indeed, although women's contribution to the making of Canadian socialism was important and women's equality was on the left's agenda, one cannot escape the overwhelming fact of women's secondary status in both the CCF and the CPC. In terms of membership, leadership, prestige, and theoretical stature, women always fell behind men. Moreover, neither party made women's equality an essential prerequisite in its vision of socialism. Why, then, was women's emancipation not the measure of these socialist movements?

Factors internal to party life, as well as external social forces, account for socialists' and Communists' inability to deal effectively with the woman question. First, neither the CCF nor the CPC grappled openly and repeatedly with the theoretical exploration of women's oppression. The Communist Party's understanding of gender inequality and its strategies for change were heavily influenced by Comintern advice, which might offer new insight on women's issues but could just as easily narrow the definition of the woman question, encourage rigid organizing tactics, or subsume work among women under what were determined to be more important Party needs. The organization of women was subject to the whim of "experts" from afar, rather than being shaped primarily from the struggles and ideas of women immediately involved in the movement.

It is true that Comintern policies were negotiated through the peculiarities of Canadian conditions and the understanding of Canadian Party leaders but, unfortunately, in their hands Marxism and Leninism became a rigid set of rules, rather than tools for inquiry, a fact not unrelated to the triumph of Stalinism in Comintern circles. Marx was used by the CPC to show the need to draw women into social production; Engels was cited as proof that private property caused women's subordination; and Lenin was quoted to caution against organizing women along bourgeois feminist lines. From the 1920's and especially the 1930's on, new interpretations of the woman question, even alternative Marxist views, were "shunned as if . . . on an invisible Index."[3] The Party thus created an economistic and static Marxism that could not explain the more complex sexual and cultural manifestations of women's oppression. In fairness to the CPC, it is true that a feminist re-evaluation and extension of Marx and Engels has been a more recent phenomenon. But even contemporary attempts to shed new light on old orthodoxies, such as Mary Inman's discussion of domestic labour, were always quickly dismissed by the Party.

The social composition of the Communist Party tended to reinforce, rather than challenge, the Party's adherence to this rigid class analysis. CPC members came largely from working-class backgrounds, and many joined during the thirties and early forties, a period of economic depression and political repression. Their daily experiences of wage labour, poverty, relief, police actions, and government indifference sparked their interest in radical ideas, and for many women these experiences confirmed an emphasis on class rather than gender identity. While the presence of a strong working-class consciousness may not automatically preclude the emergence of a feminist consciousness, in this historical context class did come to take precedence over gender. Sexual oppression was experienced, and sometimes named and criticized, by Communist women. But often, even those women who saw sexual equality as an important goal had their concerns subsumed, contained, and moulded by their education in Marxist and Leninist literature, which interpreted the class struggle as the vehicle for women's liberation.

Many CPers also came from emigrant backgrounds and the appeal of communism may have been its emphasis on class solidarity in the face of a nativist Canadian society, or secondly, emigrants' sense of connection to the vibrant, ethnic subcultures that thrived within the Party's mass organizations. These first- and second-generation immigrant women were far from passive bystanders on the political scene, for they often undertook daring political actions in support of the Party. At the same time, there is no evidence that women's cultural consciousness significantly encouraged their preoccupation with gender equality. Ukrainian women, for one thing, had immense material and cultural obstacles – from lack of economic resources to illiteracy – preventing their very participation in politics. The economic and social background of Jewish and Finnish women, on the other hand, stimulated a certain political militancy, and in the case of the Finns, some questions about traditional marriage. But there is little evidence that these women more acutely identified with feminist goals; indeed, their ethnic identification, and in the case of Jews, concern with anti-Semitism,[4] may have had the opposite effect, reinforcing cultural and class consciousness rather than gender identity.

Lastly, the Leninist structure of the CPC also hindered an emphasis on women's emancipation and prevented the integration of women into all levels of Party life. Whatever the theoretical intentions of democratic centralism, its operation within the CPC tended to cut off democratic decision-making in favour of leadership control. In certain respects, the Party's use of Leninist organization did successfully aid their work: a uniformity of purpose and a disciplined, centralized operation led to some effective organizational coups. But Leninism could also have negative consequences for sexual equality, because in the wake of the CPC's uniformity of purpose, gender differences were easily papered over and ignored.

Despite the existence of some grassroots discussion in the CPC, the Party operated as a pyramid structure with (male) leaders at the top and power flowing downward, not upward. As one woman who became disenchanted with the Party in the 1950's explained,

> When I suggested that we voice our opinion before the Central Committee had decided on the question at issue, I was seen as "disruptive." So the line was laid down: we couldn't discuss the issue until [the leadership] had . . . I explained when I left, "that's exactly what I don't want any more of!"[5]

This deference to leadership and lack of a vibrant inner-party democracy would still the voices of those less confident of theory, less assured of their social worth, and less valued by members; such people were more likely to be women. Interestingly, though, at the time few women who left the Party pointed to Leninism as a deterrent to sexual equality; instead, they objected to the Party's undemocratic organization or disagreed with specific leadership decisions.

This problem of an overbearing leadership was linked to the Leninist concept of the vanguard, supposedly the most "advanced" group in consciousness, ready and willing to share their superior insights with other Party members. Of course, as Sheila Rowbotham's critique of Leninism has pointed out, the process of deciding what was advanced and what was backward was not a neutral one.[6] In the CPC, these decisions were made by (largely male) leaders, already influenced by Comintern directives and by their own understanding of gender relations. Correct ideas were those replicating the Party's prevailing emphasis on the class struggle, and the leadership's current priorities, while incorrect ones, such as a feminist emphasis on sexual oppression, were easily dismissed as backward and dangerous. Furthermore, the whole idea of a vanguard tended to imply a very high level of commitment, including the ability to travel and organize whenever the Party called, which was difficult for a woman with family responsibilities to live up to, especially if she was currently living up to the Party's emphasis on "defending the family."

Finally, during much of the Communist Party's history, Leninism, as interpreted by the Comintern and the CPC, stressed key organizing targets: heavy industry, strikes, and a general focus on social production were given strategic priority. These priorities tended to minimize women's seasonal and "temporary" wage labour and women's work in the home; moreover, they ignored the "expression of power relations, in gender and sexuality, not directly addressed by the struggle between labour and capital."[7] Such an emphasis could only postpone a more complex understanding of women's oppression and delay actions to eradicate it.

If Leninism hindered a full discussion of sexual equality in the CPC, then one might presume that the CCF had more success in integrating the woman question into its agenda. By virtue of a more democratic decision-making process and more emphasis, at least in its early years, on local autonomy, the CCF did offer greater opportunities for criticism and flexibility. But in the CCF, too, leadership opinions, largely unsympathetic to feminism, were very influential. Moreover, the CCF was handicapped by its lack of theoretical interest in the woman question. Ironically, the CPC posed and promoted the woman question but lacked the internal democracy to let it blossom in political debates; the CCF seldom addressed the woman question, even though its more democratic organization might have facilitated more innovative discussion of gender equality. The absence of concern for women's oppression within the CCF's founding ideological traditions was one reason for this failure to address women's equality. Some Marxists in the CCF were conscious of the woman question but their political analysis often reflected the same economic determinism that characterized the CPC. Fabianism, however, rarely entertained discussion of women's oppression, while the Christian socialist and Bellamyite traditions often portrayed women as more moral and material beings, but did not delve to the roots of their oppression.

CCF policies dealt with women's issues in a piecemeal, pragmatic, and essentially reformist way: women's lower wages were condemned, for instance, and legislation offered as a panacea. But women's social and political subordination were not analysed, in the widest terms, to arrive at a theoretical understanding of oppression and to chart a course for emancipation.

To some extent, the class position and social experience of CCF members also militated against a concern with women's emancipation. An alliance of farm, working-class, and middle-class Canadians, the early CCF was largely influenced by the social context of the dirty thirties: CCF women understood and explained their conversion to socialism in terms of experiences of, or witness to, economic deprivation, not because of sexual discrimination. Even the female professionals so well represented in the CCF ranks, the teachers, were the product of very different social circumstances than those of the university-educated feminists of the 1960's. Prairie teachers who became CCFers in the depression, for example, often came from farm or rural backgrounds, had very few career and educational opportunities, and returned to economically disadvantaged farm communities to practise their profession.

Nonetheless, a feminist concern with women's equality was articulated by an influential core of women in the CCF. Not all these socialist-feminists blended and balanced their socialist and feminist impulses in the same way. While Dorothy Steeves criticized gender inequality, she was a "socialist first and foremost";[8] such women as Laura Jamieson and Beatrice Brigden, on the other hand, placed more emphasis on the need to subject all aspects of socialism to a feminist analysis.

Some of the party's socialist-feminists of the 1930's were survivors of the earlier suffrage movement who made their way into the CCF carrying, as Jamieson put it, "the zest of the suffrage struggle with them."[9] Former suffragists, including Rose Henderson and Helena Gutteridge, were already sympathetic to labour party politics by World War One, while Laura Jamieson and Beatrice Brigden made a personal transition from "feminism with a social conscience" to socialist-feminism in the aftermath of the labour revolt of 1919. This first generation of socialist-feminists in the CCF often shared similar political priorities; their outlook included some form of feminist pacifism; they avidly promoted the psychological and educational value of separate women's groups; and they urged discussion of women's issues within the larger party. Ultimately, though, their voices were a minority within the movement. The same was true of the next generation of socialist-feminists whose political teeth were cut during and after World War Two. Hesitant feminist criticisms of the immense barriers to women's equality were articulated by some members of women's committees in the 1940's, but again their views represented a minority of the CCF membership.

Although internal inadequacies and contradictions prevented both parties from addressing the woman question, this is only half the picture. The social and economic realities of Canadian society in the twenties, thirties, and forties also inhibited socialists from addressing gender equality; these external forces pressed to the very core of the CCF and CPC, aiding and abetting the parties' internal problems. Central to the social reality of farm and working-class women in these decades were the oppressive social relations of a patriarchal capitalist society. Women's political existence was affected by the material conditions of their lives, particularly by the existing sexual division of labour, which determined that women had fewer economic resources and more likelihood of being economically dependent on men. Material conditions, in part, shaped women's confining relegation to household work, which again meant women had less time and fewer resources, and perhaps even less inclination, to participate in the political world of men.

Moreover, a strong familial ideology and cultural prescriptions about "masculine" and "feminine" behaviour existed as part of, and beyond, these material realities, acting as a self-perpetuating reinforcement to women's oppression. Women, it was assumed at the time, were not merely members of the family; they were the pivot of the family. Popular advice literature of the time treated child-rearing as a suitable, indeed, *natural* role for women, and women who aspired to public careers were treated as oddities, if successful ones, and judged on their subsequent loss of femininity. CCF MP Gladys Strum distinctly remembers that the press "wrote about her hats, but not about her speeches."[10] Even in the war years, when the image of Rosie the Riveter impinged on popular culture, the maternal and domestic image was never totally abandoned.

Understandably, this hegemonic view of women's primary responsibility for domestic work and child-rearing was to some extent reproduced in the CCF and CPC. Within the Communist Party, and to a lesser extent in the CCF, a critique of the family was entertained, but it was framed primarily in economistic terms: society was criticized for failing to provide the economic security and social services needed to allow women the happy homes they so fervently desired. Maternalist rhetoric was one common theme underlining socialists' efforts to mobilize women, and even if, as some historians suggest, this was used as an expedient and practical organizing tool,[11] the rhetoric of maternalism cannot be dismissed as inconsequential, for language can play an influential role in shaping, as well as reflecting, women's understanding of reality.[12]

Socialists' use of the language of maternalism and adoption of this domestic ideal for women had contradictory consequences. By pragmatically addressing the daily work and worries of working-class and middle-class homemakers, socialists were able to interest women in such political issues as prices and education. On the other hand, the wholesale acceptance of female domesticity and the prevailing sexual division of labour were dangerous, for women's unpaid work in the home prevented them from participating equally in social and political life, and indeed perpetuated their oppression. One might suggest that socialists should have looked beyond contemporary assumptions about womanhood to carve out more egalitarian alternatives to the familial ideology of the time. It is true that, primarily in the CPC, some activists personally challenged the inequalities of traditional marriage and family life, but these experiments represented a courageous minority rather than the prevailing majority.

Other dominant assumptions about women's economic and social roles also crept into the thinking of both parties. Prevailing social views of women's wage labour, for example, saw women as secondary workers and, save for the war years, implied dissatisfaction with married women workers. Socialists, and particularly Communists, were more dedicated than most trade unionists to the rights and organization of women workers, and both parties made an important contribution to the growth of industrial unionism in Canada. But it is revealing that even from within the socialist movement came voices of frustration and dissatisfaction, as Becky Buhay and Annie Buller, for instance, criticized fellow party members for failing to take women workers seriously, to advance women into the leadership, and to press for such women's demands as equal pay.

Communists and social democrats rarely questioned the sexual division of labour within industries, and to some extent they absorbed the view of women as secondary earners and the "ideal" of the family wage. While this emphasis began to alter in the 1940's, neither party experienced a major paradigmatic shift on this issue. In everything from policy discussion to graphics, cartoons, and radical fiction, the man was given a lunch bucket and the woman a broom. On one level, this simply reflected the reality of women's lesser numbers and secondary role in the work force, but by failing to question the ideal of the male breadwinner, socialists obscured a full exploration of women's economic exploitation and in the long run worked against their own stated goals of achieving economic independence for women.[13]

Prairie socialists, some historians have argued, were cognizant of the crucial economic role that women played on the family farm; thus, in Saskatchewan, women's relatively high level of participation in the CCF reflected, in part, their important relationship to rural production.[14] At the same time, though, a sexual division of labour still prevailed on most farms, with the woman decidedly the "junior partner" in the farm economy.[15]

Women's differing economic and occupational roles might produce some variation in their status and participation in both parties. And moments of social change and economic "possibility" for women, as during World War Two, might produce new discussion, expectations, and participation of women in politics. Beneath all these variables, however, lay an inescapable problem: living in a society characterized not only by private property but also by male dominance, Communists and socialists ultimately found the latter difficult to erase from their world view.

Unfortunately, they had little theoretical or practical inspiration from other progressive movements of the period. Fragmented and weakened after the suffrage struggle, the women's movement consisted largely of middle-class reform groups, such as the National Council of Women, whose lack of sympathy for socialism made them less than attractive allies, even for some tolerant CCFers. Feminist ideas, except during the Popular Front, were largely rejected by the CPC, but the truth is that feminism was not able to offer socialist women convincing alternatives: a weak women's movement provided few theoretical challenges and strategic alternatives to socialists' treatment of the woman question. Neither did the labour movement. Organized labour, especially the TLC, did not push socialists and Communists to adopt more radical ideas on women's equality or creative strategies for organizing women. In fact, it was often the CCFers and Communists who were the unionists most dedicated to organizing women workers. Although CIO unions were more open to women workers and though both union centres took more interest in women during the war, countless issues of TLC and CCL papers addressed women with traditional women's columns of recipes, household hints, or, at best, advice on how to support your union man.

Given the secondary commitment to women's equality in the CCF and the CPC, why then did women devote themselves with such dedication to the socialist cause? As already noted, many women were radicalized around and most interested in working-class issues and class equality. But even those socialists committed to women's emancipation saw much that was positive in the CCF or CPC. The movement, they maintained, offered more avenues for women's activism and political growth and gave more attention to women's issues than did other political parties. And they were quite correct. In no other political party did one find the comprehensive platform of women's demands, or even the verbal opposition to "male supremacy" (imagine Mackenzie King even uttering the phrase), that characterized the CPC. In no other political party did one find the opportunities to direct educational work, to sit on elected provincial councils, and to organize women's committees that existed in the CCF. Moreover, however imperfectly the CCF and CPC addressed women's oppression, they did at least recognize its existence, and they often made a convincing case that gender inequality was linked to the economic deprivation endemic to a capitalist social order.

Finally, even when socialist and Communist women promoted their brand of "maternalist" politics, they quite rightly believed that their political solutions were qualitatively distinct from the ameliorative reform promoted by liberal female reformers or by the earlier suffragists. Socialist women challenged the idea of the home as a private retreat and urged women to join in a struggle to shape a new world, created anew "in the image of their own [maternal] socialist ideals."[16] Socialists' emphasis on the abolition of private ownership, on the redistribution of social wealth, on effecting public responsibility for social needs such as child care, as well as their militant participation in the struggle for social justice at home and a just peace abroad, made theirs a "militant mothering." Maternalism, though not necessarily radical by definition, could take on radical potential when married to a socialist analysis. For all these reasons, women kept the faith that, through socialism, their dreams of equality might become reality.

Historians of the early utopian socialist movement have convincingly argued that, by the late nineteenth century, scientific socialism, with its Marxist – and, one might add, Fabian – solutions, dominated Western socialist thought, displacing dreams of a utopia that had included feminism as a fundamental part of social transformation. As class-based economic issues came to dominate Communist and social democratic parties, a ''sexual retrenchment [occurred and] women's aspirations were stranded outside Socialism – to be either ignored, attacked as bourgeois deviationism, or relegated to the category of secondary issues which would be tackled once the primary battle had been won.''[17]

The CCF and the Communist Party of the twenties, thirties, and forties fit this assessment, for neither party ever fully embraced the cause of women's emancipation. Canadian socialists and Communists, however, did recognize the existence of gender inequality, debated its origins and solutions, and even attempted some campaigns to eradicate it. Moreover, within both movements there always existed a small group of women who wished for more: they struggled to awaken other women's interest in socialism, to enlarge the socialist definition of equality, to quicken the equalization of political roles. In short, they sustained the utopian dream of women's emancipation.

# Notes

## Preface

1. Charles Fourier, quoted in Barbara Taylor, *Eve and the New Jerusalem: Socialism and Feminism in the Nineteenth Century* (London, 1983), p. x.
2. For example, Juliet Mitchell, *Women's Estate* (New York, 1973); Sheila Rowbotham, *Women, Resistance and Revolution* (London, 1973); Zillah Einsenstein, ed., *Capitalist Patriarchy and the Case for Socialist Feminism* (New York, 1979); Michelle Barrett, *Women's Oppression Today: Problems in Marxist Feminist Analysis* (London, 1980).
3. This scholarship has concentrated on the U.S. and Europe. For example, Werner Thornnessen, *The Emancipation of Women: The Rise and Decline of the Women's Movement in German Social Democracy 1863–1933* (London, 1973); Jean Quataert, *Reluctant Feminists in German Social Democracy* (New York, 1978); Barbara Clements, *Bolshevik Feminist* (Bloomington, 1979); Barbara Taylor, *Eve and the New Jerusalem*; Mari Jo Buhle, *Women and American Socialism* (Urbana, 1981).
4. For example, for a completely unsympathetic view of the Communists, see Ivan Avakumovic, *The Communist Party of Canada* (Toronto, 1975), and for a largely uncritical view, Gerry Van Hauten, *Canada's Party of Socialism* (Toronto, 1977). Most social democratic historians, like Desmond Morton, *Social Democracy in Canada* (Toronto, 1977), are sympathetic to the CCF and hostile to the CPC. There are some exceptions. Norman Penner, *The Canadian Left: A Critical Analysis* (Toronto, 1977), attempts a more even-handed view of the Communists, while Michiel Horn provides a sophisticated treatment of the LSR in *The League for Social Reconstruction: Intellectual Origins of the Democratic Left in Canada, 1930–42* (Toronto, 1980). Most books on the left and labour deal with male-dominated unions, save for Eileen Sufrin, *The Eaton Drive* (Toronto, 1982), and most biographies of socialist and Communist women are incomplete and hagiographical. For example, Louise Watson, *She Never Was Afraid: The Biography of Annie Buller* (Toronto, 1976); Catharine Vance, *Not By Gods But by People . . . The Story of Bella Hall Gauld* (Toronto, 1968);

J.F.C. Wright, *The Louise Lucas Story* (Montreal, 1965); Margaret Stewart and Doris French, *Ask No Quarter: a Biography of Agnes Macphail* (Toronto, 1969).

5. Sheila Rowbotham, *Beyond the Fragments: Feminism and the Making of Socialism* (London, 1979), p. 58.

6. Sheila Rowbotham, *Dreams and Dilemmas: Collected Writings* (London, 1983), p. 174.

## Chapter 1

1. For this period, see Penner, *The Canadian Left*.

2. See Tad Kawecki, "Canadian Socialism and the Origins of the Communist Party, 1900–22" (M.A. thesis, McMaster University, 1980).

3. Exactly when the CI became completely controlled by the U.S.S.R. is debated by historians. Gus Horowitz, "Introduction" to Leon Trotsky, *The Third International After Lenin* (New York, 1974), claims that it wasn't until the mid-twenties. But a contemporary participant claims Russian control from the CI's very inception. See Angelica Balabanoff, *My Life as Rebel* (Bloomington, 1973).

4. Ruth Lestor in *Western Clarion*, July, 1911.

5. For one such debate over whether to have a women's page, see *Western Clarion*, August–October, 1908.

6. Varpu Lindstrom-Best, *The Finnish Immigrant Community of Toronto, 1887–1918* (Toronto, 1979).

7. Linda Kealey, "No Special Protection – No Sympathy: Women's Activism in the Canadian Labour Revolt of 1919," unpublished paper, 1987, p. 5. For a full discussion of socialists and the woman question before World War One, see Linda Kealey, "Canadian Socialism and the Woman Question, 1900–1914," *Labour/Le Travail*, 13 (Spring, 1984).

8. Karl Marx and Frederick Engels, "The Communist Manifesto," in *The Woman Question: Selections from the Writings of Marx, Engels, Lenin and Stalin* (New York, 1951), p. 34.

9. Frederick Engels, *Origin of the Family, Private Property and the State* (New York, 1972), p. 75.

10. Varda Burstyn, "Economy, Sexuality, Politics: Engels and the Sexual Division of Labour," *Socialist Studies/Etudes Socialistes* (1983). See also Juliet Mitchell, *Women's Estate* (New York, 1973); Ann Lane, "Woman in Society: A Critique of Engels," in Berenice Carroll, ed., *Liberating Women's History* (Chicago, 1976); Rosalind Delmar, "Looking Again at Engels' Origin of the Family, Private Property and the State," in Juliet Mitchell and Ann Oakley, eds., *The Rights and Wrongs of Women* (London, 1976).

11. August Bebel, *Woman Under Socialism* (New York, 1971), p. 9.

12. *Ibid.*, p. 1.

13. Lenin quoted by Clara Zetkin, "My Recollections of Lenin," in *The Emancipation of Women: Writings of V.I. Lenin* (New York, 1975), p. 111.

14. *Ibid.*, p. 118.

15. Lenin to Inessa Armand, in *The Emancipation of Women: Writings of V.I. Lenin*, pp. 38-39.
16. Craig Heron, "Labourism and the Canadian Working Class," in *Labour/Le Travail*, 13 (Spring, 1984).
17. On labourite women, see Wayne Roberts, *Honest Womanhood: Feminism, Femininity and Class Consciousness Among Toronto Working Women, 1893 to 1914* (Toronto, 1976). On their differences with middle-class feminists, see Carol Bacchi, *Liberation Deferred?: The Ideas of the English Canadian Suffragists, 1877–1918* (Toronto, 1983).
18. Bacchi, *Liberation Deferred*, p. 127.
19. For a feminist approach that stresses farm women's shared problems, see Veronica Strong-Boag, "Pulling in Double Harness or Hauling a Double Load: Women, Work and Feminism on the Canadian Prairie," *Journal of Canadian Studies*, 21, 3 (Fall, 1986).
20. William Irvine, *The Farmers in Politics* (Toronto, 1976), p. 123.
21. Georgina Taylor, "Equals and Partners? An Examination of How Saskatchewan Women Reconciled Their Political Activities for the CCF with Traditional Roles for Women" (M.A. thesis, University of Saskatoon, 1983).
22. See A.R. Allen, *The Social Passion: Religion and Social Reform in Canada, 1914–1928* (Toronto, 1973), and A.R. Allen, ed., *The Social Gospel in Canada* (Ottawa, 1975).
23. Salem Bland, *The New Christianity* (Toronto, 1973), p. 17.
24. FCSO quoted in Thomas Socknat, "Witness Against War: Pacifism in Canada, 1900–1945" (Ph.D. thesis, McMaster University, 1981).
25. Ruth Brouwer, "The Methodist Church and the 'Woman Question', 1902–1914," unpublished paper, York University.
26. Donald L. Kirkey, "Building the City of God: The Founding of the SCM in Canada" (M.A. thesis, McMaster University, 1983).
27. Michiel Horn, *The League for Social Reconstruction: Intellectual Origins of the Democratic Left in Canada, 1930–42* (Toronto, 1980).
28. Susan Walsh, "Equality, Emancipation and a More Just World: Leading Women in the B.C. CCF" (M.A. thesis, Simon Fraser University, 1984), ch. 2.
29. Barbara Caine, "Beatrice Webb and the Woman Question," *History Workshop*, issue 14 (Autumn, 1982), pp. 39–42. See also Sally Alexander, "Introduction" to Maud Pember Reeves, *Round About A Pound A Week* (London, 1979).

## Chapter 2

1. Richard Stites, *The Women's Liberation Movement in Russia* (Princeton, 1978), p. 344. On the transformation of woman's status in Russia, see also Dorothy Atkinson, ed., *Women in Russia* (Stanford, 1977); Gregory Massell, *The Surrogate Proletariat: Moslem Women and Revolutionary Strategies in Soviet Central Asia, 1919–1929* (Princeton, 1974); Barbara Clements, "Working-Class and Peasant Women in the Russian Revolution," *Signs*, 8, 2 (Winter, 1982); Alix

Holt, "Marxism and Women's Oppression," in Tova Yedlin, ed., *Women in Eastern Europe and the Soviet Union* (New York, 1980).

2. On the pre-war WLLS, see Bacchi, *Liberation Deferred*, ch. 8; Linda Kealey, "No Special Protection, No Sympathy: Women's Activism in the Canadian Labour Revolt of 1919," unpublished paper, 1987.

3. *London Free Press*, September 18, 1924; Report of the Conference of Women's Labor Leagues, September 17–18, 1924, London, Ontario.

4. Although the WLLS were technically expelled because of a constitutional amendment, anti-communism was the most important force behind their expulsion. *Toronto Star*, November 4, 1927; *The Woman Worker*, December, 1927.

5. Public Archives of Canada (PAC), Finnish Organization of Canada (FOC) Collection, MG 28 V 46, Vol. 141, "Program and Constitution of the Canadian Federation of Women's Labor Leagues."

6. *The Worker*, May 1, 1922.

7. *Ibid.*, June 13, 1925.

8. *The Woman Worker*, July, 1926.

9. Taime Davis, interview with Joan Sangster and Karen Teeple, July 14, 1982.

10. Lil Himmelfarb, interview with Joan Sangster and Karen Teeple, January 30, 1983.

11. Sue Bruley, "Women in the Communist Party of Great Britain, 1921–1939" (Ph.D. thesis, London University, 1980).

12. University of Toronto Rare Books Room (U of T), Kenny Collection, Box 3, "Our Tasks Among Women," Central Executive Committee Report, Fifth Convention, 1925, p. 64.

13. *Imprecorr*, 4, 71 (October 6, 1924); *ibid.*, 6, 69 (October 26, 1926).

14. U of T, Kenny Collection, "Our Tasks Among Women," p. 63.

15. Reprinted in *The Worker*, November 15, 1925.

16. U of T, Kenny Collection, "Our Tasks Among Women," p. 64.

17. *The People's Cause*, April 26, 1925. On the Willard Chocolate case, see Margaret McCallum, "Keeping Women in Their Place: The Minimum Wage in Canada, 1910–25," *Labour/Le Travail*, 17 (Spring, 1986).

18. *Vapaus*, November 22, 1933. *Vapaus* charged that a "heavenly agent [i.e., a Lutheran minister] was hovering about unemployed maids," taking advantage of their economic desperation, by acting as an employment agent, but finding them low-paid jobs.

19. U of T, Kenny Collection, "Our Tasks Among Women," p. 64.

20. PAC, FOC Collection, "Program and Constitution of the Canadian Federation of Women's Labor Leagues."

21. *The Worker*, May 1, 1922.

22. Dorothy Smith, *Feminism and Marxism* (Vancouver, 1974), p. 34.

23. Becky Buhay and unknown party member quoted in Donald Avery, *Dangerous Foreigners* (Toronto, 1979), p. 127.

24. *The Worker*, May 1, 1922.

25. Custance was prevented from running because she could not fulfil the property qualification.

26. *The Worker*, February 1, 1923. See also M. Ann Capling, "The Communist

Party of Canada in Alberta, 1922–29'' (M.A. thesis, University of Calgary, 1983), ch. 2.

27. *The Worker*, November 7, 1925.

28. *Ibid.*, March 21, 1925.

29. On the left and birth control, see Angus McLaren, ''What Has This To Do With Working-Class Women?: Birth Control and the Canadian Left, 1900–1939,'' *Social History/Histoire sociale*, XIV (November, 1981). See also Angus McLaren and Arlene Tigar McLaren, *The Bedroom and the State: The Changing Practices and Politics of Contraception and Abortion in Canada, 1880–1980* (Toronto, 1987).

30. *The Worker*, June 20, 1925.

31. *The Woman Worker*, July, 1926.

32. *Ibid.*, September, 1927. The rationale that fewer births would produce ''better children'' remained popular in the inter-war period among feminist and medical proponents of birth control. See Linda Gordon, *Woman's Body, Woman's Right: A Social History of Birth Control in America* (New York, 1974), ch. 10.

33. *The Woman Worker*, December, 1927.

34. *Ibid.*, April, 1928.

35. *The Worker*, June 4, 1927.

36. *Ibid.*, May 2, 1925, and November 2, 1924.

37. *Ibid.*, March 21, 1925.

38. Buhay's letters were written during and after trips to Russia in the early 1930's and in the 1950's. See *ibid.*, August 30 and September 6, 1930, for a description of Buhay's first trip to the Soviet Union, and U of T, Kenny Collection, Box 41, for letters written during her stay in the 1950's.

39. Interview with Taime Davis. On pre-war Finnish socialist women and marriage, see Varpu Lindstrom-Best and Allen Seager, ''*Toveritar* and the Finnish Canadian Women's Movement, 1900–1930,'' unpublished paper, 1985, p. 9.

40. For example, see references to Communists' personal lives in Lita-Rose Betcherman, *The Little Band* (Ottawa, 1982), ch. XI. Allen Seager, ''Finnish Canadians and the Ontario Miners Movement,'' *Polyphony*, 3, 2 (Fall, 1981), also points out how unmarried women could be punished by people outside the Communist movement. After the Hollinger mine disaster of 1928, the company refused to compensate the Finnish widows because they had not been legally married.

41. *Robitnysia*, December 15, 1925.

42. *Vapaus*, March 9, 1933.

43. *The Woman Worker*, April, 1927.

44. *The Worker*, July 18, 1925.

45. *The Woman Worker*, October, 1927.

46. *Ibid.*, February, 1928.

47. *Ibid.*, October, 1927.

48. Interview with Taime Davis.

49. *The Worker*, August 22, 1925.

50. *The Voice of the Workingwoman* (a precursor to *Robitnysia*), January/February, 1922. One thousand dollars was donated to Soviet famine relief; three hundred and twenty-eight dollars went to the ULFTA in Saskatoon.

51. *Robitnysia*, April 1, 1924.
52. PAC, FOC Collection, MG 28 V 46, vol. 4, file 11, Minutes of the Ladysmith's Finnish Women's Branch of the Communist Party of Canada, December 17, 1925.
53. *Ibid.*, February 19, 1925, and May 28, 1925.
54. *The Woman Worker*, February, 1927.
55. Public Archives of Ontario (PAO), Communist Party of Canada Collection, Report of the 6th National Convention, May 31–June 7, 1929.
56. *The Woman Worker*, September, 1927.
57. *Robitnysia*, April 1, 1928.
58. *Ibid.*, May 15, 1928.
59. *Ibid.*, June 1, 1928.
60. *The Woman Worker*, March, 1928.
61. *Ibid.*
62. *Ibid.*, April, 1928.
63. *Ibid.*, December, 1927.
64. *Ibid.*, July, 1927.
65. Interview with Taime Davis.
66. PAO, CPC Collection, Report from Sudbury District Executive Committee of the WLLs to Executive Committee of the Federation of WLLs, February 5, 1930.
67. Interview with Taime Davis.

## Chapter 3

1. Stewart Smith quoted in Bryan Palmer, *Working Class Experience* (Toronto, 1983), p. 205.
2. *Robitnysia*, March, 1937. For more detailed discussion of the 1929 convention and its aftermath, see Penner, *The Canadian Left*, chs. 4, 5; Ian Angus, *Canadian Bolsheviks* (Montreal, 1981), ch. 12.
3. For detail on the free speech fights, see Betcherman, *The Little Band*.
4. *Ibid.*, p. 72.
5. Davis Interview.
6. For more detail on women in the U.S.S.R., see Alena Heitlinger, *Women and State Socialism* (London, 1979).
7. U of T, Kenny Collection, Box 1, Closed Letter to the CPC from the Executive Committee of the Communist International, April, 1929.
8. PAO, CPC Collection, RG 4 C-3, General Correspondence, "Memo to all Women's Departments of District Committee and Fractions of the Proletarian Mass Organizations," 1929.
9. *The Worker*, October 26, 1929.
10. This from a content analysis of *Robitnysia* done for me by Wally Lewyckyj.
11. *The Worker*, March 8, 1930.
12. PAO, CPC Collection, Women's Department, "Memo of Women's Department

to all District Bureau and Women's Departments," June 10, 1931; *The Worker*, August 2, 1931.

13. PAO, CPC Collection, Minutes of the District Committee of the Federation of Women's Labor Leagues, February 5, 1930.

14. PAO, CPC Collection, Women's Department, WLL Constitution.

15. *The Worker*, January 31, 1930.

16. PAO, CPC Collection, General Correspondence, Letter from "Neuman" to CPC, January 3, 1931; Neuman to Tim Buck, March 26, 1931.

17. *Vapaus*, March 7, 1933; *The Worker*, September 9, 1933.

18. *Vapaus*, March 3, 1931.

19. *Robitnysia*, June 1, 1931.

20. *Ibid.*, July 1, 1931.

21. *Ibid.*, August 15, 1931.

22. On the meat boycott, see *The Worker*, April 1, 1933; PAO, Abella Tapes, Interview of Elaine Mitchell with Shaska Mandel, September 27, 1969. On a similar boycott in New York City, see Dana Frank, "Housewives, Socialists, and the Politics of Food: The 1917 New York Cost-of-Living Protests," *Feminist Studies*, 11, 2 (Summer, 1985).

23. Bessie Kramer quoted in Ruth Frager, "Uncloaking Vested Interests: Class, Ethnicity and Gender in the Jewish Labour Movement of Toronto, 1900–1939" (Ph.D. thesis, York University, 1986).

24. Penny McRae, "Annie Buller and Becky Buhay: Working-Class Agitators," unpublished paper, Carleton University, 1979. For a sympathetic treatment of Buller, see Watson, *She Never Was Afraid.*

25. PAO, Multicultural History Society of Ontario, Annie Buller Papers, Becky Buhay to Annie Buller, October, 1919.

26. William Beeching and Phyllis Clarke, eds., *Yours in the Struggle: Reminiscences of Tim Buck* (Toronto, 1977), p. 153. See also Betcherman, *The Little Band*, p. 24.

27. Michiel Horn, "Keeping Canada Canadian: Anti-Communism and Canadianism in Toronto, 1928–29," *Canada: A Historical Magazine*, September, 1975.

28. PAO, CPC Collection, Worker Correspondence, Becky Buhay's Western Tour, October 1926–March 1926.

29. PAO, CPC Collection, reel 5B 0130. I am most grateful to an anonymous *Labour/Le Travail* reader for pointing out this quote.

30. A sympathetic and sketchy biography of Gauld is Vance, *Not By Gods But By People.*

31. Watson, *She Never Was Afraid*, pp. 81–82.

32. Information on Corbin from RCMP Archives, personal history file on Jeanne Corbin, December 30, 1925; Report re Jeanne Corbin, by Jas. Ritchie, Supt. to the Commissioner, RCMP, Ottawa, notes that "I would draw you to my secret letter of Oct. 28, 1926 in which I advised that ----- [a government official] was very emphatic in assuring me that this person would not be permitted to teach in any school in this province."

33. PAO, CPC Collection, Chase River WLL to A. Cook, February 6, 1930; Aino Kahti to A. Buck, March 27, 1930.

34. *Vapaus*, February 27, 1930.
35. PAO, CPC Collection, Women's Department "Circular," December 9, 1930.
36. See *The Worker*, April 5, August 30, September 6, 1930, for her detailed favourable impressions.
37. PAO, CPC Collection, Director of the Women's Department to Annie Whitfield, October 28, 1930; Buller to Buhay, October 28, 1930.
38. PAC, CPC Papers, MG 28 IV 4, Vol. 8, Tim Buck Correspondence, Tom Ewen to Tim Buck, September 2, 1930. Stewart Smith to Tim Buck, n.d. (Smith was also in the Soviet Union at this time).
39. PAO, CPC Collection, Proceedings of the 1931 Plenum, pp. 55–56.
40. *Workers Unity*, July 15, 1931.
41. *The Worker*, January 14, 1932, April 14, 1934.
42. For a detailed analysis of this change, see John Manley, "Communism and the Canadian Working Class during the Great Depression: The Workers Unity League, 1930–1936" (Ph.D. thesis, Dalhousie University, 1984), ch. 9.
43. Quoted in Warren Carragata, *Alberta Labour: A Heritage Untold* (Toronto, 1979), p. 102.
44. *Ibid.*, pp. 102–05. See also Alvin Finkel, "Obscure Origins: The Confused Early History of the Alberta CCF," in W. Brennan, ed., *Building the Co-operative Commonwealth* (Regina, 1985).
45. Interview with Kay Hladiy, October 16, 1980.
46. *The Worker*, April 21, 1934.
47. *Ibid.*, October 17, 1931.
48. Marjorie Cohen, "Women at Work in Canada During the Great Depression," unpublished paper, May, 1979. See also Roy Rosenzweig, "Organizing the Unemployed: The Early Years of the Great Depression," *Radical America*, 10, 4 (August, 1976).
49. Ian Radforth, " 'It Pays to Strike and Fight': The Workers Unity League in Ontario," unpublished paper, York University, 1980.
50. Craig Heron, "Working-Class Hamilton, 1895–1929" (Ph.D. thesis, Dalhousie University, 1980), p. 485.
51. *Workers Unity*, July 15, 1931.
52. PAO, Abella Tapes, Interview of Elaine Mitchell with Pearl Wedro, September 14–17, 1971.
53. Dorothy Livesay, *Left Hand, Right Hand* (Erin, 1977), pp. 123–24. Livesay and Jean Watts are discussed in Chapter 5.
54. Quoted in Catharine MacLeod, "Women in Production: The Toronto Dress-makers Strike of 1931," in Janice Acton *et al.*, eds., *Women at Work: Ontario, 1850–1930* (Toronto, 1974). See Ruth Frager, "The Undermining of Unity within the Jewish Labour Movement of Toronto, 1928–35," *Polyphony*, forthcoming.
55. Mercedes Steedman, "Skill and Gender in the Canadian Clothing Industry, 1890–1940," in Craig Heron and Robert Storey, eds., *On the Job: Confronting the Labour Process in Canada* (Kingston, 1986), p. 163.
56. PAO, MHSO Collection, ILGWU Papers, Langer to Dubinsky, June 27, 1933.
57. Evelyn Dumas, *The Bitter Thirties in Quebec* (Montreal, 1975), ch. 3.

58. Manley, "Communism and the Canadian Working Class"; Frager, "Uncloaking Vested Interests."
59. Frager, "Uncloaking Vested Interests."
60. Radforth, "It Pays to Strike and Fight," p. 69.
61. PAC, Department of Labour Records, Vol. 361, file 34–34.
62. On the labourist tradition, see Craig Heron, "Labourism and the Canadian Working Class," *Labour/Le Travailleur*, 13 (Spring, 1984); Alvin Finkel, "The Rise and Fall of the Labour Party in Alberta, 1917–42," *Labour/Le Travail*, 16 (Fall, 1985).
63. For Ontario, see James Naylor, "Class and Gender in Ontario's Labour Revolt, 1914–26," paper presented at the CHA, Windsor, 1988. Naylor also indicates some of the variations in the labourite movement within Ontario. For Alberta, see Pat Roome, "Amelia Turner and Calgary Labour Women, 1919–1935," in Linda Kealey and Joan Sangster, eds., *Beyond the Vote: Women and Canadian Politics* (Toronto, 1989). This section on labour and farm women is meant only to provide a brief background to the early CCF.
64. Finkel, "The Rise and Fall of the Labour Party in Alberta." See also A. Madiros, *William Irvine* (Toronto, 1979).
65. See Roome, " 'So sweet and modest.' "
66. Naylor, "Class and Gender in Ontario's Labour Revolt."
67. *The Labour Statesman*, September 7, 1924.
68. On Brigden, see Joan Sangster, "The Making of a Socialist-Feminist: The Early Career of Beatrice Brigden," *Atlantis* (Fall, 1987).
69. PAC, Agnes Macphail Papers, MG 27 III C5, Vol. 10, "The Unique Opportunity of North American Women."
70. Public Archives of Manitoba (PAM), United Farmers of Manitoba Collection, UFWM Minute Books, June 1, 1933.
71. See Gerald Caplan, *The Dilemma of Canadian Socialism* (Toronto, 1973).
72. Saskatchewan Archives Board (SAB), Interview of Georgina Taylor with Elsie Hart, 1980.
73. *Ibid*.
74. *The Worker*, June 21, 1930.

## Chapter 4

1. *The Regina Leader Post*, July 18, 1933, listed twenty-one women out of 131 delegates. This number may not have been an exact count.
2. The Regina Manifesto. Some critics from the left describe the CCF as "liberals in a hurry." See Gary Teeple, " 'Liberals in a Hurry': Socialism and the CCF/ NDP," in Gary Teeple, ed., *Capitalism and the National Question in Canada* (Toronto, 1972). Norman Penner is more sympathetic to the CCF, seeing the Regina Manifesto as "reformist," though "anti-capitalist." Penner, *The Canadian Left*. Many writers also presume that the CCF changed over time, either from a movement to a party, or from a socialist party to a more moderate social

democratic party. See Walter Young, *The Anatomy of a Party: the National CCF* (Toronto, 1969), for the first view, and Leo Zakuta, *A Protest Movement Becalmed* (Toronto, 1964), for the second view.

3. See Patricia Schultz, *The East York Workers Association* (Toronto, 1975).

4. Interview with Sophia Dixon, November 1, 1980.

5. Interview with Avis McCurdy, May 30, 1982.

6. Interview with Mildred Fahrni, December 3, 1980.

7. Interview with Nellie Peterson, November 21, 1980.

8. On the WIL, see G. Bussey and M. Tims, *Pioneers for Peace* (London, 1965); Tom Socknat, "Witness Against War: The Canadian Pacifist Movement" (Ph.D. thesis, McMaster University, 1980). The League's statement of purpose called for a far-reaching transformation of the social order: "We work for universal disarmament, the solution of conflicts by human solidarity . . . and the establishment of social, economic and political justice for all, without distinction of sex, race, class or creed." University of Toronto, Thomas Fisher Rare Books Room, Flora M. Denison Collection, *Pax Internationale*, 5, 6 (April, 1930).

9. U of T, Kenny Collection, Rose Henderson, "Woman and War," n.d.

10. Examples of Weaver's articles are found in *B.C. Federationist/CCF News*, June 22, 1946, July 29, 1948.

11. Interview with Eve Smith, July 19, 1981.

12. Interview with D.L., November 9, 1980.

13. *Ontario New Commonwealth (ONC)*, April 27, 1935.

14. Interview with Sophia Dixon.

15. *ONC*, August 10, 1935.

16. Interview with Grace MacInnis, July 17, 1981.

17. Interview with L.M., November 29, 1980. Other women also referred to social disapproval of wives who spent long periods away from home, travelling and organizing for the party.

18. SAB, Interview of Georgina Taylor with Elsie Gorius.

19. *ONC*, November 23, 1935.

20. Interview with Mildred Fahrni.

21. SAB, Gertrude Telford papers, Vol. xxxi, Typescript, "Memories," and Vol. xx, Education.

22. *ONC*, May 26, 1935. Some oral evidence also supports this contention. See SAB, Interview of Georgina Taylor with Gladys Strum, August 14, 1981.

23. *Maclean's*, September 15, 1949.

24. PAC, Agnes Macphail Papers, MG 27 III C4, Vol. 2, Jean Laing to A. Macphail, March 28, 1940.

25. SAB, Gertrude Telford papers, Vol. xxxii, G. Telford to C.M. Fines, June 12, 1944. Telford's italics.

26. *Ibid.*, Louise Lucas to Gertrude Telford, May 5, 1945.

27. *ONC*, May 18, 1935.

28. *Ibid.*, June 8, 1935.

29. *The New Era*, January 28, 1938.

30. *B.C. Federationist*, July 7, 1938.

31. *The New Era*, May 28, 1938.

32. SAB, CCF Papers, Minerva Cooper to 1938 Provincial Convention.

33. SAB, Interview of Georgina Taylor with Margaret Benson.

34. *Manitoba Commonwealth*, February 22, 1936.

35. *Ibid.*, February 22, 1935.

36. David Lewis, *The Good Fight* (Toronto, 1981), pp. 102–03. Lewis refers to the "unintended comedy" that lightened the otherwise serious atmosphere of the convention: Brigden's report on groups to discuss birth control (which, she said, were growing by leaps and bounds) was greeted with "chortles of laughter." Also, when an aging Rose Henderson spoke of the need for a United Front, and of her long fight in the mass struggle, one delegate answered, "you look like it," again to the amusement of the convention. Lewis cites these as "amusing" incidents that eased the tension on the convention floor. The latter remark about Henderson seems in bad taste. She *was* an older woman. Indeed, she may have been ill, for she died only six months later.

37. PAC, CCF Papers, MG 28 IC I, Vol. 10, Louise Lucas to the National CCF Convention, August 3, 1936.

38. *Ibid.*, Henderson to the 1936 Convention.

39. Rose Henderson quoted in John Manley, "Women and the Left in the 1930's: The Case of the Toronto CCF Women's Joint Committee," *Atlantis*, 5, 2 (Spring, 1980), p. 104.

40. University of Toronto Rare Books Room, WMC, Box 10B, Women's Joint Committee Minutes, March 3, 1936.

41. Manley, "Women and the Left," p. 112.

42. U of T Rare Books Room, WMC, Women's Joint Committee Minutes, May 12, 1936.

43. *Ibid.*

44. *Ibid.*, April 7, 1936.

45. *ONC*, March 21, 1936.

46. U of T Rare Books Room, WMC, Women's Joint Committee Minutes, June 9, 1936.

47. Manley, "Women and the Left." Historians of the Popular Front in the U.S. make this point well. See Mark Naison, *Communists in Harlem During the Depression* (Urbana, 1983).

48. U of T Rare Books Room, WMC, Women's Joint Committee Minutes, June 9, 1936.

49. *People's Weekly Labor Annual*, 1938.

50. Interview with Hilda Kristiansen.

51. Quoted in Irene Howard, "The Mothers' Council of Vancouver: Holding the Fort for the Unemployed, 1935–38," *B.C. Studies*, 69–70 (Spring–Summer, 1986), p. 270. Howard also notes that Colley said the men were "not foreigners," presumably an anti-immigrant remark intended to increase support for the strikers.

52. Mildred Fahrni quoted *ibid.*, p. 269.

53. Interview with Hilda Kristiansen.

54. *B.C. Federationist*, December 2, 1937.

55. Interview with Hilda Kristiansen.

56. Susan Wade, "Helena Gutteridge: Votes for Women and Trade Unions," in B.

Latham and C. Kess, eds., *In Her Own Right* (Victoria, 1980), p. 198.

57. Quoted in M. Hobbs, " 'Dead Horses and Muffled Voices': Protective Legislation, Education and the Minimum Wage for Women in Ontario'' (M.A. thesis, University of Toronto, 1985), p. 36.

58. UBC, Oral History Collection, Interview of M. Karnouk with Dorothy Steeves, 182–1.

59. Interview with Grace MacInnis.

60. Manley, "Women and the Left," p. 103.

61. Interview with D.L., November 9, 1980.

62. Public Archives of Manitoba, Beatrice Brigden Papers, Box 7, Clippings, *Labor Annual*, September, 1934.

## Chapter 5

1. Gerry Van Hauten, *Canada's Party of Socialism* (Toronto, 1982), p. 111. See also Jane Degras, ed., *Communist International Documents* (London, 1971), p. 335.

2. CPC Papers, Communist Party Headquarters (hereafter CPC Papers), 9th Plenum of the Central Committee, November, 1935, pp. 139, 146.

3. *Ibid.*

4. CPC Papers, 8th Dominion Convention, 1937, pp. 56–57.

5. *Ibid.*, p. 59.

6. H. Mathieson, "Why I have Changed my Mind About Women's Branches," *Discussion*, no. 4, October 8, 1935.

7. For more on women in the Stalin era, see Tova Yedlin, "Women in the U.S.S.R.: the Stalin Era," *Atlantis*, 3, 1 (Fall, 1977).

8. For more discussion of this, see Manley, "Women and the Left."

9. *Daily Clarion* (hereafter *DC*), January 9, 1936.

10. *The Worker*, August 24, 1935.

11. *The Worker*, September 7, 1936.

12. *DC*, November 24, 1936.

13. *Ibid.*, March 16, 1936.

14. *Ibid.*, December 30, 1936.

15. Erna Paris, *Jews: An Account of Their Experience in Canada* (Toronto, 1980), pp. 162–63.

16. Sharon Strom, "Challenging 'Women's Place': Feminism, the Left, and Industrial Unionism in the 1930's," *Feminist Studies*, 9, 2 (Summer, 1983); and " 'We're no Kitty Foyles': Organizing Office Workers for the Congress of Industrial Organizations, 1937–50," in Ruth Milkman, ed., *Women, Work and Protest* (Boston, 1985).

17. Harvey Levenstein, *Communism, Anticommunism and the CIO* (Westport, Conn., 1981), pp. 40, 71.

18. See also *DC*, January 25, 1936, and May 1, 1936, for references to a Toronto Domestics Union. The party's analysis of women's ghettoization into domestic

jobs is borne out by many contemporary studies. For example, in Manitoba one study concluded that the number of domestics had doubled from the late 1920's to 1937, but that wages were almost cut in half. See A. Oddson, *Employment of Women in Manitoba* (Economic Survey Board, Province of Manitoba, 1939), pp. 44–46.

19. U of T, Kenny Collection, Box 2, "We Are Organizing Domestic Workers," *Discussion*, 1937.
20. PAC, J.L. Cohen Papers, MG 30 A 94, Vol. 11, "Kaufman Strike."
21. Stuart Jamieson, *Times of Trouble: Labour Unrest and Industrial Conflict in Canada 1900–1966* (Ottawa, 1968), p. 250.
22. For more on this strike, see Bernard Rawlinson, "Cornwall: The Diary of a Strike," *New Frontier* (October, 1936), and John Manley, "Communism and the Canadian Working Class," pp. 115–16.
23. Ann Walters had been involved with organizing textile workers with the Workers Unity League since at least 1933. She was involved in the Welland union drive but it is difficult to assess how many Communists were on the inside. It is important to remember that Popular Front strategies compelled Communists to take a back seat in labour work, sometimes restraining their bids for leadership to show their commitment to coalition politics. See Levenstein, *Communism, Anticommunism and the CIO*, pp. 50–51.
24. See *Peterborough Examiner* interviews with strikers in June and July of 1937. Interestingly, one local politician implied it was the men's wages that were the crucial issue. On August 4 he wired Premier Hepburn claiming that a minimum wage for men in the industry would "end the strike." *Peterborough Examiner*, August 5, 1937.
25. PAC, Dept. of Labour Records, Strikes and Lockouts File, Vol. 388, clippings on Peterborough strike.
26. PAC, J.L. Cohen Papers, Elmer Hickey to Cohen, September 14, 1937.
27. CPC Papers, 8th Dominion Convention, p. 57.
28. *DC*, July 22, 1934.
29. *Ibid.*, August 27, September 25, 1935.
30. *Ibid.*, December 26, 1936.
31. CPC Papers, 8th Dominion Convention, p. 7.
32. *DC*, May 7, 1938.
33. *Ibid.*, March 5, 1938.
34. *Ibid.*, November 16, 1938.
35. *Ibid.*, August 29, 1936.
36. *Ibid.*, September 14, 1935.
37. *Ibid.*, November 21, 1936.
38. *Ibid.*, November 9, 1935.
39. *Ibid.*, December 3, 1935.
40. Interview of Mary Schronk with Anna Pashka, spring, 1980, from "Women of the Communist Party of Canada," unpublished paper, Toronto, 1980.
41. Interview with Elsie Gehl Beeching, November 12, 1980. For more on the Vancouver Mothers' Council, see Chapter 4.
42. Interview of Joan Sangster and Karen Teeple with Lil (Himmelfarb) Illomaki, January 30, 1983.

43. Interview of Joan Sangster and Karen Teeple with Louise Sandler, January 30, 1983.
44. *DC*, March 3, 1935.
45. *Ibid.*, February 27, 1935.
46. York University Archives, E.A. Beder Papers, Box 9, CLWF file.
47. Some CLWF leaders, such as Beder, were not happy with the name choice. Beder claimed it signified a moderate approach that was not decisively against imperialism and for socialism. See Beder Papers, *ibid.* On the effect of the Spanish Civil War on CCF pacifists, see Tom Socknat, "Witness Against War: The Canadian Pacifist Movement, 1920–45" (Ph.D. thesis, McMaster University, 1981), p. 334.
48. Interview with Nora Rodd, November 8, 1981.
49. U of T, Kenny Collection, Rose Henderson to First Canadian Congress against War and Fascism, October, 1934.
50. U of T, Kenny Collection, Elizabeth Morton to First Canadian Congress against War and Fascism.
51. U of T, Kenny Collection, Second National Congress against War and Fascism, December, 1935. See Manley, "Women and the Left," pp. 109–10.
52. PAC, FOC Collection, MG 28 V 46, Vol. 142, Proceedings of a Conference called by the Canadian Committee to Aid Spanish Democracy, October 23, 1937.
53. *DC*, April 22, July 23, 1937.
54. Paris, *Jews*, pp. 133–34.
55. After the criticisms of mass organizations during the Third Period, Popular Front strategies now reaffirmed comrades' work in ethnic groups and encouraged their integration into North American culture. Maurice Isserman discusses at greater length the desire of second-generation emigrant Communists to embrace the Popular Front in *Which Side Are You On?: The American Communist Party During the Second World War* (Middletown, Conn., 1982).
56. Paris, *Jews*, pp. 146–67.
57. Paul Lyons, *Philadelphia Communists 1936–1956* (Philadelphia, 1983), p. 73.
58. PAO, Abella Oral History Tapes, Interview of Elaine Mitchell with Shaska Mandel, September 27, 1969.
59. Interview of Mary Schronk with Anna Pashka.
60. *Ibid.*
61. Interview of Joan Sangster with Anna Pashka, September, 1980.
62. It was wrong, of course, to stereotype all Ukrainian emigrants as "peasants," but the label was used in the Party. See also Chapter 2, note 23.
63. Helen Potrebenko, *No Streets of Gold: A Social History of Ukrainians in Alberta* (Vancouver, 1977), p. 47. For a more optimistic view of Ukrainian women socialists in the "golden years" from 1910–20, see Maria Woroby, "Ukrainian Radicals and Women," *Cultural Correspondence, The Origins of Left Culture in the U.S.: 1880–1940* (Spring, 1978).
64. *Robitnysia*, March 15, 1936.
65. *Ibid.*, April 15, 1930.
66. On American Jews and the left, see Arthur Liebman, *Jews and the Left* (New

York, 1978); Paul Buhle, "Jews and American Communism: The Cultural Question," *Radical History Review*, no. 23 (Spring, 1980). On Jewish radicalism in an earlier period in Canada, see Roseline Usiskin, "Toward a Theoretical Reformulation of the Relationship Between Political Ideology, Social Class and Ethnicity: A Case Study of the Winnipeg Jewish Radical Community, 1905–20" (M.A. thesis, University of Winnipeg, 1978).

67. The ideas for this section draw heavily on Frager, "Uncloaking Vested Interests," and on Elizabeth Ewen, *Immigrant Women in the Land of Dollars* (New York, 1985); Charlotte Baum, Paula Hyman, and Sonya Michel, *The Jewish Woman in America* (New York, 1975), ch. 5. On life in Europe, see also Elizabeth Herzog and Mark Zborowski, *Life Is With the People: The Culture of the Shtetl* (New York. 1952).

68. Frager, "Uncloaking Vested Interests"; Ruth Frager, "Politicized Housewives in the Jewish Communist Movement of Toronto, 1923–33," in Kealey and Sangster, eds., *Beyond the Vote: Women and Canadian Politics* (Toronto, 1989).

69. See Carl Ross and K. Marianne Wargelin Brown, eds., *Women Who Dared: The History of Finnish American Women* (St. Paul, 1986); Lindstrom-Best and Seager, "*Toveritar* and the Finnish Canadian Women's Movement, 1900–1930."

70. Carl Ross, "Servant Girls: Community Leaders," in Ross and Brown, eds., *Women Who Dared*, p. 46.

71. Varpu Lindstrom-Best, " 'I Won't Be A Slave!': Finnish Domestics in Canada, 1911–30," in Jean Burnet, ed., *Looking Into My Sister's Eyes: An Exploration in Women's History* (Toronto, 1986). Importantly, some British literature suggests that married women who worked outside the home were more likely to become involved in trade union or party work. For example, see Sue Bruley, "Women in the Communist Party of Great Britain, 1921–39" (Ph.D. thesis, London University, 1980).

72. J. Donald Wilson, "Matti Kurikka and the Settlement of Sointula, B.C., 1901–1905," *Finnish Americana*, III (1980).

73. K. Marianne Wargelin Brown, "A Closer Look at Finnish American Women's Issues," in Ross and Brown, eds., *Women Who Dared*.

74. Interview with Mickey Murray, October 9, 1980.

75. Interview with Josephine Gehl, November 10, 1980.

76. Interview with Claire Culhane, December 4, 1980.

77. PAO, Abella Tapes, Interview of Elaine Mitchell with Helen Paulin, September 21, 1972.

78. Interview with S.S., 1983.

79. U of T, Kenny Collection, Box 41, Becky Buhay material.

80. The comparison to an extended family was made by Marge Frantz and others: "The Second Red Scare and Women in the Communist Party," session at Berkshire Conference on Women's History, June 21, 1987. See also note 92 below for an example of the judgemental aspect of the party.

81. Elsa Dixler, "The Woman Question: Women and the American Communist Party, 1929–41" (Ph.D. thesis, Yale University, 1974), p. 194.

82. Interview with Elsie Gehl Beeching.

83. See Naison, *Communists in Harlem during the Depression*, for a useful discussion of the unique Popular Front relationship between free-floating party sympathizers and party members.

84. University of Manitoba Archives, Dorothy Livesay Collection, Box 31, autobiographical notes.

85. Livesay, *Left Hand, Right Hand*, pp. 48, 74.

86. Toby Ryan, *Stage Left: Canadian Theatre in the Thirties* (Toronto, 1981), p. 33.

87. Interview with William Lawson, September 14, 1986.

88. *New Frontier*, November, 1936.

89. Interview with William Lawson.

90. Livesay, *Left Hand, Right Hand*, p. 123.

91. Peggy Dennis, "A Response," *Feminist Studies*, 5, 3 (Fall, 1975).

92. Two interviewees referred to a party official (in both cases Annie Buller) questioning members about their personal lives in order to protect the party's image. In one case, a female comrade was urged to stay in a difficult marriage because her husband was a "bright comrade." At its worst, the party would tolerate outright hypocrisy in order to keep up public appearances. Party leader Tim Buck for many years lived and travelled abroad with his long-time common-law companion. His wife, however, presided beside him at official functions. She never refers to this in interviews about her party involvement, indicating she grew to accept the arrangement, though she has mentioned the "loneliness" of being a political wife. Though some may reject this as party gossip, I think it reveals not only the lengths to which the Popular Front was taken, but significantly, that women were more often hurt or ill-considered in Communists' attitudes toward personal relationships.

93. *DC*, October 3, 12, 1936.

94. *New Frontier*, November, 1936.

95. Dixler, "The Woman Question," p. 143, and see especially ch. 2.

96. Lyons, *Philadelphia Communists*, pp. 92, 94.

97. Margaret Gould, *I Visit the Soviets* (Toronto, 1937), p. 123; *New Frontier*, July, 1936.

98. On the antipathy of the American Communist Party to lesbianism, see R. Baxandall, ed., *Words On Fire: The Life and Writing of Elizabeth Gurley Flynn* (1987). While some American CP members claimed that homosexuals were open to blackmail and therefore "security risks," homophobia was also undoubtedly a reason for this antipathy to homosexual relationships.

99. James Weinstein, *Ambiguous Legacy: The Left in American Politics* (New York, 1975), p. 163.

100. *DC*, October 3, 1936.

101. *Ibid.*, July 1, 1936.

102. *Ibid.*, October 3, 1936.

103. Merrily Weisbord, *The Strangest Dream* (Toronto, 1983), p. 216.

104. *DC*, November 12, 1936.

105. *Ibid.*, August 22, 29, 1936.

# Chapter 6

1. PAO, Abella Oral History Collection, Interview of Elaine Mitchell with Helen Paulin, September 21, 1972.
2. Quote from the party's official history by Gerry Van Hauten, *Canada's Party of Socialism* (Toronto, 1982), p. 133. See also Penner, *The Canadian Left*, p. 99.
3. Quoted in Marvin Gandall, "Do We Need a Security Service?" *Canadian Dimension*, vol. 17, no. 6 (December, 1983), p. 7.
4. Interview with Bill and Elsie Beeching, November 12, 1980.
5. U of T, Kenny Collection, Box 41, Becky Buhay material.
6. PAC, CPC Collection, MG 28 IV 4, Vol. 39, Annie Buller's prison notebooks, 1942. Draft of a letter to William Lyon Mackenzie King.
7. Letter of Norman Penner to author, June 15, 1987. The one book on the Communist internees, Kathleen and William Repka, eds., *Dangerous Patriots* (Vancouver, 1982), makes no mention of the women jailed under the DOC Act, or of Gladys MacDonald, who was interned.
8. SAB, Violet MacNaughton Papers, A-1, file E-40.
9. Mary Prokop in K. and W. Repka, eds., *Dangerous Patriots*, p. 98. The supportive wives' committee described by Prokop is different from the committee described by Peggy Dennis in her account of the American wives' committee to aid Smith Act victims. In Peggy Dennis, *Autobiography of an American Communist* (Berkeley, 1977), Dennis claims that she drew little personal solace from the committee (p. 215). This may have had something to do with her prominent position in the party because other testimony contradicts her perceptions. For example, Deborah Gerson, "Legacy of Courage, Legacy of Pain: The Families' Committee Struggle Against the Smith Act," paper presented at the Berkshire Conference, June, 1987.
10. M. Prokop in *Dangerous Patriots*, p. 101.
11. Anne Lenihan in *Dangerous Patriots*, p. 38.
12. In the 1940 municipal election Joe Forkin had 3,012 votes and Rose Penner 3,200. In the April, 1941, provincial election Bill Kardash won with 5,889 votes. In the 1941 municipal election Joe Forkin took over Jacob Penner's aldermanic seat with 3,632 votes. *Dangerous Patriots*, pp. 107-10.
13. *Dangerous Patriots*, pp. 108-09. See also *The Tribune*, April 12, 1941.
14. Werner Cohn, "The Persecution of the Japanese Canadians and the Political Left in British Columbia, December 1941–March 1942," *B.C. Studies*, no. 68 (Winter, 1985–86).
15. Weisbord, *The Strangest Dream*, p. 125.
16. *The Tribune*, September 18, 1943.
17. UBC Archives, CCL Convention Proceedings, 1944.
18. *The Pacific Tribune*, February 3, 1945, pointed to one local of the International Woodworkers of America that won equal pay.
19. *UE News*, May 2, 1942.
20. Interview with C.S. Jackson, August 17, 1985, and a telephone conversation with C.S. Jackson, February, 1987. For a more critical view of the UE's failure

to address gender inequality, see Stan Gray, "Sharing the Shop Floor," *Canadian Dimension*, 18, 3 (June, 1984).

21. For analysis of this in the U.S., see Ruth Milkman, *Gender at Work: The Dynamics of Job Segregation by Sex during World War II* (Urbana, 1987). The same company opposition held in Canada. See UE Local 524 Archives, Brief of Genelco, Peterborough, to Ontario Regional War Labour Board, July 19, 1943. This is a twelve-page document by the company (General Electric) explaining why wage differentials should remain.

22. This was true, of course, for most unions. For an example drawn from U.S. history, see Nancy Gabin, "Women Workers and the UAW in the Post World War II Period," *Labor History*, 21, 1 (Winter, 1979/80).

23. U of T, Kenny Collection, Becky Buhay, "Women in the Struggle for Peace and Socialism."

24. United Fisherman and Allied Workers Union Auxiliary Tapes, held by Sue Radosovic, interview with Jean Pritchett, n.d.

25. Interview with Claire Culhane, December 2, 1980.

26. *National Affairs Monthly*, January, 1945.

27. Patricia V. Schultz, "Day Care in Canada, 1850–1962," in Kathleen Ross, ed., *Good Day Care* (Toronto, 1978).

28. Susan Prentice, "The Daycare Movement in Toronto: 1946–51," unpublished paper, York University, May, 1988.

29. *Ibid.*

30. *Saskatoon Star Phoenix*, March 21, 1940.

31. In the 1930's some local constituencies ignored the CCF's instructions not to co-operate with the CPC. See Peter Sinclair, "The Saskatchewan CCF and the CP," *Saskatchewan History*, XXVI, 1 (Winter, 1973). Even in 1940, Nielsen publicly maintained she was a social democrat. See SAB, CCF Papers, Nielsen to Toby Nollett, February 1, 1940. More recently, however, one of Nielsen's daughters maintains that her mother may have already decided in favour of the LPP. Personal correspondence, Christine Nielsen to author, January 26, 1984.

32. SAB, Violet McNaughton Papers, file D-53, Nielsen to MacNaughton, n.d. (Nielsen wrote under the pen name of Judy O'Grady.)

33. PAC, Nicholson Papers, MG 27 III C 26, Vol. 1, Dorise Nielsen to A.M. Nicholson, September 24, 1975.

34. In Manitoba, William Kardash was elected to the provincial legislature in 1942. Fred Rose had been elected to Parliament from Montreal in 1943. Joe Salsberg and A.A. MacLeod were elected to the Ontario legislature in 1943.

35. Helen Anderson was of Finnish origin and had worked as a domestic in B.C. before moving to Ontario, where her husband's involvement in trade union politics led them from northern Ontario to Hamilton's steel mills. Anderson was widowed by the war and by 1947 she was remarried to Vince Coulson. She ran in 1947 as Helen Anderson Coulson.

36. Prentice, "The Daycare Movement in Toronto," pp. 29–30.

37. Her opposition on the board tried to accuse her of conflict of interest on one issue because her husband was a teacher. Some CCFers on the board did try to distance themselves from this extreme red-baiting. *Ibid.*, pp. 36–37.

38. *Winnipeg Free Press*, October 27, 1947.
39. Interview with Josephine Gehl, November 11, 1980.
40. For example, Elizabeth Wilson, an LPP school trustee in Burnaby, protested a resolution that urged women teachers to resign on marriage.
41. Effie Jones quoted in Municipal History Society of Vancouver, *Your Worship, Members of Council: Highlights from Reform Movements in the Lower Mainland* (Vancouver, 1980), p. 15.
42. Dorise Nielsen, *New Worlds for Women* (Toronto, 1944), p. 110.
43. U of T, Kenny Collection, Becky Buhay, "Women in the Struggle for Peace and Socialism."
44. PAC, CPC Collection, MG IV 4, Vols. 1 and 2. Lectures given reveal a paucity of material on the woman question. Yet Buhay claimed at the 1947 school that 40 per cent of students at party schools were women. One set of attendance records for the national school does not show such a high percentage in that year.
45. *Pacific Tribune*, December 17, 1948.
46. U of T, Kenny Collection, Vol. 2, Proceedings of the 1948 Convention.
47. Interview with Claire Culhane, December 2, 1980.
48. *Ibid.*
49. U of T, Kenny Collection, Box 9, Discussion of Panel on Work Among Women, n.d. This appears to be an educational forum or a talk at a party school.
50. U of T, Kenny Collection, Box 9, National Executive Committee Meeting of the LPP, August 17, 1945.
51. Sherna Gluck, "Socialist Feminism Between the Two Wars: Insights from Oral History," in Lois Scharf and Jane Jenson, eds., *Decades of Discontent: The Women's Movement, 1920–40* (Boston, 1987).
52. Mary Inman quoted *ibid.*
53. *DC*, December 28, 1938.
54. Dixler, "The Woman Question," p. 135.
55. *Ibid.*, p. 132.
56. For examples of the recent debate, see Bonnie Fox, ed., *Hidden in the Household* (Toronto, 1980). A summary of the Marxist debate since the 1960's is Eva Kaluzynska, "Wiping the Floor with Theory: A Survey of Writings on Housework," *Feminist Review*, 6 (1980).
57. The initial reaction to Inman's newspaper articles was not so hostile. Indeed, Inman claims she received many positive letters from women readers. See Gluck, "Socialist Feminism Between the Two Wars," p. 293.
58. A. Landy, *Marxism and the Woman Question* (Toronto, 1943), p. 7.
59. *Ibid.*, p. 61.
60. *Ibid.*, p. 46.
61. *Ibid.*, p. 37.
62. *Canadian Tribune*, June 10, 1947.
63. Letter of Norman Penner to Joan Sangster, June 15, 1987.
64. Bryan Palmer, *Working-Class Experience* (Toronto, 1983).
65. Letter of Marjorie Ferguson to Joan Sangster, November 3, 1983.
66. Interview with Mona Morgan, July 20, 1981.

67. Marjorie Penn Lasky, " 'Where I was a person': The Ladies Auxiliary in the 1934 Minneapolis Teamsters' Strikes," in Ruth Milkman, ed., *Women, Work and Protest* (Boston, 1985).

68. Penner, *The Canadian Left*, p. 105.

69. PAC, CPC Collection, Vol. 9, All Canadian Conference of Women, March 9, 10, 1951.

70. *Pacific Tribune*, May 6, 1949.

71. U of T, Kenny Collection, Box 53, *Woman's Voice*, 2, 4 (September, 1950).

72. Interview with Lillian Marcus, September 3, 1980.

73. Interview with Elsie Beeching, November 12, 1980.

74. Amy Swerdlo, "Ladies Day at the Capital: Women Strike for Peace Versus the HUAC," *Feminist Studies*, 8, 3 (Fall, 1982), p. 514.

## Chapter 7

1. Interview with Margaret Mann, November 27, 1983. In 1942 the York South electorate chose a CCFer over the leader of the opposition; in 1943, the Ontario CCF became the official opposition; and in 1944, the Saskatchewan CCF swept to power. These victories were tempered by the 1945 disaster in Ontario, the defeat of some members in B.C., and the inability of the Alberta and Manitoba parties to make major breakthroughs. On the CCF in this period, see Gerald Caplan, *The Dilemma of Canadian Socialism: The CCF in Ontario* (Toronto, 1973); Jack Granatstein, "The York South By-Election of February 9, 1942: A Turning Point in Canadian Politics," *Canadian Historical Review*, XLVIII, 2 (June, 1967); Walter Young, *Anatomy of a Party: The National CCF* (Toronto, 1969), ch. 5; S.M. Lipset, *Agrarian Socialism* (Toronto, 1949), ch. 6.

2. Ruth Roach Pierson, *"They're Still Women After All": The Second World War and Canadian Womanhood* (Toronto, 1986).

3. *Manitoba Commonwealth*, March 28, 1941.

4. *The People's Weekly*, September 1, 1945.

5. *B.C. Federationist*, May 31, 1945.

6. UBC Archives, Angus MacInnis Collection, Box 24, Legislative Scrapbooks, Budget Debate, 1942, pp. 4, 5.

7. *Saskatchewan Commonwealth* (hereafter *Sask Comm*), December 14, 1943.

8. *Sask Comm*, November 1, 1943.

9. *Sask Comm*, August 16, 1943.

10. *Sask Comm*, October 14, 1942.

11. In an interesting comment made after the 1948 election, Agnes Macphail articulated this assumption that a home and a career (especially in politics) were incompatible. "I have a soft spot for working mothers, and the fight for nurseries . . . I would have liked to have children of my own, but you can't be in politics at the same time." Queen's University Archives, George Grube Collection, Box 40, Scrapbooks, *Globe and Mail*, June 8, 1948.

12. *ONC*, January 24, 1943; *B.C. Federationist*, January 21, 1943.

13. *Sask Comm*, May 12, 1943.
14. U of T Rare Books Room, Woodsworth Memorial Collection (WMC), Box 10A, Radio Script.
15. *Sask Comm*, May 31, 1944.
16. PAC, CCF Collection, MG 28 IV I, Vol. 50, pamphlet entitled ''Women Protect Your Home''; Bacchi, *Liberation Deferred*, illustration entitled ''Canada Needs a Clean-Up Week,'' p. 31.
17. *Canadian Forum*, August, 1944.
18. *ONC*, April 25, 1946.
19. *B.C. Federationist*, August 1, 1946.
20. PAC, CCF Collection, Vol. 198, Research Report, ''Women'' file. In 1942 and 1944 the one or two resolutions on women's equality presented to the national convention were dealt with rather hastily; one was rejected because ''such matters are subsumed under the [Regina] Manifesto.'' (*Ibid.*, Vol. 10, 1944 Convention.)
21. *Ibid.*, Ingle to Geneva Misener, March 17, 1948.
22. *Ibid.*, Research Report.
23. *Ibid.*, Grace MacInnis to L. Ingle, January 5, 1947 (her emphasis).
24. *Ibid.*
25. *Ibid.*
26. PAC, CCF Collection, Vol. 60, Nellie Peterson to Lorne Ingle, April 8, 1950. In 1952, a letter from Olive Valleau to Lorne Ingle confirmed that ''the National Women's Committee is no longer functioning.'' Vol. 121, O. Valleau to L. Ingle, November 4, 1952.
27. Interview with Margot Thompson, October 6, 1981.
28. Eileen Sufrin, *The Eaton Drive* (Don Mills, 1982), p. 129. See also Wayne Roberts, ed., *Where Angels Fear to Tread: Eileen Tallman and the Labour Movement* (Hamilton, 1981).
29. Interview with Margot Thompson.
30. *Ibid.*
31. Interview with Barbara Cass-Beggs, June 4, 1981.
32. For examples, see UBC Archives, Shepard Collection, Ladies Auxiliary Book, Ernie Winch to the South Westminster Ladies Auxiliary, May 16, 1945; *ibid.*, MacInnis Collection, Box 61, Saanich Women's Council Minute Book, September 22, October 6, 1942.
33. Interview with Jean Robinson, October 9, 1980. A slightly different account of this conflict appears in a letter to Marjorie Mann, from Mrs. Tait (PAC, Marjorie Mann Papers, MG 32, G 12, Vol. 1, November 2, 1948). Mrs. Tait says that she inherited the leadership of the Port Arthur women's organization from a good organizer, but one who ''wanted a separate bank account – a separate organization in all effect.'' Tait claimed that she had to therefore tread a fine line between ''Two ways . . . those who promote the financial gain aspect and those who wish to explore the reasons we are in the CCF.''
34. Interview with Nellie Peterson, November 21, 1980.
35. Beatrice Trew to Librarian, Legislative Library, Regina, n.d. Copy in possession of Georgina Taylor.
36. SAB, Interview of Georgina Taylor with Gladys Strum, August, 1981. Another

CCF leader in Saskatchewan, Carlyle King, charges in Donald Kerr, ed., *Western Canadian Politics: The Radical Tradition* (Edmonton, 1981), p. 39, that Strum lacked administrative abilities. In fact, he says he only accepted election to the vice-presidency of the party in 1944 to ''help'' Strum (who defeated him for the presidency). As Georgina Taylor points out, King's views seem somewhat exaggerated and may be coloured by his defeat for party president in 1944.

37. SAB, CCF Papers, Strum to Georgina Mathers, March 24, 1941.

38. *Ibid.*, Strum to CCF Executive, October 31, 1941.

39. Interview with Marjorie Mann, April, 1980.

40. Interview with Barbara Cass-Beggs.

41. *Ibid.*

42. Nancy Zaseybida, quoted in Myrna Kostash, *All of Baba's Children* (Edmonton, 1977), p. 256.

43. Interview with Margaret Mann, November 27, 1983.

44. Interview with Nellie Peterson.

45. UBC Archives, MacInnis Collection, Box 51, Biographical Material.

46. *CCF News*, December 16, 1948 (name changed from *B.C. Federationist*).

47. *B.C. Federationist*, July 25, 1940.

48. *CCF News*, May 30, 1949.

49. Interview with Jessie Mendels, December 8, 1980. The women's committee was revived and took on new organizing tasks in the early 1960's.

50. On MacInnis and Steeves, see Susan Walsh ''The Peacock and the Guinea Hen: Political Profiles of Dorothy Gretchen Steeves and Grace MacInnis,'' in Alison Prentice and Susan Trofimenkoff, eds., *The Neglected Majority*, Vol. 2 (Toronto, 1985).

51. A similar problem did exist in Ontario and B.C., with Toronto and Vancouver dominating those provincial committees. However, it was particularly important in Manitoba and Alberta to have rural representation, and the problem of involving rural women seemed especially acute here in comparison to Saskatchewan, where the CCF had a stronger base in the farm community.

52. *People's Weekly*, February 26, 1949.

53. Glenbow Archives, CCF Papers, Box 23, Edmonton CCF Women's Club Minutes, September 13, 1948.

54. *Sask Comm*, August 16, 1948. The party had never entertained complete accord on the benefits of separate women's organizations, or of assured female representation in the leadership (see Chapter 4). At the 1948 convention an attempt was made to ensure one female representative on Provincial Council from two member constituencies. It was defeated, just as the 1934 attempt to give women more voting rights at conventions was defeated, by the provincial leadership.

55. Georgina Taylor, ''Saskatchewan Cooperative Commonwealth Women: Reconciling Politics with Women's Work, 1932–67,'' paper presented at the Canadian Historical Association, June, 1988.

56. SAB, Gertrude Telford Papers, xxxii, copy of letter, ''Dear Worker,'' and ''Notes on Resolutions,'' and iii, Study Outline, ''Legislation Affecting the Home.''

57. SAB, CCF Papers, 13th Provincial Convention, July 21–23, 1948.

58. Interview with Margaret Mann. Similarly, in a letter to Marjorie Mann, in

Ontario, Saskatchewan's Attorney General, J.W. Corman, justified the bill, arguing that "equality . . . would take away many privileges women already possess . . . we need legislation for specific evils, like equal pay." PAC, Marjorie Mann Papers, Vol. 1, J.W. Corman to M. Mann, September 20, 1947.

59. PAC, Marjorie Mann Papers, Vol. 1, B. Cass-Beggs to M. Mann, July 12, 1947.
60. U of T Rare Books Room, WMC, Box 1, Report of Riley to the Provincial Executive, October 2, 1942.
61. Queen's University, Ontario CCF papers, William Neff Papers, Box 1, Women's Committee Report, June, 1944.
62. Interview with Alice Katool, May 31, 1981.
63. Interview with Avis McCurdy, May 30, 1982.
64. U of T Rare Books Room, WMC, Box 2, Avis McCurdy to Ontario Provincial Council, November 25, 1945.
65. The subcommittee included Barbara Cass-Beggs, Edith Fowke, Margot Thompson, and others. It was largely the same group that critiqued Ingle's brief.
66. PAC, CCF Collection, Vol. 60, Findings of Discussion Groups from Sept. 1948, by Peggy Stewart. On occasion, CCF women were also willing to co-operate with women of other political persuasions, in such events as the Women's Citizenship Dinner in Toronto, a non-partisan forum that focused on the need for more women in public life. This co-operation was not extended to women in the Communist Party.
67. Dean Beeby, "Women in the Ontario CCF, 1940–1950," Ontario History, LXXIV, 4 (December, 1982).
68. PAC, Marjorie Mann Papers, Vol. 1, Letter to Committee Members, November 10, 1948.
69. Ibid., M. Mann to Morden Lazarus, October 14, 1949.
70. U of T Rare Books Room, WMC, Box 2, Provincial Council Minutes, April 12, 1947.
71. PAC, Marjorie Mann Papers, Letter to Saskatchewan CCF Women, n.d., probably 1947, and Vol. 1, M. Mann to Margaret, October 29, 1950.
72. PAC, CCF Papers, Vol. 60, M. Mann to David Lewis, February 16, 1948.
73. Ibid.
74. Ontario CCF News, March 25, 1948.
75. PAC, Marjorie Mann Papers, Vol. 1, Mary Morrison to Marjorie Mann, July 16, 1947.
76. Ibid., Marion Bryden to Marjorie Mann, April 24, 1951, and Mann to Bryden, May 3, 1951.
77. Ibid., Women's Conference Report, 1951, and M. Mann to Margaret, October 29, 1950.
78. Ibid., M. Mann to Margaret, October 29, 1950.
79. Ibid., M. Mann to B. Cass-Beggs, June 27, 1950, and Peggy Stewart to M. Mann, February 16, 1951.
80. Palmer, Working-Class Experience, p. 274.
81. Beeby, "Women in the Ontario CCF," p. 279.
82. Birmingham Feminist History Group, "Feminism as Femininity in the 1950's," Feminist Review, 3 (1979), p. 50.

## Chapter 8

1. PAC, CCF Papers, MG 28 IV I, Vol. 460, "Report of the Women's Director."

2. Some new women's organizations of the 1960's did include many women from the Old Left. The Voice of Women, for example, included many women who had been active in the thirties and forties in the social democratic or Communist left: both Beatrice Brigden and Jean Watts Lawson, for instance, became active members. In some cases, too, younger radicals in the sixties and seventies came from Old Left families. Nonetheless, very little was written and discussed about the role of women in the Old Left.

3. PAO, Abella Tapes, Interview of Helen Paulin with Elaine Mitchell, September 21, 1972.

4. Although the Party was concerned with anti-Semitism and the Communist press often publicly supported Third World liberation struggles or the American civil rights movement, the CPC was not significantly preoccupied with other anti-racist struggles in Canada, e.g., organizing native peoples.

5. Interview with S.S., November, 1983.

6. Rowbotham, *Beyond the Fragments*, p. 109.

7. *Ibid.*, p. 96.

8. Walsh, "The Peacock and the Guinea Hen," p. 153.

9. B.C. Provincial Archives, Jamieson Papers, 311, file 9.

10. SAB, Interview of Georgina Taylor with Gladys Strum, 1981.

11. Howard, "The Mothers' Council of Vancouver."

12. See the Spring, 1987, issue of *International Labor and Working Class History* for a discussion of language and labour history, especially Christine Stansell's "Reply."

13. See Michèle Barrett and Mary McIntosh, "The Family Wage: Some Problems for Socialists and Feminists," *Capital and Class*, 9, 12 (Summer, 1980).

14. Georgina Taylor, "Saskatchewan Cooperative Commonwealth Women: Reconciling Politics with Women's Work, 1932–1967." At the same time, however, rural women in other areas of Canada did not play the same role in the CCF, so it would be premature to draw the conclusion that the only factor shaping women's political participation was their relationship to economic production. For urban as well as rural women, there were other factors as well.

15. Georgina Taylor, "Equals and Partners?: An Examination of How Saskatchewan Women Reconciled Their Political Activities for the CCF with Traditional Roles for Women" (M.A. thesis, University of Saskatoon, 1983). On farm women, see Seena Kohl, *Working Together: Women and Family in Southwestern Saskatchewan* (Toronto, 1976).

16. Barbara Melosh, " 'Peace in Demand': Anti-War Drama in the 1930's," *History Workshop* (1986), p. 85.

17. Barbara Taylor, *Eve and the New Jerusalem* (London, 1983), p. 285.

# Bibliography

## Note on Sources

When I began this work, the Communist Party of Canada kindly let me look at some of its archives, then housed at its headquarters on Cecil Street in Toronto. Since that time, these papers have been placed in the Public Archives of Canada, and I was allowed access to these in 1984. Thus, my footnotes include references both to information taken from the Communist Party of Canada Headquarters and to material from the Communist Party of Canada Papers at the Public Archives of Canada (PAC). These sources are now merged into one at the Public Archives.

## Primary Sources

I.  *Archival Collections*

Archives Board of Saskatchewan
    Violet M. MacNaughton Papers
    Gertrude Telford Papers
    Georgina Taylor Oral History Collection
    Saskatchewan CCF/NDP Collection
    United Farmers of Canada (Saskatchewan Section) Collection
Communist Party of Canada Headquarters Archives
Glenbow Foundation
    Alberta CCF/NDP Papers
    Walter Smith Papers
Hamilton Public Library, Special Collections
    ILP Records
    Municipal Election Scrapbooks
Multicultural History Society of Ontario

Annie Buller Papers
International Ladies Garment Workers Union Papers
Queen's University Archives
George Grube Papers
Ontario CCF/NDP Papers
William Neff Papers
Provincial Archives of Alberta
United Farm Women of Alberta Papers (Winnifred Ross Papers)
Provincial Archives of British Columbia
Laura Jamieson Papers
Public Archives of Canada
J.L. Cohen Papers
Communist Party of Canada Papers
Department of Labour Records
William Lyon Mackenzie King Papers
Louise Lucas Papers
Grace MacInnis Papers
Agnes Macphail Papers
Marjorie Mann Papers
Libbie and Frank Park Papers
Public Archives of Manitoba
John Bracken Papers
Beatrice Brigden Papers
CCF/NDP Papers
United Farmers of Manitoba Papers
Public Archives of Ontario
Irving Abella Oral History Collection
Communist Party of Canada Collection
Department of Labour Records
Simon Fraser University Archives
Sara Diamond Oral History Collection
Toronto City Archives
Clipping files
University of British Columbia Archives
William Bennett Memorial Collection
UBC Oral History Collection
Angus MacInnis Collection
Shepard Papers
Eve G. Smith Papers
Dorothy Steeves Papers
University of Manitoba Archives
Dorothy Livesay Papers

University of Toronto, Thomas Fisher Rare Books Room
  Flora MacDonald Denison Collection
  Robert Kenny Collection
  Woodsworth Memorial Collection
Vancouver City Archives
  Clipping files
Winnipeg School Board Division Number 1
  Winnipeg School Board Minutes
York University Archives
  E.A. Beder Papers


II.  *Government Documents*

Canada.  Department of Labour.  *Labour Gazette.*
Canada.  Department of Labour.  *Labour Organization in Canada.*
Province of Manitoba.  Economic Survey Board.  A. Oddson.
  *The Employment of Women in Manitoba.* Winnipeg: 1937. Public
  Archives of Canada. Department of Labour Records.


III.  *Newspapers, Magazines, and Journals*

*Alberta Labor News*
*B.C. Federationist*, later *B.C. CCF News*
*Canadian Congress Journal*
*Canadian Forum*
*Canadian Trade Unionist*
*The Communist*
*The Communist International*
*Frontiers*
*Imprecorr*
*The Industrial Banner*
*Labour Leader*
*The Labor News*
*The Labor Statesman*
*Marxist Review*
*National Affairs*, later *National Affairs Monthly*
*New Frontier*
*Ontario New Commonwealth*, later *CCF News*
*Pacific Tribune*
*People's Cause*
*People's Weekly*
*Robitnysia*
*Saskatchewan Commonwealth*

*Vapaus*
*The Weekly News*, later *The Manitoba Commonwealth*
*The Western Clarion*
*The Woman Worker*
*The Worker*, later *The Daily Clarion* and *The Canadian Tribune*

IV. *Interviews*

| | |
|---|---|
| Hanna Anderson | October 8, 1980 |
| Kate Bader | December 7, 1980 |
| Elsie and William Beeching | November 12, 1980 |
| Lillian Bochner | September 4, 1980 |
| Ruth Bulloch | July 18, 1981 |
| Barbara Cass-Beggs | June 4, 1981 |
| Claire Culhane | December 4, 1980 |
| Taime Davis | July 14, 1982 |
| Sophia Dixon | November 1, 1980 |
| Mildred Fahrni | December 3, 1980 |
| Gordon and Marion Fines | October 21, 1980 |
| Edith Fowke | December 20, 1983 |
| Josephine Gehl | November 10, 1980 |
| Kay Hladiy | October 16, 1980 |
| Mary Kardash | October 20, 1980 |
| Alice Katool | May 31, 1981 |
| Carlyle King | November 12, 1980 |
| Hilda Kristiansen | December 8, 1980 |
| Margaret Mann | April, 1980 |
| L.M. | November 29, 1980 |
| Avis McCurdy | May 30, 1982 |
| Grace MacInnis | July 17, 1981 |
| Lillian Marcus | September 3, 1980 |
| Jessie Mendels | December 8, 1980 |
| Eloise Metheral | November 11, 1980 |
| Eugena Moore | December 7, 1983 |
| Mona Morgan | July 20, 1981 |
| Mickey Murray | October 6, 1980 |
| On to Ottawa Group: | January 30, 1983 |
|     Taime Davis | |
|     Lil Himmelfarb Ilomaki | |
|     Alex McLennan | |
|     Ernie Solwell | |
| Nellie Peterson | November 21, 1980 |

| | |
|---|---|
| Jean Robinson | October 9, 1980 |
| Nora Rodd | November 8, 1981 |
| Stanley Ryerson | July 16, 1981 |
| S.S. | November, 1983 |
| Eve G. Smith | July 19, 1981 |
| Margot Thompson | October 6, 1981 |
| Daisy Webster | December 2, 1980 |

V. *Personal Correspondence*

| | |
|---|---|
| Margery Ferguson | November 3, 1983 |
| Christine Nielsen | January 26, 1984 |
| Toby Ryan | January 11, 1984 |

# Index

# THE CANADIAN SOCIAL HISTORY SERIES

**Terry Copp,**
*The Anatomy of Poverty:
The Condition of the Working Class in Montreal 1897–1929*, 1974.

**Gregory S. Kealey and Peter Warrian, Editors,**
*Essays in Canadian Working Class History*, 1976.

**Alison Prentice,**
*The School Promoters: Education and Social Class in Mid-Nineteenth Century
Upper Canada*, 1977.

**Susan Mann Trofimenkoff and Alison Prentice, Editors,**
*The Neglected Majority: Essays in Canadian Women's History*, 1977.

**John Herd Thompson,**
*The Harvests of War: The Prairie West, 1914–1918*, 1978.

**Donald Avery,**
*"Dangerous Foreigners": European Immigrant Workers and Labour Radicalism
in Canada, 1896–1932*, 1979.

**Joy Parr, Editor,**
*Childhood and Family in Canadian History*, 1982.

**Howard Palmer,**
*Patterns of Prejudice: A History of Nativism in Alberta*, 1982.

**Tom Traves, Editor,**
*Essays in Canadian Business History*, 1984.

**Alison Prentice and Susan Mann Trofimenkoff, Editors,**
*The Neglected Majority: Essays in Canadian Women's History, Volume 2*, 1985.

**Ruth Roach Pierson,**
*"They're Still Women After All": The Second World War and Canadian
Womanhood*, 1986.

**Bryan D. Palmer, Editor,**
*The Character of Class Struggle: Essays in Canadian Working-Class History,
1850–1985*, 1986.

**Angus McLaren and Arlene Tigar McLaren,**
*The Bedroom and the State: The Changing Practices and Politics of
Contraception and Abortion in Canada, 1880–1980*, 1986.

**Alan Metcalfe,**
*Canada Learns to Play: The Emergence of Organized Sport, 1807–1914*, 1986.

**Marta Danylewycz,**
*Taking the Veil: An Alternative to Marriage, Motherhood, and Spinsterhood in
Quebec, 1840–1920*, 1987.

**Craig Heron,**
*Working in Steel: The Early Years in Canada, 1883–1935*, 1988.

**Wendy Mitchinson and Janice Dickin McGinnis, Editors,**
*Essays in the History of Canadian Medicine*, 1988.

**Joan Sangster,**
*Dreams of Equality: Women on
The Canadian Left, 1920–1950*, 1989.